D0501934

THE EAGLE SQUADRONS

THE EAGLE
YANKS IN THE

SQUADRONS
RAF 1940-1942

VERN HAUGLAND

ZIFF-DAVIS FLYING BOOKS
New York
1979

To the gallant men who sacrificed their lives during and after service in the Royal Air Force Eagle Squadrons, this book is dedicated.

Lord, hold them in thy mighty hand
Above the ocean and the land
Like wings of Eagles mounting high
Along the pathways of the sky.

Immortal is the name they bear
And high the honour that they share.
Until a thousand years have rolled,
Their deeds of valour shall be told.

In dark of night and light of day
God speed and bless them on their way.
And homeward safely guide each one
With glory gained and duty done.

—Anonymous

CONTENTS

FOREWORD

by Lt. General Ira C. Eaker, USAF (Ret.)

Vern Haugland's book, *The Eagle Squadrons* is of intense interest to me. While in England in the summer of 1941 to study British night fighter operations, preparing to serve as chairman of the board that laid down the specifications for our American night fighter, the Black Widow, and again from February 1942 until January 1944, while in command of the Eighth Bomber Command and the Eighth Air Force—I had the opportunity to know many of the pilots of the Eagle Squadrons, particularly the originals in 71 Squadron.

Since those World War II days, I have followed the careers of many of the Eagle Aces, including Pete Peterson, later a Major General in the U.S. Air Force, Colonels Don Blakeslee and Reade Tilley.

Haugland has done thorough research of personal diaries and historical records. He deserves great credit for catching the spirit of the Eagles, as well as recording their tremendous accomplishments. He rightly notes their dedication to principle. They realized the Second World War would eventually involve the United States and that, in the meantime, they should do their gallant best to see that Great Britain survived.

The 71st Squadron took as its watchwords "Polish, Precision and Prestige." These admirable qualities they achieved quickly and held to steadfastly. I remember well the great pride we all had when Bill Dunn and Gus Daymond became the first American Aces in World War II. Within a very few months, the Eagles became recognized as one of the leading British Wings.

The author includes many interesting stories about these brash young men as they settled into British wartime life. For example, there was the matter of taxes. It was first decided that the pilots of the Eagle Squadrons must pay approximately half of their meager salaries in taxes to the British goverment. They sent a squadron commander to see the Commander-in-Chief of the Fighter Command, Air Marshal Sir Sholto Douglas, and others to protest to the Air Minister, with the result that they were exempted from British income taxes.

This book also contains many stories of their exuberance when not flying combat missions. Some of these pranks seem extreme but they illustrated, I felt, understandable characteristics. We must remember these men had little anticipation of a future other than of death in air combat. As a matter of fact, one third of them did lose their lives while members of the Eagle Squadrons. Also, their youth caused them to adopt the attitude: "If a short life, make it a merry one."

The principal thing this book of the Eagle Squadrons has done for me has been to remind me of their courage, skill and fortitude.

Haugland has quoted copiously from the reports made by pilots immediately after their battles, and this comprises one of the most valuable portions of this book. I remember well how, in September 1942, the Eagles replaced their RAF uniforms with those of the U.S. Eighth Air Force. They became the Fourth Fighter Group. For the next two years, as I commanded the Eighth Air Force, I observed how much we benefitted from having these experienced veterans with us as we adjusted to the war's requirements and hardships.

They speeded the transition of all our fighter pilots and in the coming months saved many of our bombers in their long and hazardous missions. The Eagle Squadrons were truly the first of the "Little Brothers." I shall always give them much credit, along with the gallant, invincible bomber crews, for the destruction of the Luftwaffe, which made possible the cross-Channel invasion and the winning of the land campaign.

These courageous, dedicated flying men were the vanguard, along with their RAF comrades, who destroyed, in a thousand days, the Third Reich that Hitler had boasted would last a thousand years.

PREFACE

by The Right Honorable Lord Martonmere (Formerly Wing Commander J. Roland Robinson, M.P.)

One day, early in the winter of 1940, I was asked if I would show three young Americans around the Houses of Parliament. I gladly said yes, for I had often done this for my American friends. This time, it was different: the three young men proved to be Pete Peterson, Gus Daymond and Luke Allen. Little did I realise that ten days later, I would be joining them at Kirton Lindsey as one of the Eagle Squadron team.

I had already applied for a commission in the Royal Air Force and, when accepted, was ordered to appear in uniform for my assignment to duty. The assigning officer reminded me that I had an American wife and that I was known to love the United States as I had travelled all over the country and had many American friends. It was therefore proposed that I should be assigned to the No. 71 Eagle Squadron, which was being formed for young American pilots coming over as volunteers to join the Royal Air Force. Apparently, there was no suitable officer the RAF could assign to the position who had my experience of America and Americans. This was indeed exciting news.

I took leave of absence from the House of Commons, a leave which was always given to those who wished to join the armed forces and thereafter, for the rest of the war, my appearances in the House were limited to times when I was on leave or on pass.

Life with the Eagles was a new and thrilling adventure for me. All my adult life had been spent in the House of Commons, in the company of men who, on the average, were twenty-five years older than I was. Now I was throwing in my lot with a group of young men whose average age was ten years younger than mine. What a change! It had the effect of keeping me young.

People asked what had caused these young men to come over to England to fight our battles, many at the cost of their lives. There were several answers. For some, it was sheer idealism—to fight for the cause of freedom—while many were inspired by the love of adventure. Others wanted to learn to fly and to fly quickly. The opportunity to fly came more easily in the Royal Air Force, for its wartime physical and educational standards were not as high as in the United States Army Air Force, so great were our needs. A few, perhaps, wanted to get away from home and into the world. One thing is certain: they were not mercenaries in the modern sense of the term. The pay offered to these young men who were prepared to sacrifice their lives was pitiful, so much so, that at the end of the month some of them had difficulty in meeting their mess bills.

Their period as a training squadron was soon over and there was great excitement when they became an operational squadron. They achieved many successes and their exploits became legendary, but their casualties were high. In due course, the survivors were seasoned veterans in combat and the news of their exploits reached the United States. As more and more American volunteer fighter pilots came over to England, two more Eagle Squadrons were formed, and they, too, soon became operational.

With Pearl Harbor, the United States came into the war and the Eighth Air Force was established in England. Before long all our Eagle pilots were transferred to the United States Army Air Force with the equivalent rank they had held in the Royal Air Force. I well remember the ceremony at Debden when I witnessed the change-over in which the Eagle Squadron emerged as a new unit of the Eighth Fighter Command. They came to England as boys and now they had returned to their own country's command as seasoned veterans. Their standards were high, and it was a remarkable tribute to them that two of our pilots from No. 71 Squadron—Peterson and McColpin— were, in due course, promoted to the rank of Major-General.

I felt a great affection for them all, and the friendships of the war years have proved lasting. They welded together in a great team and played a valuable part in the history of World War II. When they finally returned home, they had forged, by their personalities and example, an important link in Anglo-American relations. The link remains strong as ever after so many years, as the Eagles themselves found out when they had their reunion in England in 1976.

It is fitting that Vern Haugland should write a history of the Eagle Squadron, and I for one am looking forward to the publication of his book with great interest.

INTRODUCTION

This is the story of the Eagle squadrons of Great Britain's Royal Air Force in World War II. There were three of them, the only all-American units in the RAF. The 240 U.S. pilots who enrolled as Eagles in 1940 and 1941—including 37 who joined the Royal Canadian Air Force—did so voluntarily, determined to fight and fly in a war that was not really their own. The disaster at Pearl Harbor had not yet thrust the United States into armed conflict with the Axis powers.

The Eagles came from all parts of America. For the most part they were young, hard, lean and lighthearted. Sharing a common love of flying, adventure and danger, they were ever ready for a celebration or a fight, whichever seemed appropriate to the moment. Unquestioningly, they made tremendous sacrifices.

Initially they were recruited in the United States by furtive individuals representing anonymous and clandestine entities. They were then whisked into Canada where they boarded Britain-bound ships, under threat of grave penalties for evading the U.S. draft and violating neutrality laws: an American joining the armed forces of a belligerent nation could suffer loss of citizenship. Some of the volunteers, crossing the Canadian border disguised as tourists or salesmen, were apprehended and sent home, only to cross again at another point—in some instances only a jump ahead of the FBI. One young man from Dixie, afraid that the war would be over before he could get there, went AWOL from the Royal Canadian Air Force, stowed away on a freighter, and talked his way into the Eagles after his arrival in London.

A few of the Americans who became Eagles were already in England when the war broke out. Others were in France and, when that nation fell, scrambled aboard whatever transportation to England they could find.

Some of the applicants padded their pilot logbooks to bolster their claims to flight experience and piloting skill; they lied about their ages if they were too young and about their educational accomplishments. In such matters, they told themselves, the means were irrelevant. Only the end was important, for across the Channel Nazi divisions were waiting for the Luftwaffe to crush Britain's air defenses and open the way for invasion. For the strong-willed Americans, this was a just cause and a challenge.

Altogether the Eagles destroyed or damaged many hundreds of enemy aircraft, ships, locomotives and cargo trains, troop columns, tanks, antiaircraft guns and weapons stores. The price was high. One Eagle in every three did not live to see the United States again.

The pilots often flew on the ragged edge, near operational limits, with little regard for fuel-supply safety margins or the vagaries of fog or storm. Men were killed or seriously injured in flying accidents that might have been avoided—victims of their padded logbooks—for supersensitive weapons such as the Hurricane and Spitfire could be ruthlessly unforgiving to careless or inexperienced pilots. Now and then an old hand would simply run out of luck.

During the two years the three squadrons were in existence, sixteen of the Eagles were shot down and taken as prisoners of war, while twelve others met a similar fate on missions flown after the squadrons were transferred to the U.S. Army Air Forces. A surprising number escaped, were recaptured and sometimes escaped again. A few made it all the way back to England. One who was recaptured was shot by a German firing squad as an example to his fellow prisoners.

In the early days, there was skepticism within the RAF leadership as to how useful the American units would be. One senior British air officer considered the volunteers spoiled, temperamental and virtually unmanageable, and suggested that the units be disbanded. The Eagles themselves conceded such inadequacies; there even were times when men had to be tossed out of their squadrons.

Nevertheless, the Eagles matured and learned the meaning of combat. As each squadron met the enemy and flew operational missions, it became in turn a leader in RAF scoring, chalking up more victories than any other squadron for a specific period. The Eagles proved that they were fighting men, as good as the best, and came to appreciate that they were in a war that would profoundly affect the future course of civilization. Almost without realizing it, the members of the three squadrons became symbols to the beleaguered British of the vast, and still uncommitted, power of the United States. They helped to spark the will of Britain to hold on grimly and to await whatever miracle would bring America into the war.

Perhaps never again will the United States and Britain

share such an experience. But there remains for all time the record of the Eagles' courage, persistence, and triumph. Their own country may have been ready at one point to disown them, yet they led the way into a battle that their homeland eventually joined. They were, as one British officer said in tribute, the vanguard—a vanguard of Eagles.

THE EAGLE SQUADRONS

The major Eagle Squadron bases in Southeast England were at Biggin Hill, Debden (with its satellite, Great Sampford), North Weald and Martlesham Heath, Gravesend and Southend-on-Sea. Key points in Eagle actions were Manston, Lympne, Dover, New Romney and Beachy Head.

Cambridge

Debden
(Great Sampford)

Epping ● North Wea
Rochfor
London

Northolt ● ENGLAND
Thames River
Croydon

Biggin Can
Kenley ● Hill Lym

Southampton Hasting
Exeter Portsmouth Brighton
Bournemouth Eastbou
Plymouth Beachy Head

Torquay Isle of Wight
Bolt Head

X (REFUELING POINT)

ENGLISH CHANNEL

Cherbourg Féca
(Utah Beach) Le Havre

Channel Islands (Omaha Beach)

NORMANDY

Brest Morlaix Guingamp

BRITTANY

The Morlaix Raid: On September 26, 1942, 12 new Spit-fire IXs of 133 Squadron took off in the early morning from Great Sampford, refueled at Bolthead and flew south to rendezvous with a force of B-17s. One Spit was shot down and another badly damaged. The remaining Eagles, on their return, let down over Brest, believing that they were over the English coast. All 10 were lost to enemy fire or bad weather.

BAY
OF
BISCAY

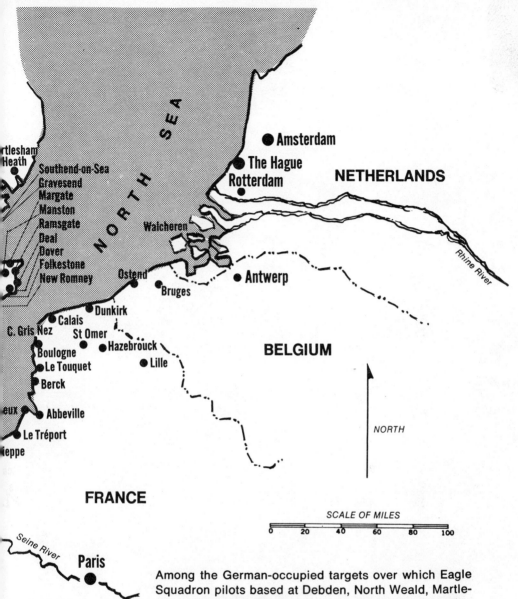

Among the German-occupied targets over which Eagle Squadron pilots based at Debden, North Weald, Martlesham Heath and Biggin Hill saw a great deal of action were Walcheren Island, the Netherlands; Ostend, Belgium; and Dunkirk, Hazebrouck, Lille, St. Omer, Calais, Cape Gris Nez, Boulogne, Le Touquet, Berck-sur-Mer, Cayeux, Abbeville, Le Treport, Dieppe, Fecamp, Cherbourg, Guingamp, Morlaix and Brest.

1

FIRST BLOOD
IN A
BORROWED WAR

The mission's code name was Circus 29. In Royal Air Force parlance, a *circus* was a large force of fighters escorting a small formation of bombers to a target in German-occupied France and back to England. The intent was not only to inflict damage on the target but, more importantly, to draw enemy fighters into action.

The target was an electric power plant at Lille, forty miles inland from Dunkirk. The twelve Hurricane fighter pilots of 71 Eagle Squadron took off from North Weald, Essex, just north of London, at 11:50 A.M. on July 2, 1941. They were Squadron Commander Paddy Woodhouse, a combat-hardened Englishman, and eleven eager, excited, untested and somewhat apprehensive American pilot officers.

On schedule at the rendezvous point twelve thousand feet above the east coast of England, the Hurricanes met twelve twin-engine Blenheim bombers. The fighters formed slightly above and to the rear of the formation and moved out across the Channel. Scanning the sky closely, the pilots saw only an expanse of blue dappled with the white clouds of summer. In the distance was the coastline of France, beyond which a haze lay over the land.

Each man knew that venturing into France with a squadron of bombers was an almost certain way to stir up an angry swarm of Messerschmitts. Already, German radar, which swept the Channel continuously, would have locked onto the approaching aircraft and sorted out the bombers and fighters, reading their altitude, course and probable target. Air raid sirens would be wailing in the French towns; fighter bases at Abbeville, St. Omer and other fields would have been alerted. Luftwaffe fighter pilots, always zealous, surely had raced out of their alert huts by now. Props would be turning on Me 109s standing in readiness alongside runways.

As. the RAF formation crossed the sandy line of the French coast, flashes of fire spurted on the ground, and shells burst well above and to the rear of the planes. Now there was no longer any need for radio silence.

"All right, lads," Woodhouse called, "keep a sharp eye out. They'll be about us soon."

The antiaircraft guns tracked the Blenheims and the fighter escort southward and passed them along to other German AA stations. Near Lille the flak became dangerously accurate, so close that the pilots could feel the concussion.

Just as the Blenheims released their bombs, the enemy fighters attacked. They swooped down suddenly, apparently in three *staffeln*—the Luftwaffe equivalent of squadrons—25 to 30 109s, each armed with two 20 mm. wing cannons and two 7.9 mm. machine guns in the nose. As the enemy pounced, the Hurricane formation broke up.

In the counterattack, it was every man for himself. Woodhouse fired five short, sharp bursts from his eight .303-caliber Browning machine guns at the oncoming Germans and then centered in on a 109 with a burst from about 150 yards. Black smoke poured out of the German plane, which rolled over and plunged earthward. His teammates saw it crash and burst into flames, but the squadron leader was too busy to watch. Continuing his attack, Woodhouse fired at four other 109s, two of which took hits.

By this time the sky seemed filled with Messerschmitts. At six thousand feet Pilot Officer Bill Dunn, flying number two to Woodhouse, opened fire from the port quarter on a diving 109. Pursuing it down, he fired three more bursts, the last from a range of only seventy-five feet, at an altitude of thirty-five hundred feet. Chips flew off the enemy plane as it caught fire. Dunn and teammate Pete Provenzano saw it crash near a crossroad.

Pilot Officer Gus Daymond, at nineteen the youngest of

the Eagles, saw two 109s attacking the bombers at eight thousand feet. The first plane fired and peeled off. As the second 109 charged, Daymond swerved and went after it, his guns chattering. The 109 turned and fired, blasting holes in Daymond's plane, and then made the mistake of changing direction. Swiftly on his tail, Daymond chased the German down to five thousand feet and fired two bursts from one hundred yards. The 109's canopy flew off. As the stricken plane swung into a sidelong dive, the German pilot bailed out.

A third pilot officer, Bob Mannix, poured fire into an Me 109 until thick smoke streamed from the plane, which dived toward the ground. Since no one could confirm a crash, Mannix claimed the 109 only as probably destroyed.

An hour and twenty minutes after takeoff, the Eagles began returning to North Weald. One after another they landed: Woodhouse, Dunn, Daymond, Mannix, Provenzano, Andy Mamedoff, Oscar Coen, Vic Bono, Bill Nichols, Virgil Olson, Ken Taylor. Eleven men only; no sign of Bill Hall. The pilots lingered around the field, their hopes dwindling. A likable, capable fellow, Hall had more flying experience than many of his colleagues. He had been a bush pilot in Alaska and at Val d'Or, Quebec.

The sadness over his disappearance lifted only somewhat after German radio reported that he had been captured and was in a hospital. Hall was but the first of the Eagles to have his life placed in the enemy's hands.

In the 71 Squadron messhall that night there was a victory celebration only slightly dampened by the absence of one pilot. In terms of air warfare, three 109s destroyed for the loss of one Hurricane was good arithmetic. These were the Eagles' first kills, and messages of congratulations came in from 11 Group Headquarters and Fighter Command. Now that they were officially blooded, the Eagles no longer represented an unknown quantity. They had done as well as any RAF squadron, and better than most.

Daymond, who had come into military flying from being a makeup man in a Hollywood film studio, told his excited squadronmates that when he realized he had shot down a German he was thrilled, yet at the same time he was confused and remorseful. He had started to watch the enemy plane, hoping that the pilot would get out, and then found himself under fire from another 109 and much too busy to worry further about his own victim.

Bill Dunn, a former cowboy from North Dakota who had learned to fly as a teen-ager in Texas, said his feeling upon destroying an enemy fighter for the first time was "one of elation. You are shooting down an airplane—you don't really think of the guy who is in it. You know that's what you were hired for—it's part of the job. You remember it could have been the other way around. Shooting down the first one sure as hell gives you confidence."

Daymond and Dunn—two fine pilots, two brave and aggressive young men. Under ordinary circumstances they might have been the best of friends, but bitterness developed between them that was to endure for decades.

───────

From six at first we soon became
A Grecian clan of wondrous fame.

(College fraternity song)

There were only three at first in No. 71 Eagle Squadron, not six. They became a Royal Air Force—not a Grecian—clan of wondrous fame. But not "soon." Not soon.

There had been a No. 71 Squadron, flying Sopwith Camels and Snipes, in World War I. The fourth British squadron to be formed from Australian volunteers, it achieved the highest score of all four, with seventy-six German aircraft destroyed. It was disbanded in Germany in February, 1919.

Reactivated in 1940 to receive American volunteers, it moved into the RAF Yorkshire station of Church Fenton 10 miles south of the city of York, 180 miles north of London and conveniently close to the brewery town of Tadcaster. The first entry in the Squadron Operations Record Book was:

19.9.40. Arrival of the first group of pilots for Eagle Squadron No. 71—P/O G. Tobin, P/O A. Mamedoff and P/O V. C. Keough having been posted from No. 609 Squadron where each had had about 50 hours operational service on Spitfires. These three officers had been evacuated from France where they had gone to join the French Air Force.

The second entry, ten days later:

29.9.40. S/Ldr. W. M. Churchill, D.S.O., D.F.C., arrived from command of No. 605 Squadron at Croydon. Arrival of P/O F. H. Tann, Adjutant. P/O A. G. Donahue arrived from No. 64 Squadron, having seen a good deal of service, having been shot down and quite badly burned.

In RAF terminology, P/O stands for pilot officer, the equivalent of an American second lieutenant. Other designations of rank include F/O for flying officer, or first lieutenant; F/Lt for flight lieutenant, or captain in U.S. terms; and S/Ldr for squadron leader, or major. Wing commander corresponds to the American lieutenant colonel; group captain corresponds to colonel.

Arthur Gerald Donahue, the fourth American pilot to join 71 Squadron, arrived at Church Fenton on September 29, 1940, with Englishmen Walter Churchill, who assumed command of the new unit, and Tann. Donahue, fresh off the family farm near St. Charles, Minnesota, had been assigned to the all-British 64 Squadron upon his arrival in England on August 4, 1940. The very next day he tangled with enemy fighters and barely managed to bring his crippled Spitfire home. On August 8 the squadron intercepted thirty raiding German planes, and Donahue damaged and possibly destroyed a Messerschmitt.

In his third engagement four days later, cannon shells tore away his elevator and control cables, and incendiary bullets set his Spit afire. Donahue bailed out, and British soldiers later found him with his legs, hands and face badly burned. In little more than a week of action with the RAF, Donahue had become something of a war hero in England. Seven weeks later the durable youngster was out of the hospital and in the new Eagle Squadron.

During October a few more men joined the new squadron: two American pilot officers, Philip H. "Zeke" Leckrone, a farm youth from Salem, Illinois, and Luke Elbert Allen, from Ignacio, Colorado, and two British officers, Flight Lieutenants George A. Brown and R. C. Wilkinson, who would lead two of the squadron's three four-plane formations, known as flights. And then more Americans, Squadron Leader William Erwin Gibson Taylor, a former aeronautical engineering student at New York University, and Robert V. "Bobby" Sweeny of London, winner three years previously of the British amateur golfing title. These were would-be combat pilots—but with no equipment, not even one airplane to fly. The single aircraft that had been provided them, a Miles Magister trainer, was unserviceable.

Donahue could stand the enforced inaction no longer, and on October 23, 1940, at his own request, he was allowed to go back to an all-British squadron that had flyable equipment. The 71 Squadron Operations Record Book entry on that date: "At this point the entire personnel were completely browned off because of the enormous lack of interest in the equipping of the squadron with any aircraft."

Just twenty-four hours later, the Ops Record Book exulted: "This was a momentous day, for three Brewster American fighters arrived and the pall lifted." Another Brewster arrived the following day.

Enthusiasm over the single-seat, single-engine Brewster F2A Buffalo faded quickly. Developed for the U.S. Navy and not well adapted to land-based operations, the plane had a disconcerting tendency to float on its approach to a landing. Leckrone overshot the field, turned his plane over on its back, and was taken to a hospital with a slight concussion. An inspection panel in the fuselage of Churchill's plane came open in flight, and the rush of air on the aileron made it almost impossible for him to maintain control. Churchill had to make an emergency landing at nearby Linton airdrome.

The pilots also found the Brewster to be too slow, too limited in altitude capability, too lightly armed and too vulnerable structurally for use in combat. The plane also lacked self-sealing fuel tanks. The tanks were an integral part of the wing, and a single bullet in the wing could set it afire. There were no spare parts available, and the plane's sheet metal and hidden parts made maintenance difficult.

Concluding that the little airplanes were deathtraps, Churchill decided quietly to get rid of the three that were still operational. He ordered Wilkinson, Mamedoff and Tobin to take off in the Brewsters and come right back to land without locking the tail wheels.

This startled the pilots, because standard instructions for the Buffalo were to make sure the tail wheel was locked for landing, but they soon had a fair idea of what Churchill had in mind. A Buffalo landing with its tail wheel unlocked usually would ground loop. In a ground loop at high speed the plane would tilt to one side and dig its wingtip into the ground. A damaged wing meant a fuel tank wrecked virtually beyond repair.

Each pilot landed with the tail wheel unlocked, as ordered. The automatic result was a series of devastating ground loops. In one stroke the entire Brewster "squadron" was wiped out, but no one was hurt. The RAF remained discreetly silent about the disappearance of the American Buffalo from its inventory.

Before deciding to eliminate the Brewsters, Walter Churchill had received assurance that better equipment, the

Hawker Hurricane I, was on its way. The first British low-wing fighter and the first operational RAF aircraft capable of top speeds above three hundred miles an hour, the Hurricane had been the mainstay of the defense against German bombers in the Battle of Britain. It had a wing span of 40 feet, was 31 feet and four inches long and 13 feet one inch tall. Its 1,030-horse-power Rolls-Royce Merlin III twelve-cylinder liquid-cooled engine gave it a maximum speed of 328 mph at 20,000 feet, a maximum range of 505 miles, and a service ceiling of 34,200 feet. Eight wing-mounted machine guns provided a devastating flow of explosive ammunition capable of slicing the wing off a Messerschmitt 109.

Accordingly there was this entry in the 71 Squadron official diary for November 7, 1940:

> Everything good happened today.
> Nine Hurricanes arrived, delivered by No. 85 Squadron. The commanding officer, S/Ldr. Townsend—most attractive fellow, stationed at Gravesend—was leading his squadron into battle daily despite one foot in plaster cast, having had several toes taken off by a cannon shell. Further eight pilots posted from No. 5 F.T.S. (Flying Training School) Sealand arrived.

That "most attractive fellow" leading the Hurricane flight, the first fit-for-combat aircraft to be delivered to an American unit in World War II, was Peter Townsend, who was later to become well known as equerry to King George VI and as a frequent escort of Princess Margaret.

The newly arrived 71 Squadron pilots, all pilot officers, were Pete Peterson, Indian Jim Moore and Gus Daymond; Charles Edward Bateman, of Stephentown, New York; and Californians Stanley Michel Kolendorski, from Bell; Byron Kennerly, Pasadena; James Leland McGinnis, Hollywood; and Edwin Ezell Orbison, Sacramento.

Two weeks after the introduction of the Hurricanes and after additional fighters had been delivered, the squadron was transferred 40 miles southeastward to Kirton-in-Lindsey, near Lincoln but still 130 miles north of London. The first thing the Americans noticed was that RAF fighters "beat up" the station every morning—making simulated low-level attacks to give gun crews on the base some realistic training. This had never happened at the previous location. Furthermore, the Ops Record Book observed: "The squadron after first flight was very pleased with the field, as it is much larger than Church Fenton. There is a much bigger mess, and a happier atmosphere reigns here."

Nevertheless Kirton, like Church Fenton, Coltishall, Dux-ford and other nearby bases, was still within the area assigned to the RAF's No. 12 Group, the organization responsible for the air defense of the industrial Midlands. The Americans were hoping that 71 Squadron soon would be moved into 11 Group, defender of the London area where most of the excitement and action prevailed. They were not to attain that goal for five more long months.

At Kirton the emphasis was on formation flying, convoy patrols, and air combat practice using gun cameras. The squad-ron was ordered to readiness for the first time on January 4, 1941. That same day No. 71 formed its first *Balbo*—an exercise with twelve planes in close formation.

On the following day the squadron experienced its first fatality. Keough, Orbison and Leckrone were flying in close formation, at an altitude of more than twenty thousand feet, when the latter two collided. Keough followed Leckrone down all the way, shouting to him over the R/T—the radio tele-phone. Leckrone didn't reply and made no attempt to bail out. Orbison managed to land safely in spite of a damaged left wing.

The Operations Book said of the idealistic Leckrone:

> Zeke was quiet and reserved, and had over 100 hours on Spitfires (in 616 Squadron). He will be a great loss to us, for his influence was a sobering one. If the death of one of the pilots can help a squadron, Zeke's will help this unit for, if nothing else, it will tend to impress on the other pilots the attention they must pay to detail in these practice flights. It is true of this squadron, as of most others in the RAF, that they are inclined to treat all this practice flying as a bit of a bore.

In the midst of funeral services for Leckrone, four new Eagles arrived: Californians Victor Robert Bono, of Novato, Nat Maranz (later he changed the spelling to Marans), of Tibu-ron, and William H. Nichols, Woodland; and James Keith Alexander, of Huntington, West Virginia.

So the grim business of war began, with its inevitable grief. The flow of pilots to the Eagle Squadron was moving, but it was not easy. At the beginning of the venture, in fact, the formation of an Eagle Squadron had often been in doubt, had in fact been an adventure in itself, first given life by the determination of two imaginative and stubborn men.

2

GETTING THERE
—AND WHY

The early birds among the Americans who made their way into
Britain's Eagle Squadrons did so through the maneuverings and
diligent efforts of Charles Sweeny, a well-heeled American
sportsman, businessman and socialite living in London, and his
uncle, also named Charles—Colonel Charles Sweeny, of Salt
Lake City, Utah—a famous, even notorious, globe-trotting soldier of fortune. Also taking part in the preliminary arrangements, mainly in terms of providing financial assistance, were
the Londoner's younger brother, Bobby Sweeny, winner of the
British Amateur Golfing Championship in 1937, and their father, Robert Sweeny, an international financier.

The Sweeny project, though short-lived, was a start. It
gave way almost immediately to a larger, better organized program backed by the Royal Canadian Air Force, a recruiting
committee set up in Ottawa and New York City under the
command of Air Vice Marshal Billy Bishop, Canada's leading
air ace—Bishop had been credited with shooting down seventy-
two enemy planes in World War I. He induced an American
wartime flying colleague—Clayton Knight, of Rochester, New
York, a well-known military artist, portrait painter and magazine illustrator—to head the recruitment force. A wealthy Canadian, Homer Smith—who just happened to be a cousin of

Charles and Bobby Sweeny—was commissioned a wing commander in the RCAF and named to administer the recruiting organization that became famous as the Clayton Knight Committee. By the time the U.S. entered the war in December, 1941, the Knight Committee had processed fifty thousand applications and had approved sixty-seven hundred Americans for duty with the RCAF or the RAF. About 10 percent of the RCAF enrollment at that time consisted of American volunteers—and 92 percent of the Americans who became Eagles were products of the Clayton Knight Committee.

The Sweeny family derived its fortune from yet another Charles Sweeny, father of the Utah colonel and of industrialist Robert Sweeny. This Charles Sweeny had struck it rich in the goldfields of Idaho and British Columbia. His eldest son and namesake was dismissed from the U.S. Military Academy at West Point because of a hazing offense. Young Charles went to South America as an engineer and then branched out into quasi-military ventures. He was said—over a ten-year period—to have provided weapons and trained military personnel for uprisings in Mexico, Venezuela, Honduras and elsewhere. He enlisted in the French Foreign Legion in 1914, at the age of 32, and fought in the American Expeditionary Forces as a colonel. Later he served with the Poles as a brigadier general in the Russo-Polish War. Charles Sweeny also organized an air squadron of Americans and other pilots for the French Army in the Riff War, and became chief of the Sultan of Morocco's air force. He also fought against the Fascists in Spain on behalf of the Loyalists.

When the Nazi invasion of Poland and the Soviet Army's coordinated invasion of Finland touched off World War II, the ubiquitous Col. Charles Sweeny appeared in France once again. Two months later he was in Canada to begin recruiting 150 American pilots for a French Air Force detachment to be modeled after the famed Lafayette Escadrille of World War I. Sweeny found himself cramped by the U.S. neutrality law, by the hostility of some major pro-German U.S. newspapers, and by a general indifference on the part of the American public. Nevertheless, by May of 1940 he had sent thirty-two volunteers to Paris just in time for them to become caught up in the chaos that led to the fall of France in the third week of June. Four of the American volunteers in that group were killed, nine became prisoners of the Germans, and the others made their way elsewhere. Of six who escaped to England, five—Andy

Mamedoff, Virgil Olson, Gene Tobin, Vernon Keough and Newton Anderson—became Eagles.

In London, meanwhile, Colonel Sweeny's nephew, the younger Charles Sweeny, had helped organize a motorized squadron, made up of leading members of the American community, as an "American Mechanized Defence Corps." "We were an ill-equipped outfit," he recalls, "until my father arranged a shipment of 50 Thompson submachine guns to our unit through a friend who was chairman of the Colt Firearms Groups. After that date we were the best equipped unit in London."

RAF historical records in London contain a June 27, 1940, letter from Charles Sweeny to Sir Hugh Seeley, of the Air Ministry, urging that an American Air Defence Corps be formed "under the command of my uncle . . . as an adjunct to my American Mechanized Defence Corps which has completed its first unit of 50 members for the London Defence under the direction of Lt. Gen. Sir Sergison Brooks." In an accompanying memorandum marked "private and confidential" he pointed out that the American recruiting organization of his uncle, "known and unofficially approved in the highest quarters in Washington," was still in existence despite the collapse of France. Sweeny added that a considerable number of experienced American pilots had been interviewed and approved and could readily be made available to the proposed Air Defence Corps. Colonel Sweeny had estimated, he said, that ten thousand American volunteers with flying experience could be recruited if they were assured that they could serve without loss of citizenship and if adequate financial help could be arranged.

In furtherance of his proposal, Charles Sweeny called upon Lord Beaverbrook, minister of production, and Brendan Bracken, personal assistant to Prime Minister Winston Churchill, and then made a presentation before the Air Staff and Air Marshal Sir Sholto Douglas, chief of Fighter Command. The Air Ministry thereafter authorized the project.

"In effect the squadrons, which I called Eagle Squadrons and which took their insignia from my U.S. passport, were born on that day," Charles Sweeny says. "In those dreadful times England stood alone. Anything that might contribute to the participation of the U.S. was well received."

Bobby Sweeny recalls that the cost of recruiting the original Eagle pilots and of bringing them to England had been borne "entirely by my brother and myself and our friends."

Among the latter was heiress Barbara Hutton, then known as the Countess Reventlow, whom Bobby often had escorted around London. "Barbara gave $15,000 to the Eagle Fund, as it was known," he said. "In all, $100,000 was raised amongst us."

According to Bobby's brother, Charles:

"My uncle, Colonel Sweeny, had had an extraordinary career, and I thought he was the perfect man to set up as a non-flying Commander of the first Eagle Squadron. He was my boyhood hero. I had considerable difficulty in arranging his appointment with Harold Balfour, Under Secretary of State for Air, but finally my uncle was granted a rank of Group Captain.

"Balfour, incidentally, was against having an independent U.S. unit in the RAF, as it conflicted with his Empire Training Program in Canada which was under the command of Billy Bishop, an old friend of my family. However, he finally gave his approval.

"Sir Archibald Sinclair, Secretary of State for Air, in fact confirmed the formation of the Eagle Squadron before we had any pilots. I was astonished when the Air Ministry called me within a few days to inform me that my first pilots had arrived —Mamedoff, Tobin and Keough.

"I was amazed because nothing concrete had yet been done. I made an appointment to dine with these three volunteers at White's Club. They were refugees from the debacle in France. They wanted to fly, and they agreed to enter flying training and then be transferred to an Eagle Squadron to be formed.

"It was quite an historic moment."

———

The day after England and France declared war on Germany, RCAF Air Vice Marshal Bishop, in Ottawa, telephoned Clayton Knight in Cleveland, where the artist was covering the National Air Races for a magazine, and asked him to take charge of screening American pilots who might soon volunteer for duty with Canada's Air Force. Bishop pointed out that most Canadian trained fliers were already in service and added that the Commonwealth air training program was faltering for lack of cadets.

Knight agreed to help out where and when needed. He had enlisted in the American Air Service in 1917 and later flew first as an aerial observer for the British Second Army and then as a fighter pilot for the Royal Flying Corps. Shot down on October 5, 1918, he spent the last days of the war in German hospitals. Knight became doubly well known to aviation enthusiasts for his illustrations in the air war books of such writers as Elliott White Springs, Floyd Gibbons, Norman S. Hall and Bert Hall in the 1920s. Bishop felt that if anyone could persuade young Americans to fly for Great Britain, it would be Clayton Knight.

During the six months of the so-called Phony War, when the opposing ground forces in Europe were curiously inactive and there were only occasional air clashes, few Americans sought to become involved. However, when Hitler's motorized columns poured across the frontiers of neutral Belgium, Holland and Luxembourg in the Spring of 1940 and flooded into France, and when Churchil became prime minister, many Americans underwent a great change of sentiment.

On the basis of a manpower survey showing that one-fourth of America's unemployed pilots lived in California, Knight and his working partner, Homer Smith, interviewed pilots and flying students in Los Angeles, San Francisco and San Diego. Mindful of U.S. neutrality restrictions, they proceeded cautiously, relying largely on word-of-mouth communication and discreetly placed notices at key airfields. A typical bit of publicity was this item in an aviation magazine:

> Ernest L. Benway, Room 1101–2, Hollywood Roosevelt Hotel, is given as a contact if you wish to join the Canadian Air Force. He is described as an ex-American Airlines pilot whose home is in Glendale, Cal. He claims to have been a test engineer for a British aircraft firm as well.

Knight and Smith met with aviation people in major cities in other states and returned to Ottawa with a list of three hundred potential volunteers for the RCAF. Recruitment for the RAF was not yet on their program. Alerted that the War Department was becoming concerned about their activities, the two men went to Washington to assure leaders of the Army and Navy air forces that (1) there would be no luring away of pilots already in U.S. service; (2) there would be no soliciting of the airplane mechanics so badly needed at home; and (3) there was little likelihood anyway that the U.S. and Canada would be competing for the same men. The Canadians, for example, accepted fliers with 20-40 vision correctable with goggle lenses, while the U.S. insisted upon 20-20 vision. Canadian rules governing age limits and marital status were also more liberal.

Knight said later that General Henry H. Arnold, chief of the U.S. Army Air Corps, agreed that there was no problem and told him:

"According to the rules I'm working under, if a flying cadet gets fractious, goes in for low stunt flying, gets drunk even once, or we discover he's married, we've got to wash him out. If I was fighting a war, they're the kind I would want to keep. I wouldn't be surprised if a lot of our washouts look you up."

Advised that the FBI had no objections so long as pilots were not actually solicited, Smith decided that a sub rosa operation was no longer necessary. He opened a Knight Committee Headquarters in the Waldorf Astoria Hotel in New York City to respond to "unsolicited" applications for pilot interviews.

Knight described Smith in these terms:

"An out-sized individual who bubbled with enthusiasm and brimmed with energy, Homer was the happy executor of a personal family fortune that stemmed from the Imperial Oil Company of Canada. Handsome, likable, gregarious, Homer had lived for years in Palm Beach and New York, and seemed to know every VIP in the country. Best of all, he was a comrade in arms, having flown for the Royal Navy Air Service in World War I."

Other aides of Knight and Smith included Harold Fowler, a British ace of the First World War, and banker-businessman Pierpont "Pete" Hamilton, a nephew of J. Pierpont Morgan.

Pilot interest was so great that Knight Committee offices had to be set up in a dozen other cities. To be eligible, applicants had to have at least three hundred hours of certified flying experience, a Civil Aeronautics Authority license to pilot a two-place airplane, and the equivalent of a high school diploma. Men under twenty-one needed the consent of a parent or guardian.

"Busy as we were with our volunteers for Canada, we suddenly found ourselves with two other assignments," Knight later told Eagle Squadron members. "We began interviewing volunteers for the RAF and for the Ferry Service. We got into business for the RAF almost by accident."

The British Embassy in Washington had become unhappy with the tactics used by the Sweeny recruiting organization in the U.S. "Unlike the CK Committee, the Sweenys sought newspaper publicity, entertaining their volunteers at champagne parties and in nightclubs to the glare of flashbulbs," according to Knight. "The RAF decided to use our operation to screen

Sweeny's pilots. Homer Smith came up with the perfect solution: send the Sweenys to London immediately and let British censorship handle their publicity. Thus Colonel Sweeny, Robert Sweeny and a small contingent of fliers arrived in England in August and September, 1940. In October a discreet announcement reported Sir Archibald Sinclair as saying Group Captain Charles Sweeny had been made honorary commander of a newly formed Eagle Squadron with William E. G. Taylor, a former U. S. Navy pilot, as its head."

Why would American pilots choose to rush off from a nation at peace to risk their lives in a borrowed war? Two of the men who became Eagle aces in the RAF and who then went on to become two-star generals in the U.S. Air Forces—Chesley Peterson and Carroll "Red" McColpin—have voiced almost identical opinions.

"Six or seven of us volunteered together—and out of a sense of adventure, primarily," Pete Peterson said. "But everyone I knew in the group had a fairly deep innate sense of patriotism. We felt strongly that the United States was going to get into this war sooner or later. We knew what side the Americans would be on. And we were committed to the principles of the British and of the French, their allies at that time."

Red McColpin put it this way: "Most of us were in the 19–23 age bracket. At twenty-seven I was one of the oldest. Each of us had his own reason for joining. Some had washed out of flying school because of the rigid discipline. Others simply could not take the long routine in the U.S. services to become military pilots, when they were already experienced aviators.

"For myself, I reasoned that since I had flown most of my life and knew there was going to be a global war, why not start flying for England, a country that needed help and believed in our precepts of democracy, and one that would be our ally soon in any case? I knew America was on the verge of war. When the Battle of Britain started, I decided that I couldn't just stand by and do nothing."

Leo Nomis, son of a World War I pilot who became a noted Hollywood stuntman and was killed in 1932 doing aerobatics in a biplane, observed: "I think all of us, with very few exceptions, were simply adventurers and romanticists, and perhaps idealists. Few were patriots, but it probably worked into that later for those who got a real taste of what the war was, and were permitted the chance to view liberty from a distance."

Robert G. Patterson, who learned the fundamentals of flying by cadging rides with pilots while serving as a Navy aviation machinist mate and who mastered the fine points in light planes rented from civilian owners: "I joined the RAF not primarily for patriotic reasons. We all knew a war was coming. I used this as a quick way for some flying excitement."

Harold H. Strickland, at thirty-eight one of the eldest of the recruits: "We were all motivated by the thought of high adventure, the excitement of combat flying, and a desire to help the British. I hesitate to use the expression 'romance,' but it was there. It was the romance of highest adventure, a sort of trademark among fliers everywhere. Adventure could have been found in any of the British armed services where thousands of other Americans had volunteered, but we could *fly.*"

────

The greater the amount of flying experience, the easier it was for a man to get into the Eagle squadrons. For example, while still in his teens, McColpin designed and built his own airplane and then taught himself the basics of stick flying and aerial acrobatics. By the time he was twenty-two, McColpin considered himself a seasoned pilot, capable of flying anything that had wings.

Becoming a member of the Royal Air Force was a lot easier than McColpin expected. After the Air Ministry in Ottawa ascertained that he did possess a pilot's license, they immediately provided him and ten other Yankees with one-way ship tickets to London.

Cadman Padgett—a favorite Eagle amusement was the call, "Never fear when Padge is near"—had no difficulty either. He had learned to fly in Maryland in 1938 and a year later, with a friend, purchased a new J-4 Cub Coupe. They flew it frequently, especially to favorite places in Florida and Canada. An interview at the British Embassy in Washington started him off to one of the RAF-preparation centers, the Spartan School of Aeronautics in Tulsa, Oklahoma.

Ervin Lloyd "Dusty" Miller received his wings at a flying school in San Diego in 1937 while serving in the Navy as an enlisted man. After leaving the Navy, he had qualified as a commercial pilot in Sacramento. Vernon Parker was a civilian pilot at Del Rio, Texas. Barry Mahon had qualified as a private pilot at Santa Barbara, California, in 1938. George Sperry had what he considered a good job, "$40 a week and expenses, not a care in the world, free as a bird," assembling Aeronca training planes for a fixed-base operator at Oakland airport, test flying them, and delivering them to users throughout California. Harold Strickland trained in World War I Curtiss JN-4H biplanes at the Army Air Service Primary Flying School at Brooks Field, Texas, in 1925 when Charles Lindbergh was a cadet at the Advanced Flying School at nearby Kelly Field. He had logged more than twenty-one hundred hours of flying time when he quit a thoroughly enjoyable job as flight supervisor for the Indianapolis district of the CPTP—Civilian Pilot Training Program—of the Civil Aeronautics Authority.

The CPTP was a highly successful federal program—offering ground training at colleges and universities, along with flight training by established civilian instructors—designed to create a reserve of college-age pilots, both men and women. Many of the future Eagles became inducted into aviation through the CPTP: Don Young—later to become an airline jet pilot—at Kansas State College; Charles Cook, at California State Polytechnic, San Luis Obispo; Eric Doorly, at Rensselaer Polytechnic; Moran Morris and Edwin Dale "Jessie" Taylor, at Oklahoma's Southeastern State College; Bill Geiger, at California's Pasadena City College; James Gray at the University of California at Berkeley. Gray, who also became an airline pilot after the war, recalls that he had joined the Army Reserve Officers' Training Corps hoping to get into the Air Corps but was assigned instead to an ordnance unit. That was when he decided to join the RAF, although his military instructor had warned him that the average life span of a fighter pilot on combat duty was less than five weeks, whereas ordnance officers never got into combat and had the best deal in the armed services. Years later Gray reflected that "nearly all of my classmates who followed the instructor's advice died on Corregidor or in the Bataan Death March."

Several future Eagles failed their initial flight training courses but refused to give up their plans to become pilots. Edward Thomas Miluck, who had left the University of North Dakota and his basketball scholarship at the end of his junior year, was rejected by the Army Air Forces at Randolph Field in San Antonio but went on to join the RAF by way of Love Field in Dallas.

Strick Strickland's "hopes, dreams and plans for a flying future came to a crashing halt, at the most miserable moment in my entire life, or so I thought then," when he was dropped from Primary Flying School at Brooks Field after almost forty hours of dual and solo flying time for "lack of inherent flying ability—so I picked up the pieces of my world and went back to the Army Meteorological Service"—until his next opportunity came along.

Pete Peterson altered his birth records in 1939 to show that he was twenty-one instead of nineteen and thus eligible to serve in the Army Air Corps. Having dropped out of Brigham Young University in Utah at the end of his sophomore year, he took primary flight training at San Diego and then went to Randolph Field for basic instruction—and flunked out. "When I saw 'lack of flying ability' on my record I thought that maybe the instructors were right," he recalls. "I thought I would never step into an airplane again." His instructors could never have dreamed that this Idaho farm youth—"You could see the hay sticking out of his ears," one officer said—would become an Eagle ace with six enemy planes to his credit; would add three more kills after leaving the RAF for a total score of nine enemy aircraft destroyed, seven probably destroyed, and six damaged; would be shot down four times but would never remain long out of action; would become at age twenty-three the youngest full colonel in the U.S. Army Air Forces; and would attain the rank of major general.

After his failure at Randolph Field, Chesley Gordon Peterson went to Santa Monica, California, and found work with the Douglas Aircraft Company. Several other young men who had flopped at flying school worked there, and they formed a wash-out club with R. A. "Indian Jim" Moore, of Fort Worth, Texas, as president, and Peterson as vice president. The Los Angeles newspapers picked up the story. The cheerful young men were more amused than embarrassed by the publicity.

"Half a dozen of us at Douglas learned that Col. Charles Sweeny was at a Santa Monica hotel organizing a squadron to fight in France," Peterson recalled more than thirty-five years later. "I knew him by reputation. He was from my home state of Idaho, and he had a ranch in the Magna-Tooele area of northeastern Utah. In my little home town of Santaquin, Utah, there were two men who had joined the Spanish Civil War and fought in the Lincoln Brigade. They told us fascinating stories about Sweeny recruiting for the Spanish Loyalists."

The boys from Douglas met Colonel Sweeny and found him to be a very impressive man—ramrod straight, with a clipped voice and a prominent chin. Sweeny told them his liaison man in Los Angeles, J. Everett Weddle, would let them know when they would be needed. The signal from Weddle came in February, 1940.

They boarded the train and headed, they thought, for the war. "One of the group was from Chicago. "When we got there," Peterson recalls, "he decided to get off and say goodbye to his folks. He never came back to us. We could only assume that his parents intervened when they found out where he was going and called the FBI. At any rate, when we got to Windsor, Ontario, across the river from Detroit, we were met by two men. They read out our names, and when we responded they told us to get on the train going back to where we had just come from, or we would be thrown in jail. They were from the FBI. The Neutrality Act had just gone into effect, and they were really bearing down. One of them said that if they ever caught up with Sweeny he'd never get out of jail.

"When we got back to Los Angeles, Weddle told us the Colonel wanted to try a new plan. It would involve posing as Red Cross workers, and as civilians we would have to carry passports. Everything would have to be kept quiet. At the time it seemed rather ridiculous to do everything so furtively. Weddle would tell us to be at a certain place at a certain time. When we'd get there he would tell us to disappear and wait until we heard from him again.

"Finally, one night, at the back of a house in what was really a small shed, we met a man with a long beard, looking like Jeremiah straight out of the Bible. He was introduced to us as Sedley Peck, a Lafayette Escadrille ace who had remained in France after World War I and was working with the Red Cross in Paris. We were to go to France as ambulance drivers, then join the French Foreign Legion. It was strictly a sub rosa operation by Sedley, as an individual. It would certainly have placed the Red Cross under suspicion. In April or May, 1940, the plan fell through.

"The Colonel by this time had returned to Toronto and the original plan: to go by train straight through into Canada, be processed there, and then proceed on out by ship. We took the bull by the horns. At Chicago we separated and went by different trains, and crossed into Canada individually. Cars picked us up in Ottawa.

"Germany's invasion of France, May 10, changed our plans again. Now we were to go directly from Canada to England. In Canada we worked through Group Captain Banting, head of Empire training there. We were all lying like hell about the amount of flight time we had.

"Seven of us finally sailed out of Halifax on the *Duchess of Richmond* the first week in July. In addition to Jim Moore and me there were Byron Kennerly, Bud Orbison, Dean Satterlee, Jim McGinnis and Paul Anderson. Paul was to become one of our first casualties. He was the son of the chief of the San Francisco bureau of the FBI. He went into London one night and was attending the show at the Cafe de Paris, a huge nightclub, when a bomb demolished it, killing him and a large number of other people."

Tall, freckle-faced John A. "Red" Campbell, who started flying lessons at the age of fifteen with money earned working for a fixed-base operator at National City Airport near San Diego, applied to Knight Committee representative Benway in Hollywood but was sent home because he was only eighteen. Three days later, after his nineteenth birthday, his parents signed his application form. Reporting to the Polaris Flight Academy at Grand Central Airport in Glendale, California, he joined several future Eagles.

Early applicants to the Clayton Knight Committee had to follow procedures almost as devious as those imposed upon Sweeny candidates. Dusty Miller, responding to a small typewritten notice on a bulletin board at the Sacramento airport, telephoned and was told to come to a certain room in Oakland's Hotel Leamington without reporting to the reception desk.

When he knocked, the door opened only a crack. He was asked to identify himself, and then was admitted. After a flight test he was assigned to a refresher course at Spartan Aeronautics in Tulsa, his native city. Thirty civilian pilot volunteers were assembled there, amazed that in a neutral nation they were being paid by Britain and were flying U.S. Army trainers.

The final briefing at Tulsa concerned how to leave the United States legitimately. Miller was to notify his draft board in Sacramento that he intended to go to Canada for a week on a vacation. After crossing the border, he would be an RAF pilot officer and would not need to contact the draft board further.

George Sperry and Walter Soares were friends and fellow fliers at San Francisco Bay Airdrome at Alameda when they became interested in the RAF. Soares had learned to fly in 1938, in a 40-horsepower Taylorcraft. Sperry received his commercial license from the same instructor in 1940. Also in 1940,

Soares was landing his newly purchased Taylorcraft at Oakland Airport when a Navy fighter descended almost on top of him. The propeller blade missed Soares' head by about six inches. The Navy assumed responsibility and paid Soares enough to enable him to buy another plane. Soares chose to use the money for more flying time toward a commercial ticket.

Clyde Pangborn, one of the most widely known American pilots, announced that he was interviewing fliers at the Leamington Hotel. Sperry and Soares went to see him.

"For two hours Walt and I listened to Pangborn's tales of early-day barnstorming and of his famous flight from Japan to Washington, and his other exploits," Sperry says. "He gave us the soft sell on what was happening over the skies of Britain and France, and both Walt and I decided to give it a try.

"I told him I had had a mastoid operation in the past year, and this had kept me out of military flying. Pangborn replied that mastoids were a lot of malarkey and would not interfere with my flying for the RAF."

Soares was sent to Tulsa and Sperry to Dallas for training in British flying procedures. Sperry's RAF instructor for aerobatic flying at Dallas was Joe Ben Lievre, a French fighter pilot during World War I. Lievre had gone to Kelly Field in 1917 to teach cadets to fly Jennies and had stayed on in San Antonio after the war.

Sperry had the pleasure of Joe Ben's company in the air for several hours, with the instructor swearing in French all the while. Every maneuver had to be performed at minimum air speed for development of "feel," and every time Sperry stalled out of a slow roll his teacher would beat the side of the Fleet trainer with his fists, uttering unprintable French. Sperry finally satisfied him by becoming the only American who could perform a Cuban eight and remain in a stall throughout.

Harold Strickland recalled that when he took his primary flight training in a Curtiss Jenny in 1925, some fifteen years earlier than Soares or Sperry or the others, the exhaust stacks of the Hispano-Suiza engines made such a racket, and the plane's wires and struts whistled and vibrated so loudly, that hand signals were the only way to communicate in flight.

"When the instructor slapped his right cheek, that meant that the plane was skidding to the right, and when he clenched his left fist, that meant that he wanted some left rudder," Strickland said. "But when he tapped the top of his head he meant, 'For God's sake, let loose of the controls!' "

The recruits were advised to carry as few personal
effects as possible upon leaving the United States: one suit
or trousers and sport coat for daily wear; one pair of good
shoes and one pair of work shoes; three shirts, at least one
with white stiff or semistiff collar; four suits of underwear;
three suits of pajamas; four pairs of socks; one felt hat; one
pair of leather gloves; neckties, handkerchief, toilet articles
including soap; four medium sized bath towels; and one
suitcase or leather bag.

The trip out was sometimes melodramatic. One of the
groups traveling by rail to Canada included Bill Geiger, Bob
Mannix and Wally Tribken. Geiger recalled that his father
came out from New York to ride the train back with the would-
be Eagles:

"Bob Mannix had a very romantic and passionate goodbye
with a pretty brunette at the railroad station in Los Angeles and
came on board the train carrying an eight-by-ten picture of her.
Bob spent the next two days holding the photograph and moan-
ing and groaning about how much in love he was and how
terrible it would be to be separated from her. 'I don't know how
I'll be able to live without her,' he said.

"When we got to Chicago my father said, 'Bob, I can't
stand this any longer. I will pay for the telephone call you are
about to make to her. I hope this will help you survive for at
least the next few weeks.'

"Mannix looked at my father and said, 'Mr. Geiger, I can't
do that. I don't know where she lives. I don't even know her
last name.' "

Upon arriving at their station in Canada, eight startled
cadets were told by an RAF group captain, "His Majesty has
accepted you as sergeant pilots after you swear allegiance to
him."

Bob Reed, of Carroll, Iowa, looked around the room and
drawled, "Fellows, that bakery I have back home looks good
to me. I don't think I want to become a British subject."

Joe Durham announced that he felt the same way, because
he had a little golf course in Arkansas he intended to go back
to. They were all ready to go home until the group captain came
back to say that he had given the Americans some wrong
information and was very sorry. "You will be commissioned as
pilot officers rather than becoming sergeant pilots," he said.
"And you will not have to give up your American citizenship
unless you so desire."

A few of the Americans found their way into the Eagles without benefit of Sweeny or Knight. Richard Lear "Dixie" Alexander, a professional middleweight boxer and minor league baseball player, was one. He had been an outfielder in the Cincinnati Reds' farm system for eight years before finding out something that the pitchers knew six months after he started playing ball: he couldn't hit a curve ball.

Rejected by the Army Air Corps because he had only a high school education, Alexander enlisted in the RCAF in October, 1940, as an aircraftsman second class. He was told that if he passed the qualification tests he could enter pilot training in Canada. Even if he failed that course, he would be given a chance to qualify as an observer or gunner.

At Windsor, Ontario, the pay was about $2.25 a day. The Canadians were the highest-paid service in the world, including the RAF, throughout the war. When Alexander flew with the RAF as an RCAF sergeant and flight sergeant, he was paid substantially more than the pilot officers and flying officers of his squadron who were on the RAF payroll, which sometimes caused friction.

After a tour of duty as a private in the U. S. Army Infantry, after attending the University of Minnesota, after graduating from the Minneapolis Commercial Art Academy, and after punching cattle and herding wild horses in Montana, North Dakota and South Dakota, Bill Dunn became one of the first Americans to serve in World War II. When the war broke out in Europe, Dunn went to Vancouver, British Columbia, and joined the Seaforth Highlanders Regiment of the Canadian Army. He went to England with the Seaforth's 1st Battalion, a part of the 3rd Brigade of the 1st Canadian Infantry Division, serving as a mortar platoon sergeant. In early June of 1940, with the advanced party in France and the full regiment ready to follow to Brest, the German advance caused the evacuation of the British and Canadian forces back to England. There Dunn learned that the British Air Ministry, critically short of pilots, had invited Army men with five hundred or more hours' experience to apply for transfer to the RAF.

"I didn't have 500 hours—I had about 130 or 150," Dunn recalls, "but somehow the pencil slipped a little and my figure one looked like a five."

There was another American in the battalion, a corporal named Jimmy Crowley. Dunn and Crowley both put in for the RAF, were accepted and dispatched to flight training school.

At least Dunn no longer had to carry "that damn mortar all over the countryside."

W. Brewster Morgan, who had been taking flying lessons at Honolulu's John Rogers Airport, went to Shanghai in 1939 to begin premedical training at St. John's University. He arrived there the day war was declared between Great Britain and Germany. There was chaotic fighting in the streets between British and German troops and between the French and the Italians. Young Morgan planned to join the RAF but learned that the nearest recruiting center was in Chungking. He returned to his studies in Hawaii and, in the fall of 1940, enrolled in premedicine at Columbia University in New York City. Through an acquaintance, a nephew of P. M. Hamilton of the Knight Committee, he learned that he had logged enough flying time to qualify for flight training in Canada. Accordingly, he obtained a draft board permit to leave the country for seventeen days. Morgan went to the RCAF recruiting office in Montreal and signed up. Assigned initially to bombers, he talked his commanding officer into approving a transfer to Hurricane flight training.

——

The most unconventional approach to RAF Eaglehood was taken by Hubert Layton "Bert" Stewart, a boisterous, ebullient, funloving, foolhardy and sentimental furniture salesman from Raleigh, North Carolina. Stewart impulsively quit his job the day after Great Britain declared war on Germany, and rushed up to Ottawa to apply to the RCAF. He presented his logbooks, which had been doctored somewhat. Stewart's ardor cooled instantly when he was told that he must renounce his U.S. citizenship. He went home crestfallen. In May of 1940, however, after learning that the rules had been changed and that he need only promise to *obey* the Canadian government, he returned to Ottawa and enlisted as a sergeant pilot.

Stewart went to Camp Borden, Ontario, and started training in single-engine aircraft. The recruiting officer had assured him that in view of his considerable flying experience, he would be granted a commission on completion of the course. Under the impression that the surest way to get over to England was to become an instructor who could relieve fighter pilots needing rest, Stewart signed up for a training course in instruction. The teacher of the course promptly crushed Stewart's hopes. "There's little or no chance of you going to England," the instructor said. "You'll probably be in Canada instructing for the duration of the war."

Stewart protested to his commanding officer: "That's the reason I enlisted in the RCAF—to get over to England." The reply was, "Sorry, our hands are tied. We have orders from HQ. You will go to Moncton, New Brunswick, for twin-engine instructor training."

Fuming with frustration and resentment, Stewart was waiting at the Toronto station for his train when he struck up a conversation with two Americans who introduced themselves as Oscar Coen and Bill Hall. They had been accepted as RAF pilot officers and were on their way to Halifax.

"I talked it over with them, decided to hell with Moncton, and tossed my gear on the train to Halifax," Stewart says. "Then I simply went aboard ship with their group. I had no idea what the outcome might be, but I decided the chance was worth the try."

It turned out to be ridiculously easy because of the inefficiency of the embarkation authorities. After two days on the boat, the draft disembarked, and Stewart went with them to Debert, Nova Scotia, where they stayed for six days. While they were at this station, Stewart attended every parade without being detected.

When the draft was moved back to Halifax for embarkation, Stewart traveled with them again, making no attempt at concealment. During the trip to England he took an active part in the routine duties and even helped in the entertainment program. With his Southern drawl he was a master at telling jokes.

In England, Stewart accompanied the RAF group to its quarters at Uxbridge, near London. He didn't report in, but lagged back. Since he had not been paid, he borrowed money to get into London.

He went to the U.S. Embassy to ask what could be done to an American citizen who was in England without proper authority. He was told that he could be deported, but not back to Canada—only to the United States. With that information, he returned to Uxbridge and told the adjutant about his problems. The outraged RAF flight lieutenant took him to the station commander, a World War I pilot, Wing Commander Castings, who turned out to be sympathetic. Castings sent the young American to stay with a friend in a nearby town while the matter was sorted out.

In a letter dated March 4, 1941, to Headquarters, RAF Personnel Receiving Center, Uxbridge, Middlesex, written while he was in this temporary seclusion, Sgt. Pilot Stewart said:

"My sole ambition is to become a member of the American Eagle Squadron at present fighting in England. With this object in view, I earnestly plea for leniency in taking my above mentioned actions into consideration, and sincerely hope that it will be realized that they were carried out with the best of intentions and the heartfelt desire to do my part in ridding the world of this menace to democracy."

Ruffles and flourishes! Three days later Stewart was posted to the RAF Operational Training Unit at Sutton Bridge. Completing that course with above average marks, he was sent on to a newly established second Eagle Squadron, No. 121.

3

INTO
THE RAF

Royal Air Force records identify Gene Tobin, Andy Mamedoff and Shorty Keough as the original Eagles, the first to join the initial American unit, No. 71 Squadron, when it was formed in September, 1940.

Eugene Quimby Tobin and Andrew B. Mamedoff were flying friends at Mines Field, which would later become Los Angeles International Airport. Tall, red-haired Tobin, age twenty, had paid for flying lessons by working as a guide and messenger at the Metro-Goldwyn-Mayer film studio.

Mamedoff had grown up in Thompson, Connecticut. His family had fled from the Russian Bolshevist revolution. After performing at air shows on the Atlantic coast for several years, Mamedoff had acquired a small airplane. He tried to develop a charter service in the Miami, Florida, area and then transferred his one-plane operation to Southern California.

Learning through the Mines Field grapevine that a Colonel Sweeny was recruiting fighter pilots to fly for Finland for $100 a month, Tobin and Mamedoff volunteered and were accepted. Before they could even begin to make plans, however, the Finns were out of the war, and the two men were told they would fly instead for the French Armée de l'Air.

They were given train tickets to Montreal and instructions

to report at the Mount Royal Hotel. At the hotel's reception desk there were no letters, no messages. The desk clerk gestured toward a slightly built man in the lobby.

"He's been asking for messages, too," the clerk said. "Nothing for him, either."

When the Americans introduced themselves, the fellow stood up to his full height of four feet ten inches and identified himself as Shorty Keough, pilot and professional parachute jumper from Brooklyn, New York. He too was trying to join the French Air Force and was waiting for enlistment instructions. At fairs and air shows, he had bailed out of airplanes about five hundred times.

A messenger arrived belatedly with money and tickets for the night train to Halifax. On arriving in Halifax the men were to wait at the station until the crowd had thinned out. They were to talk about airplanes and flying loudly enough to be readily identified.

At Halifax the three Americans were led through back alleys to an office in a dark building on the waterfront. They were given twenty-five hundred francs each—the equivalent of about fifty dollars—and pink identity cards that omitted their nationality but showed they were en route to France.

After joining other American recruits in Paris, they quickly discovered that the French authorities had no time for them. Hitler's motorized columns had poured through the Low Countries and into France.

Tobin, Mamedoff and Keough spent four frustrating weeks in Paris and Tours, the city 150 miles south of Paris to which the French government had fled. At Tours two Czech pilots invited the three Americans to join them in a plan to steal two French Potez-63 twin-engine bombers and fly them to England. The plan misfired: both Czechs were killed by French guards, and the Americans narrowly escaped into a forest. They made their way by foot, by freight train, and by army truck toward the Spanish border. At St.-Jean-de-Luz they barely managed to jump aboard the last ship out of France—for the French had signed an armistice with Germany on June 22, 1940.

In London the British Air Ministry at first told the Americans that the RAF could not use them because they lacked combat training. Then the authorities reconsidered. On July 5, 1940, the three pilots were assigned to four weeks of indoctrination at No. 7 OTU, the Operational Training Unit at Ha-

warden, Cheshire. Along with other international candidates—
Poles, French, Belgians, South Africans, Australians, Canadians—they initially flew in the Miles Master advanced trainer
and then in the Supermarine Spitfire. Finally, they were sent to
609 Squadron at Warmwell in Dorset, across the Channel from
Cherbourg.

On July 10, 1940, the Luftwaffe opened a daylight bombing campaign against Britain, attacking shipping for the most
part. They stepped up the ferocity of their assault early in
August. Hitler then ordered a major offensive against England,
the Attack of the Eagles, to begin on August 13, *Adler Tag*—
Eagle Day. The plan was to destroy Britain's airfields with
daylight raids and to demolish her factories by night bombings.

On Eagle Day more than fifty German Stuka divebombers
attacked airdromes in the area of the Portland naval base.
Spitfires of 609 Squadron shot down five enemy planes. Two
days later, as a rerun of *Adler Tag,* an estimated two thousand
German aircraft hammered British targets. The RAF Fighter
Command flew nearly one thousand sorties, and the three
American pilots saw action for the first time. Tobin scored hits
on a Messerschmitt and saw it fall away out of control. Mamedoff and Keough fired at enemy aircraft but could make no
damage claims. For the day, the RAF counted forty-five German planes downed, at a cost of twenty-six British fighters.

Day after day, night after night, the German onslaught
continued. In one engagement Tobin attacked Me 110 fighters
escorting Junkers 88 bombers and was credited with destroying
two. The following day the cannon shells and machine gun
bullets of a German fighter smashed the tail wheel of Mamedoff's Spitfire and pierced the plane's armor plating and seat.
Mamedoff managed to land safely, uninjured except for severe
back bruises. In another encounter Mamedoff and Keough
combined the fire of their sixteen machine guns to shoot down
a Dornier bomber.

At dawn on September 7, 1940, the Germans sent aloft the
greatest aerial armada the world had yet seen. In the first major
attack on the capital itself, almost one thousand aircraft struck
at the heart of London, setting the city and its docks ablaze,
killing more than three-hundred persons, and injuring thousands. The Blitz was on, but the shift of the attack, from factories and airdromes to population centers, eased the pressure on
England's fighters and airfields.

On September 15, 1940, the Germans hurled their maximum aerial might against the British. The losses to the Luftwaffe were so punishing, however, that for the first time Germany lost the initiative. Hitler had to call off the planned invasion. England thereafter would celebrate September 15 each year as Battle of Britain Day.

On that day Gene Tobin shot down a Dornier bomber and probably destroyed an Me 109. Four days later he, Mamedoff, and Keough were off to Church Fenton to bring into being No. 71 Squadron. A new chapter of Anglo-American comradeship in arms was about to begin.

———

In the early part of its existence 71 Squadron was saddled with a command problem. For the first four months there was cause for debate among the Eagles as to who was in charge, the Englishman, Walter Churchill, or the American, William E. G. Taylor. Both held the rank of squadron leader. Even after Churchill's departure on January 23, 1941—"for treatment after an attack of neuralgia," the squadron logbook said—there were differences of opinion over whether Taylor or an American subordinate, Chesley Peterson, was actually running the unit.

There had been talk in the early summer of 1940 that William Mead Lindsley Fiske III, of London, a popular transplanted American sportsman with a number of highly placed British friends, might head up an interceptor squadron of U.S. pilots if one were formed. Fiske, the son of an international banker living in Paris, was a scratch golfer at Cambridge, had set a record for the Cresta bobsled run at Saint-Moritz, and had captained the team that won the Olympic bobsled championship at Lake Placid, New York, in the early 1930s. At the age of nineteen, he had driven the first Stutz car to be entered in the twenty-four-hour race at Le Mans.

"Billy Fiske should have been our first squadron leader, and it had all been arranged with the Air Ministry," Bobby Sweeny recounted. "Unfortunately, he was killed—the first American to die in active service against the Nazis."

Charles Sweeny agreed: "Undoubtedly, Billy Fiske had all the qualities of leadership which would have made him an outstanding officer if he had lived. I talked over with him my ideas for an Eagle Squadron and he was very receptive."

Fiske entered the RAF Volunteer Reserve in March, 1940, and joined the 601 City of London Squadron in July. On August 17, 1940, as he returned to Biggin Hill from one of his first operational flights, a German fighter set his plane afire, and he was fatally burned. Fiske was buried in St. Paul's Cathedral in London, where a memorial plaque says simply, "An American citizen who died that England might live."

Bill Taylor had been an ensign in the U.S. Navy and was a first lieutenant in the U.S. Marines on vacation in England in September, 1939. Four days before the outbreak of war, he received permission to join the Royal Navy for which he flew from the British aircraft carriers *Glorious* and *Furious* in operations off Norway.

Taylor was in Washington in the spring of 1940, temporarily attached to the British Naval Attaché and to the British Purchasing Commission in New York City, when he made the acquaintance of Bobby Sweeny and Col. Charles Sweeny. The Sweenys decided that the tall, aristocratic-looking and highly qualified flier would be ideal to command an all-American RAF unit. Bobby's brother, Charles, who was in London, concurred.

The three men went to England by ship together. Taylor recalled that in front of newsreel cameras at a large press "do" at Northolt airdrome he was transferred to the RAF and made a squadron leader. Bobby Sweeny was commissioned a pilot officer and given the title of adjutant of 71 Squadron, and Sweeny's uncle was made a group captain and appointed honorary commander.

According to Taylor, "The three of us went to pay our respects to the Air Officer Commanding 12 Group, in the Midlands, where 71 Squadron was forming at Church Fenton. The AOC was Air Vice-Marshal Trafford Leigh-Mallory, and he received us coolly.

"He said he was very strongly opposed to having a squadron of Americans. He had had experience with them in the First World War and found that individually they were charming, but as a group they were completely undisciplined. I kept my mouth shut except to say that the squadron's formation was already a *fait accompli.*"

Taylor and Bobby Sweeny joined 71 Squadron at Church Fenton on October 4, 1940, only to discover that Squadron Leader Churchill and Flying Officer Tann, both British, had arrived five days earlier and had taken office as squadron commander and squadron adjutant, respectively. Taylor said he was not disturbed by the apparent duplication in command, since it was natural to have RAF officers indoctrinate Americans. Almost at once Taylor was sent to RAF Station Hawarden for

Spitfire training. Bobby Sweeny settled in at 71 as assistant adjutant.

By the time Taylor returned from training, 71 Squadron had made its move to Kirton-in-Lindsey. Churchill was still firmly in charge. Among his qualifications were that he had commanded a squadron in the desperate air combat over France before the Dunkirk evacuation, had organized two squadrons of Polish fighter pilots for the RAF, and had been decorated with the Distinguished Service Order and the Distinguished Flying Cross.

Bored by his role as a figurehead CO and skeptical over whether Churchill was teaching the pilots manners, discipline, or fighter tactics, Taylor went to Fighter Command and asked to be sent to "one of the best fighter squadrons in 11 Group."

With Taylor posted temporarily to RCAF Squadron 242 for further training under the famous Douglas Bader, Pete Peterson became the tacit spokesman for the Americans. In Peterson's opinion, "Churchill was designated 71 squadron commander from the very beginning, on the reasoning that if anyone could get along with the Poles he could get along with the Americans. Group Headquarters decided to go with a known quantity, Churchill. This left Bill Taylor a bit out in the cold. We were told, 'You now have two squadron commanders,' but we knew who the real CO was. Bobby Sweeny's position in the squadron was just about as tenuous as Taylor's. We already had an adjutant when Sweeny arrived. And there was no such title in the RAF as the one he took, assistant adjutant."

Taylor returned to 71 Squadron a second time and found the command situation unchanged. "I was still a figurehead in the squadron, a really infuriating position to be put in," he says. "I had heard that a number of Polish, Czech and French squadrons had been formed but actually had British CO's. I finally went to the Air Ministry and saw Balfour, the Parliamentary Under Secretary of State for Air. I complained bitterly about what I termed a double cross. I reminded him that I had been told I was to be given the squadron, and so had the press. I said I wanted sole command of it or permission to return to the Royal Navy. I don't know what wheels turned after that, but soon AVM Leigh-Mallory was transferred south to 11 Group, and Churchill was made a wing commander and disappeared. I was finally CO."

The squadron was declared operational shortly after Taylor took command, late in January, 1941. Its first operational patrol, in foggy weather on February 5, was tense but uneventful, as were those that followed almost daily. The pilots, flying in relays, concentrated on covering Britain's shipping lifeline—convoys moving into and out of the English Channel. Usually the weather was atrocious, and the flying became dull and monotonous. Even if visibility conditions were near minimums at the RAF fields, it was essential to maintain an air guard against German fighters, bombers and torpedo-carrying aircraft. Convoy routes had to be kept open, especially in poor weather. Seen from over the water in clouds or haze, the horizon line became deceptive or nonexistent, and the risk was great. The pilots knew that war was a trade-off and that they were expendable in comparison with high priority cargo vessels and crews.

At the same time they found humor in their work. Leo Nomis tells this story about Mike "Moe" Kelly—J. M. Kelly, of Oakland, California—who was not yet nineteen when he volunteered for RAF duty:

> On Moe's first convoy patrol right after we arrived, the weather was foul—rain and bad visibility, as usual. Kelly had heard and absorbed all the horror stories at OTU about the Hun jumping on one suddenly out of sun and clouds, and on this first patrol he was overly imaginative, wary and nervous.
>
> So it was that after about a half hour of patrolling, with Kelly staring big-eyed at the surrounding overcast, expecting a black-crossed monster at any second, the rain condensation began to leak slightly through the canopy. Kelly was unaware of this, in his neck-craning peering position, until a drop of ice water hit him on the back of the neck, the only bare section between the bottom of his helmet and his Mae West.
>
> What followed was told forthrightly by Kelly after the patrol returned (he never concealed anything) and was substantiated by the Section Leader, who had the hell scared out of him. In Kelly's expectant mind, the drop of cold water instantly became a white-hot machine gun bullet. He was sure that what he feared—a surprise attack—had occurred. A Jerry had got him.
>
> Assuming that the water traveling down his spine was blood, Moe proceeded to take on all the actions of a riddled man. His finger flipped open the R/T (radio-telephone) switch, and he shrieked convincingly that he was hit.
>
> This type of call coming out of radio silence has a strangely unsettling effect upon others who are on the same channel. Needless to say, the Section Leader went through agonizing stick-racking moments before it was discovered that they were surrounded by nothing more than falling rain. Kelly, somewhat surprised that he hadn't died yet and fascinated at the curiously

painless development, was brought out of his theatrical state at last by more water coming through the canopy and making the obvious evident.

Moe told the story with gusto back on the ground, amid much laughter. He was a light-hearted and happy-go-lucky boy. How he survived the war no one will ever know.

The risks usually presented a far grimmer aspect. During a patrol on February 9 Bud Orbison apparently became disoriented in thick clouds and spun in from about four thousand feet. Six days later Shorty Keough failed to return from a scramble in which a three-plane section had been ordered aloft after a warning of possible attack. A coast guard unit found the tops of some size five flying boots.

"Nobody but little Shorty could wear such small boots," the Ops Record Book noted. "There can be little doubt that Shorty's plane dived into the sea at a great speed and that he was killed instantly."

Pete Peterson commented, "Shorty had fairly normal legs, but his trunk was so short he had to sit on two pillows in order to see over the windscreen. Apparently on his last flight he forgot to turn on his oxygen and blacked out simply for lack of air."

Three fatal accidents in forty days of no combat was not an encouraging sign. Reports reached the squadron that Henry H. "Hap" Arnold, commanding general of the U.S. Army Air Corps, had visited Sholto Douglas in London and had been told by the Fighter Command's leader that 71 Squadron's performance was unsatisfactory.

According to Peterson, "We learned later that Douglas had told General Arnold that we were prima donnas, and that Arnold had replied that if we did not show improvement very soon, the RAF should consider releasing us and sending us home.

"Some of the fellows took a bit of umbrage at this, but I put it to them that if the Old Man thought we were prima donnas, why, let's be the best prima donnas there are. I told them this was the highest compliment the commanding officer of the U.S. Army Air Corps could pay us, because it meant that literally we were the best—and we knew it. Our performance later in the U.S. Fourth Fighter Group certainly proved that prima donnas can last out a whole war and still be best.

"General Arnold's position regarding Americans serving with the RAF as a squadron can be rationalized from his World

War I experience. He was never a tactical pilot, but he had seen American pilots in that war seconded to French and British squadrons. It took a good deal of time for the American squadrons in that war to be formed as a unit, and meanwhile the American officers flying with the French and the British, especially in the Lafayette Escadrille, stole the glory away from what was then known as the Army Air Service. I don't believe General Arnold liked that very much, and on this basis he formed his opinion as to American volunteers within the RAF."

Going over the head of 71 Squadron Leader Churchill, Peterson went to see Air Marshal Hugh Saunders, who had succeeded Leigh-Mallory as 12 Group Commanding Officer. He told the Air Marshal that the Eagle squadron was becoming demoralized. "You will have to send us to 11 Group and let us start fighting." Shortly thereafter, on April 5, the squadron moved to Martlesham Heath in 11 Group and started functioning as an operational unit.

The first taste of battle for Eagle squadron pilots—and it was barely that—occurred on April 13, 1941. Jim McGinnis and Sam Mauriello pursued a Junkers 88 bomber which eluded them in clouds.

There followed an unfortunate incident described in the squadron's logbook in this wry note:

> Squadron scramble during evening. P/O Alexander has probably drawn first blood for the squadron and P/O J. Flynn has the distinction of being the first shot down in combat. He landed his shot-up plane near Manston, as he was uninjured.

The terms "first blood" and "first shot down in combat" were applied sarcastically. Near Calais James Keith Alexander fired at a Messerschmitt 109 that was pursuing John F. Flynn. Alexander damaged not only the German plane but Flynn's Hurricane as well. The 109 flew off, trailing heavy smoke. Flynn managed to struggle across the Channel to a safe landing.

There was a derisive comment in some of the other squadrons that at long last the "bloody Yanks" had shot down a plane—one of their own. Another Eagle, Wendell Pendleton, later put the incident in better perspective in a *New York Times Magazine* article.

> A Messerschmitt shot past and John Flynn couldn't resist tailing him. Instantly another Messerschmitt was on his tail.
> Alexander turned out of formation then, to protect Flynn,

and tailed the Messerschmitt, and another Jerry promptly followed Alexander. Flynn used his head, however, and went to circling. Or maybe it was the Messerschmitt ahead of Flynn that started to circle.

Anyhow, there was a gigantic merry-go-round in the sky there for a time, Flynn chasing Jerry, Jerry chasing Flynn, Alexander chasing the Jerry that was chasing Flynn, and another Jerry chasing Alexander—five planes altogether playing ring-around-a-rosy.

Flynn's plane was hit at least 130 times by machine gun bullets and cannon shells. His wing ammunition chambers were exploded. He got a bit of shrapnel in an arm. Despite this, he managed to glide back across the Channel to safety and was back with us as good as ever within a month.

Actually, the first Eagle to fire his guns at the enemy—even before the Alexander-Flynn mixup—was nineteen-year-old Gregory Augustus Daymond, the baby of 71 Squadron, who had been flying since he was thirteen. Gus Daymond sighted his first German plane, a Dornier bomber, a few days after McGinnis and Mauriello had their brief glimpse of the enemy. Daymond fired and missed as the Dornier dived. Already at full throttle, Gus applied emergency boost, but nothing happened, and the Dornier darted away.

Back at home base, Daymond discovered that the emergency power switch had been wired shut. A red-faced crew chief explained to the irate pilot that the Hurricane usually was flown by Mike Kolendorski, a fiery Pole from California whose hatred for the Germans was so great that he frequently used boost override to take off wildly after false targets. "We got so tired of having to do major maintenance on the engine after every one of Mike's sorties that we wired the boost switch closed," the mechanic said. "We forgot to remove the wire this time."

About a month later the twenty-six-year-old Kolendorski allowed his lust for Nazi blood to cloud his judgment one last time. After he was reported missing over the North Sea, his body washed ashore at Rockanje, south of the Hook of Holland.

"Mike broke formation to go after sucker bait," reported Peterson. "It was our first time out over the Channel, and the weather was cloudy. It was evident that he got trapped and shot down. We confirmed this later through German sources. He never got to use his parachute, but crashed in his plane.

"I had always maintained that Mike would be the first in the squadron to win the DFC, or the first to be killed. He was the first Eagle to be killed by enemy action."

The transfer to Martlesham Heath did not soften the impact of the unfavorable remarks made by Hap Arnold and Sholto Douglas. In fact, the members of 71 Squadron remained stunned by them. They felt that after interminable weeks of training and flying routine missions, they at last had learned quite well how to handle their equipment and engage an enemy that had been difficult to find. Bill Taylor in particular, now that he finally had full command, was determined to whip 71 Squadron into shape. Most of the pilots shared his feelings.

"I knew that Winston Churchill had overridden the Air Staff in the first place to have the squadron formed for propaganda purposes, and I knew that somehow I *had* to make it a good squadron," Taylor said thirty-five years later. "Its failure would have reflected on us all as Americans, would have made the other fighters sneer at us, and not the least, would have done my reputation no good. So I bore down on the lads hard, and I knew what I was doing, and it worked.

"We were to report the squadron at readiness at thirty minutes before first light every morning. I told all the pilots I wanted them to come to dispersal shaved, buttons shined, uniforms pressed, shoes or boots shined and inside their pant legs, inspect and run up their planes, and report at readiness forty-five minutes before first light.

"There was a loud moan, and ten days of griping, until the boys saw the results. No. 71 Squadron had all sections lighted on the readiness boards at Group and Fighter Command Ops rooms *every* morning while the rest of the boards were still black. It didn't take very long for the word to trickle back that 71 appeared to be the keenest squadron in 11 Group."

Taylor said the pilots began to take a new interest in themselves, their appearance, their flying. "They had heard that fighter pilots in the First World War always left the top button of their tunics unbuttoned, so all of the Eagles started doing it. I stopped that and told them they would be entitled to unbutton when they had shot down their first plane. More grousing. I am sure they unbuttoned every time they went to London but not when I was there."

A disturbing number of flying accidents in bad weather soon made it obvious that most of the pilots had had no training in blind flying. "I requested and got a competent blind-flying instructor to go over all of my pilots. The accidents stopped, except when one of the pilots would disobey orders and try to do a victory roll over the station—even though neither he nor anyone else saw any real action until after I was detached—and fly into the ground. So we never did get up to full strength in my day."

Members of 71 Squadron asked permission to fly "rhubarb" low-level strafing missions, as other squadrons were doing. Taylor refused, explaining that he wanted the squadron to have a full complement of pilots first. "At least one of my pilots went to Walter Churchill to complain, then Churchill to Group," Taylor said. "Group sent a group captain over to talk to me. I think he just wanted to size me up. About a month later I was called over to 11 Group to see Leigh-Mallory, its new commander. He told me that I had overrun the number of operational hours permitted, between my Navy and RAF time, and that at thirty-six I was too old to command a fighter squadron. Group had decided to make me a wing commander, he said, and put me in charge of a fighter training unit.

"From my own perhaps not very bright point of view, I had had the RAF. Both the U.S. and British navies had asked me to come back. I received my American commission first. I was back in the USN again.

"It isn't very pleasant to make everyone think you are an s.o.b. But before I left 71 Squadron I felt that if it wasn't the best one in Fighter Command, it was at least the third best. I was very, very proud of it. And my heart was broken when it was taken from me, whether or not it was my time to go."

With Taylor's departure, on June 7, 1941, the RAF restored 71 Squadron to the command of an Englishman—Squadron Leader Henry de Clifford Anthony "Paddy" Woodhouse. Far from penalizing Peterson, a mere pilot officer, for having been so bold as to appeal directly to the 12 Group Command for the squadron's transfer to 11 Group, Fighter Command rewarded the aggressive Utah towhead with a double promotion to flight lieutenant, the equivalent of a jump from U.S. second lieutenant to captain.

In May, 1941, less than a month before the change in command, No. 71 traded in its Mark I Hurricanes for the more powerful, more versatile Hurricane IIA. The pilots were delighted with the newer plane's improved maneuverability. It had an eight-hundred-foot turning radius at ten thousand feet, considerably better than that of the then-current German fighters, and it could take off and land in extremely short distances. It carried the same armament as the Mark I—eight machine guns capable of fourteen seconds of continuous fire. The Eagles found it to be a sturdy and extremely stable gun platform.

At Martlesham Heath 71 operated as a lone squadron and had it good for two months. As the Eagles flew out on solitary sweeps, both their performance and their morale began to improve. The Americans now could work as part of a wing.

In June 71 was sent to North Weald just north of London, near Epping, flying as one of the three squadrons in that wing for the rest of the year.

The Squadron's Operations Record Book for June 22, 1941, said of the transfer to North Weald: "Rather a disappointing move with regard to buildings and equipment, but apparently quite a good station."

All of the pilots exulted over the change. Now they would be in the center of things, flying wing to wing with their hard-pressed, hard-working comrades of the all-British squadrons.

4

SQUADRONS NO. 121 AND 133

Eagle Squadron No. 121 came into being on May 14, 1941, at Kirton-in-Lindsey, the base which No. 71 Squadron had vacated six weeks previously. There were now too many American pilots in England wanting to fly fighters to be accommodated in a single squadron.

No. 71 Squadron had taken the motto "First from the eyries." For its badge it displayed the American bald eagle bedecked with three nine-pointed stars symbolizing the states from which its earliest members had come.

No. 121 selected the slogan "For liberty" and used an American Indian warrior's head with feathered bonnet as a badge.

Taking care to avoid the kind of command confusion that had caused difficulties at 71 Squadron, the RAF chose Peter Powell, one of the heroes of the Battle of Britain, to manage the new American unit. Squadron Leader Robin Peter Reginald Powell had shot down seven German planes and shared in the destruction of two others in the first seven months of 1940.

Two particularly well qualified British flight lieutenants were selected as Powell's deputies. They were Hugh Kennard, brought in from Squadron 306, and Royce Clifford Wilkinson, who had held a similar post at 71 Squadron since its founding.

Wilkinson, a former sergeant pilot, had shot down nine enemy planes and shared credit with five other pilots for destroying two more in combat over France from May to October, 1940. He had been decorated with the Distinguished Flying Medal and bar.

Fighter Command declared No. 121 operational on July 21, only two months after its founding. The three Englishmen in charge of the new Eagle squadron could look back on major changes. Less than a year previously the RAF Hurricane pilots fighting in France had been ordered to fly all of their serviceable planes back to England. Wilkinson was to have been evacuated by army truck because the only Hurricane remaining at his base was considered out of commission. One end of its two-bladed propeller had been shot off, leaving it a foot short. Wilkinson decided that the Germans were so close his only hope for escape was by air, so he sawed twelve inches off the other blade and flew the plane to Britain.

After the Dunkirk evacuation there had been a lull in fighter activity from the time of the French appeal to Germany for an armistice in mid-June until the start of the Luftwaffe's massive daylight offensive in mid-August. The Battle of Britain was won in large part because the Powells and Kennards and Wilkinsons of Fighter Command fought defensively. Their main purpose was to seek out and destroy enemy bombers.

Then, in September, when Germany's plan for an invasion had clearly been foiled, the enemy launched the Blitz—night-long bombing attacks on London and other major population centers. This offensive reached its climax on the night of December 29, 1940, when incendiary bombs burned out a large part of London. Not until May, 1941, did the broad-scale nightly bombings of British cities come to an end.

To prepare to take on their share of the fighting, the American pilot officers went through tough indoctrination at specialized British flying schools, called Operational Training Units or OTUs, before being posted to operational assignments. Joe Durham, the Arkansas golf pro, and Eddie Miluck, the North Dakota basketball star, had special memories of a superlative instructor at OTU No. 56 at Sutton Bridge, Francis Joseph Soper. In eight days of action in May, 1940, Soper, a former sergeant, had shot down ten enemy planes. Before his death in October, 1941, Soper was to raise his score to 14 1/2.

"Soper quickly recognized my need for special training, and eventually he shaped me into an acceptable fighter pilot,"

Durham recalls. "The six weeks of flying training that I received under the constant surveillance of this great man was responsible for my survival in scores of later aerial combats."

Miluck called Soper, then twenty-two years old, "the marshal from Budenny" because of his huge, red, handlebar moustache. At their first meeting, the instructions from Soper were: "See the crew chief, read up on the instructions for the Hurricane, and when you feel you've got it, try some circuits and bumps. See me here when you get back—and for God's sake, don't prang it!" "Circuits and bumps" are what American pilots call "touch-and-goes," or practice takeoffs and landings.

Barry Mahon, of Santa Barbara, was mightily impressed upon arriving at the OTU mess to meet "Joe Pak, flight lieutenant, double DFC, in his early twenties and a veteran of several years of combat."

"The British wasted no time in their training program," Mahon said. "The very next day we were given a few hours of ground school and then an exhibition of the operation of the flaps and landing gear on a Hurricane that had been jacked up for that purpose.

"Next a couple of trips around the field in a Miles, and then there it was—a Hurricane that looked forty-five feet tall, ready to take me up alone. Just climbing up to get to the cockpit was frightening, but I figured that if they thought I could fly it, I guess I could. So with a deep breath I pushed the switch, and the Rolls-Royce engine coughed into life. The engine was a giant compared with any I had tried before. It even had torque while I was taxiing.

"Surprisingly, it flew exactly like the Spartan Executive with just a little more problem on takeoff. The early Hurricane model had a peculiar hydraulic landing-gear lever located, unfortunately, at the bottom of the airplane. This entailed changing hands on the stick to use it, and also putting your head out of sight in the cockpit. It must have been amusing to watch.

"Coming back on the landing approach, again there was the routine with the hydraulic system to get the wheels down, and then after the selector was moved, to get the right degree of flaps. I took no chances and set everything up on my way out from my turn on to final, and came in to what surprised me as probably the best landing I had ever made. From then on I was hooked."

Shine Parker received forty minutes of dual instruction in the Miles Master the day he arrived at Sutton Bridge and then was sent up for an hour of practice landings and takeoffs. The Master, at 170 mph the world's fastest trainer, was for all practical purposes a Hurricane fighter.

"The next morning I looked forward to more instruction," Parker says. "Instead, we were assigned high-altitude exercises in the Hurricane I with a 1,250-horsepower Rolls-Royce engine, quite a jump from Cubs. These we flew for the rest of the course.

"The Hurricanes were in such poor mechanical shape and so obsolete they were unfit for combat. We lost eight of our student class to accidents—four Americans, two British, one Free French and a South African."

As had been the case in 71 Squadron, pilots of 121 were disappointed with Fighter Command's order of priorities on equipment. Of fifteen war-worn Hurricane I fighters initially assigned to the new squadron, only six were serviceable. After seven weeks 121 finally received what it considered suitable aircraft, nine Hurricane IIBs. Primarily, 121 flew convoy patrols and provided the basic protection for the city of Hull—"a lot of flying, not much shooting."

As the RAF struggled in the late autumn of 1940 to recover from its Battle of Britain losses, it started sending small-scale patrols over the German-occupied territory of northern France. At first these patrols consisted of a few bombers accompanied by one or more squadrons of fighters. In the early summer of 1941 increasingly powerful fighter formations gave the RAF a fair degree of air supremacy over much of northern France. British bombers now were able to make effective daylight attacks on harbor installations, docks, power plants, and factories linked to the German war effort. Thus it was that in 121 Squadron's first enemy contact, on August 8, Sel Edner and Jack Mooney damaged a Junkers 88 bomber.

If the tide was turning, the Eagles, including Carroll Warren McColpin, were not surprised: "From the first until the last day that I was in England, I knew that the British were going to win the war," McColpin wrote thirty-five years after he had donned the sky blue uniform of the RAF—the special uniform with the Eagle shoulder insignia and the initials *ES*.

"Why did I know this? They told me so."

The sandy-haired, out-going young man from Buffalo, New York, who had built his own airplane and taught himself to fly, had arrived by ship in Liverpool with ten other Americans in the midst of a German bombing raid. Overhead, the misty afternoon sky became filled with whirling black specks and small ominous clouds of flak. The ground shook as bomb after bomb found its mark. The horizon became singed with red and orange hues as city blocks erupted in fire and smoke.

"What we wanted to see," Red McColpin later wrote, "were the flaming remnants of German planes twisting down from the sky. We were not disappointed. We saw several shot down by Spitfires and another by artillery."

McColpin trained for five weeks at 56 OTU, Sutton Bridge, and then was offered the posting to 71 Squadron that routinely was made available to American fighter pilots. He refused it. He had known too many of that squadron's pilots in the States. The publicity they had received was unacceptable. Furthermore, 71 Squadron was not yet in combat.

McColpin was sent instead to the No. 607 (County of Durham) Squadron, Auxiliary Air Force, that had just been moved to Wick, Scotland, to protect the Scapa Flow Naval Base. Among the pilots in the conglomerate 607th were two Americans, two Frenchmen, two Norwegians, a Czech, a Pole, an Australian, and a South African.

During the month McColpin spent with 607, Rufolf Hess, Hitler's private secretary, was captured nearby after he had bailed out of his plane. His mission: Anglo-German peace.

"Two of us pilots from 607 and two from another squadron were up that night," McColpin was to say. "Both of us from 607 fired at enemy aircraft, but we made no claims. Later we learned that it was Hess' plane we had attacked, but we never found out whether it had been shot down or he had bailed out."

McColpin's first taste of action with the Scottish squadron came on a reconnaissance patrol when he broke out of a cloud layer at about twenty-eight thousand feet and found himself within a few feet of ramming a German Dornier 17 medium bomber. No shots were fired.

His first shots in anger were against a Ju 88 one dark night at fifty feet over the water of Scapa Flow harbor. He claimed no damage of that plane. McColpin recounts, "It was rugged flying. We flew without Mae Wests because there weren't enough to go around. The RAF did have some Mae Wests down south but not enough to equip people where we were. We had some radar but we did not have radar control. We were never allowed to talk on the air. We had parachutes but we only wore them in good weather; usually we folded them up and sat on them. We never flew high, and we knew that if we had to bail out we would not live." The water was too cold for the fliers to survive any bail-out even if they carried the proper equipment. They flew patrols all night in ice and snow. Pilots who were lost—four of them in the month McColpin was there—were never located.

McColpin joined 121 Eagle Squadron the week it was formed. He recalls the experience:

> In the months that followed the activation of 121 Squadron the terms "liberty" or "pass" became obscure. When you weren't flying, you were getting ready to. Should the weather turn lousy, you stayed put on alert and used all of your spare time planning for the next mission.
>
> It seemed a little incredible, at times, that I was in a foreign country and fighting a war very far from America's shores. Sometimes when I look back on my first flights with the Eagles, I wonder how I managed to survive.
>
> In those days we did not have radar and we could not use radio because of regulations on silence. The most elaborate navigational aids were buoys used to direct shipping in rivers, harbors and channels. Night operations were a gruelling test of navigational abilities, especially flying only 50 to 100 feet above the ocean waves.
>
> There are many words to describe alert duty. After a while, I could count every board and nail in our alert shack. For the first eight months, I never knew what it was like to have time off.
>
> As time moved on a pilot began to think of himself as invincible. "Maybe everybody will get clobbered but me," he would say to himself. "I have this fighting down to a science."
>
> Pulling alert was, for all practical purposes, like an actor waiting to go on stage, a fireman waiting for the alarm bell. For us, it was waiting to go on a defensive or offensive mission.
>
> If you flew offensive sorties you were given a briefing and told where you were supposed to be and when. You were also told whether you would be flying rodeo, fighter sweep or rhubarb.
>
> In rodeo, the trick was to draw as many enemy fighters up as possible, regardless of the odds, as a diversion for friendly bombers. At first contact everyone broke from the formation into individual combat on his own initiative and formed a beehive—a vertical air space from 30,000 feet to the deck containing both enemy and friendly fighters.
>
> Going the escort route for the bombers was considered somewhat routine. It was like a policeman protecting a caravan of trucks from being robbed.

Of all the missions, the rhubarb was the most fun. Flying a few feet off the ground, you shot up railroads, troops, tanks, ships or anything else of military value.

An offensive alert was rough on the nerves because of the waiting. On the other hand, defensive duty usually demanded more skill than flying combat missions over France, Belgium or Holland. You never knew when or where the enemy was going to strike. You had to move at lightning speed. Weather and darkness were a big factor.

One early morning the Luftwaffe attacked York, 40 miles from the 121 Squadron base. Two pilots were on five-minute alert. The rest of us were on standby, sleeping in our barracks. It took less than 10 minutes from the sounding of the alert for 12 of us to be in the air and on our way.

In those days it was standard procedure to be wheels-up within five minutes after the first gong. The Eagles usually did it in less than three. At one time our base held the record scramble time of one minute and 20 seconds flat.

Upon arriving in our designated area, we used the coordinated efforts of British artillery and their searchlight system to find our birds of prey. Before dawn, we had shot down two Junkers 88s and possibly two Dornier 17s.

In the dark it was great sport shooting at and being fired upon by the enemy. If you couldn't see too well at night, you were in deep trouble.

Sometimes I get to thinking about my first kill, not because I had taken the life of another human being but because it reflected how inexperienced we were in warfare and violence.

My reaction to the encounter, where luckily I was the winner, was much like that of one of my buddies, Flying Officer Weak-Eyes Anderson, so named for the thick lenses he wore.

On landing after his first contact with the enemy, Newt Anderson jumped from his cockpit and hurried to look at the damage done to his aircraft. Surveying some rather large bullet holes near the tail section, he blurted, "You know what that damn fool was trying to do? He was trying to kill me!"

Two colorful individuals in 121 Squadron were Joe Durham, the long, tall drink of water from Fort Smith, Arkansas, and Fred Scudday, a chubby, dark-haired, good-natured Texan.

Scudday had a reputation for Southern lethargy because he would often sit in the sun or in the ready room with his hat tipped over his eyes. But he changed completely when he was in the air and became a first-class fighter pilot. He and Durham were very close buddies.

In their first crack at the enemy as a team, Durham and Scudday had been scrambled and directed across the mouth of the river Humber and out over the North Sea. They felt some disappointment when a long convoy of merchant ships came into view. It looked like another boring convoy patrol—until they noticed the gun flashes from one of the accompanying destroyers.

Scudday shouted, "Tallyho! Bandits at two o'clock, on the deck." Durham looked in the right direction and saw the black and white crosses and clear outline of a Ju 88. His account of that battle was that "the pilot must have spotted us before we discovered him. He had turned away from his attack on the ships and was flying out to sea. I gave Fred a few seconds after he started his dive to attack, to make certain he would be clear of my guns. Then I made my pass.

"Scudday's first burst of fire tore away the top gun turret of the bomber and caused the port engine to explode in a ball of smoke and flame. There was no question that the Junkers was already mortally wounded when I pressed the firing button for my guns and added the *coup de grace*. As I made my climbing turn to rejoin Fred I noticed that the enemy bomber had vanished into the sea, without a trace."

The two pilots had drifted somewhat north of their original course. Base Operations messaged them a "good show" and ordered them home. They were now flying directly toward the balloon barrage protecting the city of Hull. Durham was getting uneasy about it and was wondering why Scudday had not changed course to fly around the city when the big Texan called Base Ops and asked for a homing. After a brief pause Base Ops called in an excited voice, "Orbit your present position and ascend to angels 10 [10,000 feet]. Repeat—orbit your present position and climb to angels 10."

"It all became clear to me," Durham recalls. "Scudday, the big lug, knew that Operations, plotting our course all along, would realize as soon as it received the request for homing instructions that at 3,000 feet we were headed into the center of cables supporting balloons floating 6,000 feet above Hull. He had flown in that direction deliberately, just to stir up some excitement in Operations. This was no time for practical jokes. I breathed a prayer that the operations officers would not see through his little act. Thankfully, they did not."

Loran Lee "Gunner" Laughlin, of Morgan Hill, Texas, was the first member of 121 Squadron to lose his life. Squadronmate Reade Tilley describes him: "Gunner was a solidly built, curly-haired, ruggedly handsome man with a Scotch-Irish face—a very friendly, quiet-spoken, dependable fellow. We were on a practice formation flight, with sections of the squadron flying at low altitude, 200 to 300 feet off the ground. Suddenly Gunner went into a very gradual dive. At first no one thought anything of it until, unexpectedly, here was a steady, reliable guy dropping out of formation. The feeling changed to one of concern when he got near the ground, and then to sheer horror as it became obvious he was going in. The aircraft exploded."

Flying accidents continued to be a serious problem for 121, just as they had been for 71 Squadron and for every fighter unit. Every practical safety measure was applied, yet losses could not be avoided.

Warren Shenk, of Royersford, Pennsylvania, and Bradley Smith, of Yonkers, New York, collided during a mock dogfight over the city of Lincoln. Both men bailed out and landed safely, but their planes crashed into the streets, killing a motorist, a cyclist and a woman in a house.

Squadron Leader Powell forced the two pilots to attend the victims' funerals and to apologize to the city fathers. For a long time thereafter, the Eagles refrained from going into Lincoln when they had leave.

Smith brooded about the tragedy and was tortured with feelings of guilt. "He really got to be paranoid," one of his fellow Eagles wrote. "He used to sit and stare at the floor, and you could see him coming to a boil. He would start mumbling and then he would get into a rage and shout. One time he jumped up suddenly and hurled a chair through a window, for no reason that was evident to the rest of us. Eventually he had to be sent home."

Powell, dark-haired and of medium build, had a surprisingly boyish face that belied his relatively high rank and his impressive combat record. One of the Americans described him as "a stand-offish, English type with an aristocratic Cranwell RAF College attitude—not a popular CO." Other members of the Squadron strongly disagreed.

"Peter Powell was nothing less than inspirational," said Reade Tilley. "As each new pilot arrived at Kirton Lindsey, Peter would take him up to determine his capabilities. At first there would be just a few normal turns, then aerobatics and an all-out tail chase and dogfight. If you managed to get on his tail and stay there for a while he was delighted. His initial estimate of you as a pilot was made this way.

"He was a most unlikely person. Turn his collar around and he would be the picture of a village parson. We were surprised to learn that he had been a soccer star, and belying his appearance of innocence was the fact that he could out-party and out-fly just about everybody. He was ready at any time, day or night, to demonstrate these qualities. Some of his achievements in combat had earned him the soubriquet Mad Peter, 'mad' being the contemporary British expression for anyone whose actions suggested he was utterly fearless."

The squadron's two British flight leaders were similarly admired by the American pilots. Wilkie Wilkinson had a thick Yorkshire brogue that confused his Eagle listeners until they became accustomed to its rhythms. Wilkinson also quickly became a master of the nightly poker games and crap shooting in the officers' mess.

In the early days of the Eagles, much of the air combat was over Kent, the county from which Flight Leader Hugh Kennard came.

"I used to wonder what made Kennard, a low-pressure guy on the ground, such a tiger and ruthless go-getter in the air," says Tilley. "Many years later, when I was in the U.S. Strategic Air Command, Kennard invited me to the family home, a beautiful estate near Canterbury. For the first time I understood why those missions were so important to him. He was flying and fighting right over his own home territory."

Safety became an obsession for Powell, as his pilots overextended themselves into dangerous, even fatal, situations while training. In a lecture to his pilots, Powell lashed out about reckless flying:

"Last month 83 aircraft were destroyed in low-flying accidents. There probably have been more RAF casualties—more deaths in low-flying and other stupid accidents—than the number of enemy that we have killed in recent months, and more of our pilots were killed this way than were lost in action against enemy fighters.

"If any of you destroys the 84th aircraft in low flying and if you are not killed doing it, I'll do the killing for you. Go kill Germans instead of each other."

This squadron leader had a highly effective way of reprimanding his pilots in a "very level voice." "When Powell got through," one Eagle recalls, "you were unable to defend yourself from someone so calm and collected. He made sure you understood every word he said."

John Campbell recalls one sweep over France by the squadron as "pure chaos—a real terrifying experience:"

At the time we were converting our fighters from their dark green and olive drab to gray and what we called duck-egg blue on the under side, for sea camouflage. We painted orange stripes down the leading edge of the wing to identify the RAF aircraft of our three squadrons at Kirton-in-Lindsey—121 Eagle Squadron, the English 165, and Paddy Finucane's Australian squadron.

Only half the planes had their camouflage changed when we were sent out to escort the bombers. The Germans had already started to change theirs, too, so it was a real dilemma to try to identify planes by their camouflage paint.

We were on patrol between St. Omer and Dunkirk—we in the center, and the Aussies above us. Every time we did a turn they would lose altitude. Finally all three squadrons came together. We scattered every which way and then came back together again.

Just as we were doing another turn we were bounced by a bunch of 109Fs. The squadrons came together in a big ball of airplanes, with the Germans coming on about the same time. We kept swarming, trying to get ready to open fire, but nobody dared to shoot because we couldn't tell friend from enemy.

On the whole mission I never fired. We were scared to death. We lost two planes from one of the other squadrons, due to flak. If the Germans had been on the ball, they could have wiped us out.

Powell knocked one 109 off firing from a distance of 400 yards. He nailed it and it went down, smoking.

On another mission, September 15, 1941, my wing man and I sighted what appeared to be Dornier 17 bombers chasing one of our convoys. It is hard to believe, looking back on it. We saw two bombers making a run on a ship, and we could see the puffs from bombs. I said to my buddy, "I'll take the closest one, you go after the other."

I dove on my plane and was ready to let go a burst at it when I saw that it was not a German but a Hudson bomber with British markings. This poor guy must be trying to protect the ship, I told myself. The other bomber must be German.

I looked around for my wing man and couldn't see him, and I worried that maybe the other bomber had shot him down. Then I looked over and saw the other bomber making a run on the ship. To my astonishment, it was another Hudson.

I called Operations and told them my problem. Ops said, "I think they are friendly and are making practice runs on a derelict ship sitting on a reef. But follow them. We have some reports on bandits (enemy aircraft) in the area."

I still thought there was a chance these were Germans flying Hudsons. But both planes headed back toward the English coast, went in and landed. My wing man, meanwhile, had landed north of Hull with engine trouble.

It turned out that the guy in front had been following me with his guns. He thought we were just giving him some practice, but he had his guns trained on me just in case. That is as close as I came to getting killed by or killing someone on our side.

On this same day, September 15, 1941, Campbell lost his roommate and best friend, Earl "Tootie" Mason, of Roosevelt, Minnesota, and Elrose, Saskatchewan, Canada.

"Tootie—a feisty, aggressive little guy with thinning hair —dove in beating up some ground troops in an army coopera-tion exercise," Campbell said. "He and Bert Stewart went down and were doing some rolls, and as he pulled up, his Hurricane did two and a half rolls, and hit a tree. Apparently Tootie saw the tree when he was inverted, pushed the nose up and rolled to get past it, and went in on his back. He was one of our best pilots and one of the most popular."

Less than a month earlier Mason and four of his fellow sergeant pilots—Stewart, Tilley, Bradley Smith and Tommy Allen—had been commissioned pilot officers.

Bert Stewart gives an anguished account of his friend's death.

Tootie and I went out to do an exercise with some British tanks. I was leading the flight. After we had finished our exercise we started playing, as pilots will, a kind of follow-the-leader.

We were doing some aerobatics over the tanks—rolls, and just generally cutting up. I went down and did a slow roll maybe 50 feet off the ground, and slipped out of the roll and almost hit the ground myself. I came very close to writing myself off.

It crossed my mind immediately to call Tootie and tell him, "Don't do it." Before I could call him I saw him roll into the ground.

I have never been shook up that bad before or since. I came back to the base very, very badly disturbed. I went to the offic-ers' mess and proceeded to drink about a quart of whiskey in the early afternoon.

Ken Kennard came and said, "Stew, you are going to have to get back in the air today or you will never fly again."

I felt just about as guilty as if I had taken a gun and shot Tootie. But between Kennard, Reade Tilley and Pat Patterson, we went out on a late evening patrol.

When we took off, Patterson did a reasonably steep turn into me. I was flying close formation, and I was forced to stay right with him. When we came back in it was dark, and I had a hell of a time getting the plane on the ground. Tilley, circling over the field, helped talk me in to a landing. That flight was the only thing that saved me.

For many years afterward I had a guilty feeling about having killed Tootie. In retrospect, he might have been leading and I might have been the one to auger in. While I still have thoughts about it, I don't feel any more that I am guilty of actually having killed him.

———

With two Eagle Squadrons in operation and beginning to win respect within Fighter Command, the increasing flow of Knight Committee recruits from primary flight-training schools operated by the RAF in the United States and by the RCAF in Canada justified the creation in England of yet another all-American fighter pilot unit in the summer of 1941. On August 1 No. 133 Squadron was established at Coltishall, near the Essex base of Duxford. During the following weeks it was shifted to three other bases in the area —Duxford itself, Colly Weston and then to Fowlmere, five miles south of Cambridge.

The squadron took the motto "Let us to the battle" and adopted a badge showing a bronze eagle and seventeen white stars against a blue background (in heraldic terms: "On a hurt semee of mullets an eagle displayed").

Unlike the earlier Eagle units, No. 133 started out with relatively advanced equipment—eighteen Hurricane IIB fighters with high-altitude Rolls-Royce Merlin XX engines fitted with two-stage manually operated gear-drive superchargers. The Mark IIB was armed with twelve .30 caliber machine guns, compared with eight on the early model Hurricanes of 71 and 121 Squadrons. The new plane also had the model 522 VHF radio which soon was to become standard for Allied fighter aircraft.

To command the new Eagle unit the RAF selected Flight Lieutenant George A. Brown, the Englishman who was the most experienced in working with the American volunteers. Brown had been assigned as a flight leader to No. 71 at its very beginning. He and Wilkinson had demonstrated during long months of service their skill in handling the American pilots. When Wilkinson was transferred to 121 Squadron, Brown had known that he soon might be tapped for leadership of a new Yankee unit.

One of the first members of 133 Squadron, George B. Sperry, of Alameda, California, remarked years later that Brown proved to be an excellent leader who "understood Americans and how to get the best out of them. Nevertheless, to most of us, Squadron Leader Brown seemed standoffish and reserved. I have never forgotten his opening words at the pilots' meeting the morning after we arrived.

" 'Gentlemen,' he said, 'no Englishman is more appreciative than I to see you American volunteers over here to assist us in our fight. It is going to get a lot tougher as time goes by, so take a good look around this room. A year from now most of you will be dead.' At the moment, his statement left us rather dumfounded. Looking back a year later I realized how almost right he was."

Adjutant of the new squadron was Pilot Officer J. G. Staveley-Dick, described by Sperry as "an English lawyer with the proverbial pipe clenched in his teeth, appearing always to be in a state of amazement at his close association with such odd-ball Americans."

The commander of A Flight was Flight Lieutenant H. A. S. Johnston, a former civil servant with the British Foreign Service, "a true bubble-and-squeak type. He worked all of us each and every day, somewhat along the lines of training we had undergone already, but with a great deal more purpose toward developing teamwork and individual efficiency."

Fighter Command transferred another member of 71 Squadron along with George Brown to 133 Squadron—Andy Mamedoff, one of the original Eagles. Mamedoff was given the coveted post of B Flight commander, the first American to be awarded this kind of responsibility in another American unit.

Flying Officer J. M. Emerson—"a fabulous character, millionaire cattleman from Argentina, playboy, polo player," Sperry said—became the squadron intelligence officer; and F/O R. T. Wood, a quiet, reserved Englishman, was appointed engineering and maintenance officer.

"Woody's efforts resulted in the setting of a record in the

RAF for the greatest number of serviceable aircraft available at all times."

Most of the members of the new squadron had only recently arrived in England, and many of them were overconfident.

"My six years of flying experience had given me complete confidence in my ability to do anything that could be done in an airplane in the form of aerobatics," Sperry said. "At 56 OTU, before going to 133, I quickly discovered that my knowledge of flying added up to next to nothing. I knew how to fly, but I had much to learn about flying fighters and about the *why* of flying.

"I knew little about identification and about correction of flying faults. I was fairly ignorant of the problems of stability, trim, and the balance of controls. Within a week after starting training in Hurricanes, I had changed from a self-satisfied pilot to a very deflated novice. Luckily I had 70 hours of instrument flying experience. The British complained that the Americans did not know how to use instruments. And we learned that flying fighters called for a cold, reasoned observation and assessment of maneuvers, so as not to exceed the aircraft's design limitations. Piloting had to be much more accurate than was needed for weekend flying jaunts in California."

The Americans signing in at 133 exchanged stories of their experiences en route. Don Dawson Nee, of Whittier, California, said his ship from Halifax, the Dutch freighter *Maaskerk,* had developed compass trouble and was unable to sail with its convoy. "Just as well," Nee said. "We were told later that the convoy lost 18 ships to enemy action."

Leroy Gover, of Loveland, Colorado, had an even more stressful transatlantic crossing. "We sailed from Halifax on a very decrepit old ship which rendezvoused with 44 other vessels. A German submarine torpedoed two of the ships right alongside ours. I was on watch at the time, and they just blew up and went down immediately. That really made everyone nervous. We had been ordered to sleep with our clothes and life jackets on, which made sleeping almost impossible. After the two ships went down so suddenly I took a look below decks, where I wasn't supposed to be, and found that we were carrying ammunition. That night I took my clothes off and went to bed for a good night's sleep. I figured that if we were torpedoed there'd be no chance anyway, so why not enjoy the trip."

Dusty Miller, the former civilian pilot from Sacramento,

had a CO in operational training at Llandow, Glamorgan, Wales—a bristly-moustached World War I ace named Taffy Jones—who was particularly safety-conscious and demanded accident-free flying.

"Taffy kept the new American intake waiting for hours in an isolated hut on the airfield where the walls were plastered with photographs of coffins covered with the Stars and Stripes," Miller recalls.

"All Jones said, in his stuttering fashion, was that he did not wish to see any of us ending up like those fellows. It was he, however, who on his annual birthday anniversary flight landed a Spitfire with a flat tire. He did a slow uncontrolled graceful turn toward the control tower and ran head-on into a parked plane.

"The CO's remarks on the dangers of flying soon came home to us in an emphatic way. A preceding class was celebrating its passing-out of OTU with a station fly-past and beat-up. One of the instructors, a Battle of Britain celebrity called Pickles, had the tail of his plane chewed off by the propeller of a fellow instructor. Pickles didn't get out, but the other pilot did. That poor chap was stoned for a week.

"The demise of Pickles brought us our first experience with an RAF military funeral—a slow march to the cemetery, a quick march back to the Station."

Sent aloft daily in flight and squadron formations, the pilots of 133 quickly learned the rudiments of strict air discipline. The first practice missions of an operational type were conducted under the supervision of the squadron's flight commanders and CO. They consisted of low-level tours out over the North Sea, along the Dutch coast under the cloud ceiling, and daily convoy patrols along the North Sea shoreline.

One practice interception with a Duxford squadron developed into an explosive dogfight all the way down to the deck. Both commanding officers and all four flight commanders had to shout orders to their teams to break it off.

On a practice mission September 27, 1941, Walt Soares and his wing man, Charles S. Barrell, of Hamilton, Massachusetts, collided while turning on final approach and were killed. It was 133 Squadron's first fatal accident.

Shortly before leaving 71 Squadron for his new assignment with 133, Andy Mamedoff had become the first of the Eagles to take a war bride, Penny Craven, a member of the Craven cigarette family. Best man Vic Bono suggested to the squadron that since most of the pilots were on readiness and unable to leave the base for a social occasion, they might take their Hurricanes up and honor the couple with a fly-past right after the church ceremony at Epping.

Two of the pilots, Bill Geiger and Ed Bateman, flew over the little town first. The bridal party rushed out from the inn where Robbie Robinson, 71 Squadron intelligence officer, was host at the luncheon. The other pilots came thundering over a few minutes later.

"It was market day," Bono recalled. "Never before had planes flown over at such a low altitude. Pigs and lambs scattered everywhere, leaving the marketplace a wreck."

Fighter Command decided that 133 Squadron should take further instruction at Eglinton, Northern Ireland. "We never did forgive the RAF for this move to the island of never-ending rain," Sperry said. "It cost the lives of four of our members."

Fifteen pilots left Fowlmere in their Hurricanes on October 8, 1941, and reached their first refueling stop, at Sealand, in less than an hour. Storm clouds settled in. Only six pilots made it to the next planned stop at Andreas RAF station on the Isle of Man. Three landed at an intermediate field. Two turned back to Sealand. The other four perished—R. N. Stout, of Kansas City, Missouri; Hugh McCall, of South Pasadena, California; W. J. White, of Topeka, Kansas; and the flight leader and bridegroom, Andy Mamedoff.

At Eglinton, 133 Squadron moved into what one member called "a vast sea of mud surrounded by knee-deep lakes of water," a base built for Coastal Command. The Eagles found the station personnel none too friendly at having to put up with a group of highly disgruntled American fighter pilots.

The station was dispersed into sites over a large area about eight miles from Londonderry, making it uncomfortable and poorly suited to the purposes of its temporary occupants. The quarters for the pilots were at least a mile away from the officers' mess. The bathhouse next to the mess was reserved each day between 1 and 5 P.M. for the WAAF detachment assigned to the station.

This arrangement would have worked out well had the women cleaned the bathtubs and vacated the premises by 5 P.M. Instead, they ignored the deadline, rarely bothered to clean the tubs, and left soggy, soiled towels and bathmats scattered around, even after their commanding officer had assured the men that her girls would obey the rules. When the situation had failed to improve, a week later, the Eagles took direct action. Several of them, sweating and tired of waiting in line, marched into the bathhouse at 5:30, ordered everyone out of the tubs, and supervised a cleanup of the quarters by the WAAFs. From that day until the Eagles left the station, the bathhouse and its clean tubs were ready for male use promptly at the designated hour.

The squadron was to remain at Eglinton through most of 1941. There were the seemingly inevitable accidents that marked air training everywhere. George Russell Bruce, of Winnipeg, Ontario, returning from a convoy patrol on October 23, buzzed the officers' mess, slow-rolled down a tree-lined road, clipped a wing, crashed and was killed. Four days later Gene Coxetter, of Chevy Chase, Maryland, was killed in a flying accident at Rasharkin, about forty miles east of Londonderry.

There was another kind of hazard—this one political. R. L. "Bud" Wolfe, of Ceresco, Nebraska, practice-flying a Spitfire, reported to Ground Control that he was on top of an overcast, low on fuel, and on a dead-reckoning course for home. His radio receiver had gone dead, so he could not hear any instructions.

Ground Control asked other pilots on training flights to try to give him visual guidance, but they were unable to find him. In his last transmission, Wolfe said he was out of petrol and was going over the side.

He landed only ten miles from home base but on the wrong side of the border. The squadron received word within two hours that Wolfe had been interned in the Irish Free State.

Later in October the squadron also lost George Brown, who was promoted to a post at Fighter Command Headquarters. He was succeeded as 133 Squadron leader by Eric Hugh Thomas, of Tunbridge Wells, Kent, an RAF career officer since 1936.

Three American squadrons were now in place and in business. All had now suffered baptism-by-loss. And like a forest full of predators, the war loomed still larger before them.

5

INTO
ACTION

The news reports of the war's first violent encounter between American and German pilots—the July 2 engagement over Lille—centered on the exploits of Gus Daymond. Radio commentators and newsmen began to refer to him as the first American in the war to bring down an enemy plane. Understandably, Bill Dunn in particular resented this. The Hurricanes had taken off for Lille at 11:50 A.M. and had all returned to Martlesham at 1:10 P.M., so from a practical standpoint the three victories of Daymond, Dunn and their English leader could have been considered simultaneous. According to personal combat reports released by the British Ministry of Defense in 1972, Dunn had timed his air victory at 12:35 P.M. The destruction of the German plane had been confirmed by Mannix and Provenzano. Daymond had listed his kill at 12:40, five minutes later.

Queried on the matter, Dunn said, "I was told at the time that I had shot down the first enemy plane as an Eagle Squadron member, but what the hell—I'm not going to argue over these things again." Royal D. Frey, of the U.S. Air Force Museum, said in an article in the Air Force's *Airman Magazine* in August, 1967, that Dunn's Me 109E was "the first enemy aircraft destroyed by an Eagle Squadron pilot." To outsiders the matter may appear inconsequential, but within 71 Squadron the seed had been planted for a bitter contest.

Four days after the first-blood engagement, 71 Squadron again fought off enemy fighters attacking British bombers on another raid upon targets near Lille. Dunn and a Polish pilot, P/O Leon Jaugsch, of 306 Squadron fired at an Me 109 at the same moment. The enemy plane dived straight into the ground, and the two pilots shared credit for its destruction. On the same mission, however, Daymond shot down another Messerschmitt, thus taking a half-plane lead over his rival. Dunn shot down another Me 109E on July 21, shortly after leaving Lille. "The pilot, in a gentle dive, jettisoned his hood," Dunn said in his combat report. "He probably bailed out, but I did not see him do so." Then Daymond regained the lead by shooting down a Dornier 17Z bomber that was preparing to attack a convoy off Orfordness promontory on August 3, 1941. His combat report:

> He dived to near sea level when I attacked. I opened fire at 250 yards, and had to use emergency boost to keep up with him. I fired a three-second burst. The rear gunner fired back. His aim was inaccurate, and his fire was high and to starboard. The return fire ceased after my second burst. I saw my bullets strike below the aircraft, and raised my aim and fired all my remaining ammunition high. The port motor started smoking. The aircraft hit the water, bounced 50 to 75 feet into the air, and plunged into the sea leaving a spot of oil on the surface. I saw no survivors.

Six days later Dunn destroyed another Me 109E to lead the scoring 3 1/2 to 3. Everyone in the squadron knew that an undeclared but tense contest between two daring and highly skilled pilots was underway.

As the rivalry developed, other painful events became part of the public's awareness of the Eagles. One International News Service dispatch from London credited quick thinking by Victor Bono for saving another Eagle, Virgil Olson, from death or capture and imprisonment in a Nazi internment camp. On August 19, Olson's plane had been attacked by a Messerschmitt. The INS gave this account:

> Bono plunged into the fight and shot down the German plane. Then the Californian saw that Olson, his craft damaged, apparently was going to attempt a crash landing—in France. "Keep going; you've got plenty of height," Bono radioed.

Olson took his advice and managed to glide his plane far out over the English Channel, where he bailed out and parachuted safely down to the water. A little later an English rescue boat picked him up and took him in to Dover.

The rescue account, however, was in error. Apparently an excited newsman had made some optimistic assumptions, for Olson was never found.

Bono, a funloving individual who stencilled his plane *Pro Bono Publico,* said later that when he saw that Olson's plane had been hit as they left the Calais area, he flew alongside and asked, "How do you feel? You look all right."

"I probably was the last guy to talk to him," Bono said. "He wasn't smoking or anything. When I said, 'You all right?' he answered, 'Yeah.' Then he said, 'I gotta get out of here,' and started to climb out of the cockpit.

" 'Don't get out,' I called. 'Head back to the coast. I'll stay with you.' He kept on trying to get out, and I yelled, 'Don't go; don't go. You're all right. You can climb back in.' But he was over the coast by then and probably had his earphones off and didn't hear me."

Olson was the squadron's parachute officer. It was his responsibility to make sure that the planes were equipped with the required parachutes and dinghies. What the other pilots did not learn until later was that Olson had made the flight without the dinghy that could have saved his life.

And then came the Spit—the Vickers-Armstrong Supermarine Spitfire. Most of the Eagles and the other RAF fighter pilots still regarded it, years after the war, as probably the finest propeller-driven airplane ever produced. Eagle Squadron 71 received its first Spitfires—fourteen Mark IIAs—at North Weald on August 20, 1941, after nine months of flying Hurricanes.

Slender, almost frail-looking alongside the stocky, sturdy, hunchbacked Hurricane, the Spitfire was speedier and could climb faster and higher than the Hurricane, although it could not quite match the Hawker fighter's maneuverability and firepower. More to the point, the Spitfire was equal to, if not better than, the Me 109 in most regards.

The Spit IIA was about a foot and a half longer, six inches lower and, at sixty-three hundred pounds, considerably lighter than the Hurricane. Its wing span was seven feet less than that of the Hurricane. The maximum speed of the Spitfire IIA, 370 miles an hour, represented a gain of almost 50 mph over the Hurricane. The rate of climb was 2,600 feet a minute, the ceiling 32, 800 feet, and the range 395 miles. The Spit's stalling speed was 79 mph flaps up and 71 mph flaps down. The IIA had the same armament as the Hurricane. It was powered by a 1,175-horsepower Rolls-Royce Merlin XII engine driving a three-bladed, two-speed propeller instead of the two-bladed, fixed-pitch airscrew of the original Spits.

As their knowledge of combat techniques increased, RAF fighter pilots needed a choice of weapons against different targets. The eight machine guns they had been using provided devastating firing power, but they wanted greater explosive potential against large, armor-plated enemy bombers. In September, one month after delivery of the Mark IIAs, 71 Squadron's wish was granted in the form of the Spitfire VB, which had the more powerful Merlin 45 engine and, best of all, a choice of weapons—four .303 machine guns and two Hispano 20 mm. cannons. A three-way firing button on the control column enabled the pilot to fire the machine guns or the cannons or all the weapons together.

Initially, there were pilot complaints that the cannons would fire several rounds and then quit. The feed and ejection system was corrected, and the mixed armament became a permanent fixture. The VB remained in operation throughout the rest of 71 Squadron's existence.

At Kirton-in-Lindsey, 121 Squadron traded its Hurricanes for Spitfire IIAs in October, 1941, and then turned them in for VBs the following month. The newest squadron, 133, acquired Spitfire IIAs in October and later the VA. In September, 1942, 133 became the only Eagle squadron to be given the Spitfire IX, which basically was the Mark V with a strengthened engine mount and a stiffened rear fuselage.

Bill Dunn still likes to talk about the Spit—his glowing description is typical:

> I've flown Hurricanes, Typhoons, P-39s, P-51s, P-40s, P-47s, et cetera, and the Spitfire was the absolute best.
> It is the only aircraft I've ever flown that had absolutely no bad habits. You can't even scare yourself in it. You can do a high speed stall, and it will do about a half flick and you can kick it out of a spin. You can do a low speed stall, and about the same

thing will happen. You can bring it up on a stall, and then flutter down in a falling leaf without ever getting into a spin. It's got a very high rate of climb, it's very maneuverable, very fast—so fast that you could close the throttle and you'd still feel yourself sliding through the air.

If you wanted to slow up, you had to put the propeller in fine pitch, which acted sort of like a brake. There were just no bad habits in that airplane at all. If you were coming in on a precautionary landing, for example, you could dump the gear and flaps and make your final approach at about 75 miles an hour. Over the fence was about 70, drop in at 65 miles per hour, and you'd stop rolling in a few hundred feet. Yet you could pour the coal to it on takeoff—a high boost, which would be about equal to 108 inches in an American aircraft—and by the time you crossed over the perimeter of the airfield you'd be doing well over 200 miles an hour. Then you could stick the nose up and climb so steeply that the leading edge of your wing blanked out the horizon. A lot of guys climbed right over onto their back.

————

On August 13, 1941, a week before delivery of the first Spitfires, Squadron Leader Paddy Woodhouse was promoted out of 71 Squadron to command the 36-plane, three-squadron Tangmere Wing. Douglas Bader, much admired for his frequent engagements in combat despite his artificial legs, had been forced to bail out of his crippled plane over France on August 9 and had been captured by the Germans. Fighter Command decided that only a man of Woodhouse's stature could take Bader's place as wing commander.

Most of the members of 71 Squadron had not reacted well to Woodhouse when he arrived in June to succeed the American skipper, Bill Taylor. They quickly learned that Woodhouse was a perfectionist and would brook no questioning of his orders. Paddy had come from the command of 610 Squadron and, only two months previously, had shared credit with another English pilot for bringing down a Ju 88 bomber. However, by the time Woodhouse moved on to Tangmere he had won the unquestioning respect and affection of the Eagles at North Weald. The Americans all agreed that he had been a superb teacher and leader.

Another Englishman, E. R. Bitmead, followed Woodhouse briefly as 71 Squadron leader. He had been injured in a flying accident and found within a week that he had not recovered sufficiently to lead the American unit. After Bitmead's departure another exceptional Briton, Squadron Leader Stanley T. Meares, a Battle of Britain veteran, took charge of 71 Squadron on August 22, 1941.

———

One week after its conversion to Spitfires, 71 Squadron took part in a battle over France that almost cost the life of its leading scorer, Bill Dunn. The engagement did in fact mark the end of Dunn's career as an Eagle, but not before he had established a claim as the first ace—the first man to shoot down five enemy aircraft—among the RAF's American pilots. In his score keeping, Dunn naturally had counted only planes shot down in air combat. Before joining the RAF, when he was still a mortar platoon sergeant with the Seaforth Highlanders in England, Dunn was credited with shooting down two Stuka divebombers while manning a machine gun.

Dunn's last mission with the Eagles was a thing of fury. On August 27, 71 Squadron was part of a 100-Spitfire force escorting nine Blenheim bombers on an attack on the steelworks at Lille. More than thirty Messerschmitts attacked from above. One Spitfire was hit and headed for home, trailing smoke. Another Spit blew an Me 109 in two. After the battle, Dunn wrote:

> I dived on one of two Me 109Fs, fired from a distance of 150 yards, and fired again to within 50 yards. Pieces of the aircraft flew off, and engine oil spattered my windscreen. The plane looked like a blow torch with a bluish white flame as it went down.
>
> Tracers from another 109F behind me flashed past my cockpit. I pulled back the throttle, jammed down the flaps, and skidded my plane sharply out of his gunsight. The German overshot me by about 10 feet, and as he crossed overhead I could see the black cross insignia, unit markings, and a red rooster painted on the side of the cockpit.
>
> The 109 was now in my range. With a burst of only three seconds I had him out of commission. A wisp of smoke from the engine turned almost instantly into a sheet of flame. The plane rolled over on its back. As it started down the tail section broke off. I had claimed my second victim of the day.
>
> I fired at another Me 109 and saw smoke come from it. Just as I started to press the gun button again my plane lurched sharply. I heard explosions. A ball of fire streamed through the cockpit, smashing into the instrument panel. There were two heavy blows against my right leg, and as my head snapped forward, I began to lose consciousness.
>
> My mind cleared again, and I realized that the earth was

spinning up toward me. I tugged back on the control column and pulled back into a gradual dive toward the English Channel, 50 miles away.

I checked the plane for damage. The tip of the right wing was gone. The rudder had been badly damaged. The instruments on the right side of the panel were shattered.

There was blood on the cockpit floor. When I looked at my right leg I saw that the toe of the boot had been shot off. My trouser leg was drenched with blood; I could feel warm, sticky fluid seeping from under my helmet to my neck and cheek. I gulped oxygen to fight off nausea.

Releasing my shoulder harness, I started to climb out of the cockpit. For some reason, I paused. The engine was still running all right, and the plane seemed flyable. I slid back into my seat; I would try to make it home.

Crossing the Channel, the engine began to lose power. I switched on the radio telephone and called May Day. Within a few moments I had an escort of two Spitfires.

They led me across the coastal cliffs to the grass airfield at Hawkinge, near Folkestone. The escorting pilot signalled to me that my landing gear had extended.

I dropped smoothly onto the newly mowed turf, and taxied to a waiting ambulance. An airman climbed up on the wing and shouted that I was in the wrong area and must taxi over to a dispersal hut if I wanted fuel and ammunition. Then he saw my bloody face and helmet and called the medical officer.

I awoke 30 hours later in a bed in the Royal Victoria hospital in Folkestone and learned that the front part of my foot had been shot away, that there were two machine gun bullets in my right leg and that another had creased the back of my head. I spent three months recuperating there and at the RAF hospital at Torquay.

As Dunn recovered from his injuries, Gus Daymond shot down his fourth enemy plane, an Me 109F, on a bomber escort mission September 4, 1941. Fifteen days later he downed another Me 109F and thereafter was usually referred to in news stories and RAF publicity releases as the first American ace of the war. No one was around to push Dunn's kill claim of August 27, which would have meant acedom and a score of 5 1/2 victories.

———

Impatience among the pilots showed in various ways. William H. Nichols, a very keen, very eager new member of 71 Squadron, fretted over an early autumn lull in the action and told Pete Peterson that he wanted to go immediately on a rhubarb—a two-man low-altitude search for targets of opportunity.

"Bill was my wing man," Peterson recalled many years later. "He didn't really know what he wanted, except that the two of us should go hunting. So off we went, around the north of France, and couldn't find a train, a plane, a gun. Bill said, 'I've just got to shoot something. Those cows down there—how about them?' I said no, and when we got back to base I gave him hell for talking too much on the radio.

"In the next couple of days we got in a lot of fighting—started sweeps and found all kinds of action. Then it was slow again for the next four or five days.

"I was sitting in the hot sun at North Weald reading when Nichols came up and said, 'I hope I get a scramble. I have to get more fighting in this next week.' I asked why, and he said it was because he was going home the end of next week. Noticing that I was surprised, he explained that he had come into the RAF through the Clayton Knight Committee.

" 'They signed me up for only one year, and the year is up at the end of next week,' he said."

Peterson went to the Air Ministry in London and asked for background data on Nichols.

"The group captain showed me Bill's contract, and it was the same one I had signed," Peterson said. "It called for service for the duration of the war and not more than a year thereafter. I went back to Nichols and said, 'I'm sorry—you've simply been sold a bill of goods.' Bill merely shook his head.

" 'I signed up for a year,' he insisted. 'I want to get fighting for the week I have left.'

"As it turned out, he did not have a week left."

The action *was* picking up. The three squadrons of the North Weald Wing—71 Eagle and two British outfits—were ordered out on a fighter sweep over France on September 7. No bombers were involved, so the mission appeared likely to be not much more than a practice flight. There had been little action over this part of enemy-occupied area. The Me 109s, saving themselves for attacks on bombers, rarely came up to do battle when only fighter sweeps were intruding.

It was the first sweep with the new Spitfires. Squadron Leader Meares noted that two of his pilots—Hillard S. Fenlaw and Forrest P. "Pappy" Dowling—were recent bridegrooms. Others on the mission included Peterson, Gene Tobin, Bill Nichols, and M. W. "Jack" Fessler, Meares' wing man. Because of mechanical difficulties, there were only nine planes instead of the normal twelve as 71 Squadron started over France.

About seventy-five miles inland, near the planned turning point, the English ground radar controller advised the formation that there were enemy bandit plottings to the rear, between the Spitfires and the French coast. The plottings turned out to be approximately one hundred Me 109s which had waited for the RAF planes to fly inland before coming up to overwhelm the invading force.

The battle quickly turned into the fiercest engagement the Eagles had yet encountered. The 109s attacked the Spitfires of 71 Squadron from above, at twenty-nine thousand feet, and then returned to higher altitude rather than continuing downward to the other two squadrons.

Peterson shot down his first enemy plane; other 109s probably were destroyed. But Tobin and Fenlaw were killed; Nichols bailed out of his burning plane and was taken prisoner; and Dowling barely made it home in his crippled Spit. Fessler narrowly escaped death from anoxia, as he later recounted:

Usually the 109s would attack with three or four aircraft in line astern. We would turn very tightly into them at the proper moment, but gradually they were picking us off. It soon became obvious that things could not go on this way, or there would be none of us left.

At this point Squadron Leader Meares said over the R/T, "Every man for himself now, chaps." We were at about 22,000, having been constantly losing altitude during the attacks. As we descended, the other two squadrons below us went down lower.

During every attack and tight defensive turn my oxygen mask kept slipping off my nose and mouth down onto my chin. I constantly had to push it back up to breathe properly. To do this, my left hand had to leave the throttle.

At about 21,000 feet four 109s were starting an attack on Meares and me. Meares was in a tight defensive left turn toward them, and I was close behind. It was about a 20- or 30-degree diving tight turn, full bore.

As the first 109 started firing at Meares I could see that he would pass between us, giving me a momentary chance to fire. I had to wait a short moment, to avoid hitting Meares. As soon as the 109 was sufficiently clear I began firing, and was hitting him with my cannon and machine guns. At that instant I passed out.

My only thought, as consciousness left me, was that my

momentary delay in turning, in order to fire at the 109, was just long enough for the second 109 in the attack to get me. I was still firing as I faded out, and my last thought was, "I've had it. I've just been shot down."

I regained consciousness in a vertical dive—actually, past the vertical—heading straight for the earth with the throttle wide open. My sun glasses were floating in the air before me. For some reason, my gloves were off. My head was buffeting on the Plexiglas canopy, and that probably is what aroused me. As I awakened I could see a cloud deck rapidly approaching; I recalled it had been 10,000 or 12,000 feet over France that day.

"I've been shot down," I told myself. "I'm heading straight for the ground, wide open. I'm not dead yet, though. But I surer than hell will be shortly if I don't pull out of this dive."

I could not read the cockpit instruments. My vision for distance was all right, but my eyes would not focus close up. I could not see the spade grip of the stick, but I could see the swivel point.

I tried pulling back on the swivel, but without effect. Then I leaned forward as much as possible, put both hands around the swivel, locked my fingers together, and pulled and leaned back with my whole body. I passed out again.

The next time I came to I was still in the same position, with hands clasped around the stick and my body pulling back. I was horrified to see that I was not more than house-top high off the ground, but I was flying level across slightly rolling countryside. The airplane was trimmed slightly nose down, so it wanted to descend even further. I dared not release the back pressure on the stick, lest the plane fly itself into the ground. Quite a predicament!

In perhaps a minute or two—my timing was vague—I gained enough strength in my arms to release one hand and to trim the airplane out of its nose-down tendency. My eyesight was still poor. I could not read any of the instruments, but I did note the relative position of the airspeed needle—which later turned out to be the equivalent of 540 mph.

The engine was still wide open and roaring loudly. I knew I would have to throttle back, or the engine would destroy itself. I also suspected that an enemy plane had followed us down and might be about to try to finish us off. For that reason I started weaving and looking around. Seeing no other aircraft, I throt-tled back. I found no blood on myself, and decided I had better head back for England.

How much gas did I have left? Would I make it back? And which way was home? Since I still could not focus on the cockpit instruments, I was unable to read my compass. Then it came to me—"keep the sun on the left to get back to England."

Off I headed, the sun on my left, staying very close to the ground to avoid ack-ack, radar and ground machine gunners. As I passed over the French coast ground positions at house level, I could clearly see the gunners in their pits. But I do not recall that any of them fired at me, nor did I see tracers or ack-ack. Half way across the Channel I could see both coasts. Suddenly I was unsure which was the English coast and which the French.

Again I remembered—"sun on the left"—and made for England. Still unable to see well enough to read a map, I landed at a sod field, Shoreham emergency airdrome. I came to a halt 50 feet from the far end of the field, and a few feet from a ditch.

Two airmen greeted me. I felt miserable; my head was splitting; I still did not fully realize I had not been shot down. I didn't really know what had happened to me, but I knew I wasn't bleeding.

A quick survey of the airplane showed no evidence of bullet holes. But my seat was shattered, although still holding together somewhat. A hole in the fuselage skin, aft of the cockpit in the belly, turned out to be the radio box which had sheared its mounting and had gone almost all way through the aircraft skin. The antenna was broken off.

I asked the airmen to check the engine screens for metal, and if they found no engine damage to service the plane so I could fly it home, without radio. While they did this I went to a pub a block off the field and had first a Scotch, then another, then a couple of aspirins, then some tea. Beginning to recover, I had a beer.

The booze was taking effect when I returned to my plane, which had been inspected and refueled, and I took off for North Weald feeling no pain. Over the home field I dived on our hut, did a victory roll, pulled up, and then came in and landed.

The squadron leader had already reported me missing in action. He had returned to base more than an hour earlier, after seeing me going straight down into the cloud deck with no indication of a pull-out, and he had assumed I was a goner. We actually lost five pilots that day, our blackest day.

The squadron engineering officer, inspecting my plane, found a four-and-a-half-degree *set* in the wing spars, and wrinkled upper wing skin. The calculated G force required to shear the radio brackets was 10.4 times gravity. Apparently I had had a ride at the real terminal velocity possible with a Spitfire. The only effect on my person was that my shoulder muscles ached for a couple of weeks. The airplane never flew again.

Fessler's remarkable recovery from unconsciousness in the cockpit, his determined battle to regain control of his plane, and his courageous flight back to England warmed the hearts of his teammates. They were equally delighted with the superb flying that enabled Forrest Dowling to get back from the mission—his first sweep—alive. A colleague called Dowling's survival "another classic of Divine Providence."

Shells from an Me 109 had ripped into his Spitfire and had sent it out of control. Dowling managed to regain level flight thousands of feet below, only to find another 109 streaking after him. The second plane followed him halfway across the Channel, with the Spitfire becoming increasingly difficult to manage. Among his other difficulties, Dowling had to hold the control column back in his lap to maintain a pitch attitude of about twenty degrees below the horizon.

Dowling made it across the Dover cliffs with little altitude to spare and headed for the first open bit of farmland. The field was crossed with hedgerows, and he had no choice but to slam into one. The hedge merely covered a sturdy stone fence, which the plane hit with shattering force. When the dust had cleared, Dowling remained seated in the cockpit, with most of the rest of the Spitfire strung across the field behind him. His principal injury was a broken collarbone.

Under the leadership of Meares, 71 Squadron was gaining experience and acquiring the three P's—polish, precision and prestige. According to Bill Geiger, "We were probably the top close escort squadron in the RAF. We certainly did more than anyone else. I think we had something of a record in that we never lost a bomber due to fighter action in the summer of 1941."

As a typical Eagle, Bill Geiger had flown about thirty combat missions, most of them in close escort of bombers, and fifty or sixty convoy patrols. Now it was September 17, 1941, just twelve days short of his twenty-second birthday, and Geiger was among the Spitfire pilots assigned to escort twenty-four Blenheims on the largest daylight raid over France then undertaken by British bombers. Another of the fighter pilots on the mission was a jaunty eighteen-year-old from Los Angeles, Tommy McGerty, who had told his parents he was a Link trainer instructor so they wouldn't worry about him.

Although the Blenheims inflicted considerable damage, so

did the German fighters. Both McGerty and Geiger were shot down off Dunkirk. McGerty was killed, and Geiger became a war prisoner. How does it feel to be shot down? Geiger gives this account:

Ever sit in a steel drum in a calypso band while they're playing "All day, all night, Mary Anne; down by the seaside, sifting sand?" Well, I did; only it was a small Spitfire and not a steel drum, and I was 15,000 feet over the English Channel. But that's what it sounds like when you get hit.

There is the smell of cordite to go along with the noise. The instrument panel disappears in front of you and the gun sight blows up in your face. There is no radio any more, and you are very, very much alone.

This all happened on September 17, 1941, just a few moments after Gus Daymond reminded me that there were three 109s on my tail. We always wondered what it would take to make up your mind to bail out.

The decision comes very easily, very quickly when the plane won't fly any more and when it's on fire. You say to yourself, "Let's go. Let's get out of here *now.*"

It's at about this point that the voice takes over. I'll call him Know-it-all, because he seemed to have all the answers. It was a voice very familiar to me; sounded like my own, in fact, only it was rather calm and deliberate and didn't seem too concerned over my predicament.

The British flying helmet had a split up the back and a little strap that went across the back of your head just above the nape of your neck, so that supposedly it would fit anyone. I had always felt that if we had to take the helmet off fast one could grab the oxygen mask, give a sharp tug forward, and the strap would split and the helmet would come off quickly and easily.

At this point the voice started telling me, "Grab the oxygen mask and pull." I did, and sure enough, off came the helmet.

The voice said, "Tuck it down beside the seat so it won't wrap around your leg as you get out." I did. The voice then said, "Pull that little black ball over your head on the canopy." I did. Nothing happened. I banged the canopy a couple of times; it gave a little "chunk" and then just sat there.

A Spitfire cockpit is very small and the canopy is very close on all sides. In fact, normally we slide the canopy back with our elbows. I proceeded to make like Kung Fu inside the canopy, bashing it with elbows, fists, wrists, anything available. Nothing happened.

I was now heading for the water in a slightly inverted spin, and time was running out. Old Know-it-all was very quiet indeed. At one point I brought my hands down into my lap. I thought, "I'm going in with it." I told myself (and this was very important at the time), "It won't hurt." I remember a feeling of curiosity: What is it going to be like to be dead? Somehow, it didn't seem that it would be all that bad. It was almost like I was going on a new adventure.

I noticed that the corner of the canopy was sticking out. "If I stick my elbow in there and push hard enough, perhaps I can bend it out to a point where the slip stream will grab it and pull the canopy off," I told myself. In went the elbow. Sure enough, off went the canopy.

Old Know-it-all started talking again. "Bring your feet up so they won't get caught under the instrument panel. Pull the pin in the Sutton shoulder harness. Get your hands up on top of the windscreen." Surprising how easily I popped out of that cockpit.

Again, the voice. "Stand at attention to stop the tumbling." The British parachute fits rather snugly between the legs, with a twin strap that comes up to about the belly button area. The instructions are to open the chute while dropping feet first, but when I had listened to the lecture on parachute use I had decided I would go down head first. Old Know-it-all reminded me of this.

I arched my back slightly, looking over my head until I saw the water. Then Know-it-all said, "Look for the rip cord; don't feel for it." I looked; it was there. I grabbed it, pulled it, and threw it half-way to England. There was a gigantic tug, and then dead silence. "Thank you, Jumpsack," I said.

Swinging gently to and fro, I reached down and removed one flying boot, dropped it, and watched it sail away below me. I removed the second one. Know-it-all said, "Hold on to that, and drop it when you think you're about 20 feet above the water. Might help you judge distance, that last minute before you cut the chute loose."

The entry into the water was a thing of sheer beauty. I got rid of the chute the way it is supposed to be discarded. By this time, however, Old Know-it-all had deserted me. He and I had never gone to the lecture on the fighter dinghy operation. We had never gone to the swimming pool to learn how to open the dinghy in water. Now I had to figure that out for myself.

The Mae Wests we were wearing in those days did not have the CO_2 bottle. The life vests had to be blown up with lung power. My first discovery was that the Mae West did not keep me high enough in the water to let me get much air. It became essential to open the fighter dinghy as quickly as possible.

I grasped the valve on the dinghy CO_2 bottle and tried to turn it. It wouldn't budge. I tried again, unsuccessfully. In desperation I returned my attention to the Mae West and decided to try to inflate it. I put the little hose in my mouth and blew, but I was getting more water than air. Frustrated, I went back to the fighter dinghy and noticed a small pin running through the valve. I pulled the pin out, turned the valve easily, and the dinghy inflated. I climbed into it and at last was in a position to breathe without difficulty. Fighter dinghies do not keep you high and they do not keep you dry, but they do give you a little air.

I started looking around for the paddles and particularly for the little pump that should keep the dinghy inflated. After more searching I found that I had climbed into the dinghy while it was upside down. Back into the water I went. I flipped the dinghy over, climbed back in, and there were all the survival articles promised. Several frozen hours later I noticed a small line hanging over the stern. Retrieving it, I discovered I had left my sea anchor out. Clearly I had not traveled more than 100 yards through the water, but the rowing I had done at least served to keep the circulation going.

As it was getting dark the crew of an E-boat plucked me from the sea and took me to the French coast. I spent the night at St. Omer. At four o'clock the next morning an officer and four soldiers escorted me out of my room and down through the streets.

They are going to shoot me, but they won't shoot me in town, I told myself. They will take me out in the country. I will stand up against a stone wall behind a farmhouse, and this will be the spot.

I had not heard from Old Know-it-all for some time. He said nothing now. I decided on my own that if I were to be shot at I would not be a stationary target. My captors would see one of the fastest moving human beings on earth. I started eyeing every alley, every side street. Several times my mind told me I was running, but my body did not follow. As we neared the fringe of the town I said to myself, "There isn't much time left. If you are going you'll have to go very soon."

We came to a covered truck with many German soldiers around it, and a number of men sitting in the back. I was ordered up into the back part and found myself looking a German soldier right in the eye.

"You are an American, aren't you?" he asked, in perfect English with a slight American accent.

"Yes," I replied. "Don't worry," he said. "They are going to send you to Dulag Luft. For you the war is over."

It was a very, very cold morning. I was bathed in sweat. This was the beginning of three and one-half years; three and a half years where every day was like a week, every week like a month, every month a year.

———

Squadron rosters changed constantly as various Eagles were transferred to other units or sent off to become instructors or were grounded for reasons of health or unsatisfactory performance. One man literally stumbled into being an Eagle. Wayne A. Becker told his companions that he had been a Pan American pilot. While in England, he had gone on a binge and at the end of it found himself in the RAF. He became engineering officer of 71 Squadron.

"Becker was a good pilot, but they would not let him fly, because he was the best engineering officer in the RAF," Bert Stewart recalls.

"Every time he went on a toot he would call up Sholto Douglas or anyone else available and shout, 'Let me fly or I quit.'" One Sunday morning, Tribken and Beck and I went in to breakfast and the WAAF waitress served Wally and me ham and eggs, the special meal for fighter pilots. In front of Beck she set a plate of hobble and squish—old cold potatoes and Brussels sprouts.

" 'Where's my bacon and eggs?' Beck growled.

"The waitress replied, 'Those are only for operational pilots.' Becker's fist hit the table so hard the dishes bounced.

" 'That does it,' he roared. 'I'm through.' And he rushed out to phone Sholto Douglas. Eventually he got a transfer to the Commandos.

Flying accidents continued to take their toll. It finally became necessary in September, 1941, for 71 Squadron to draw upon the two other Eagle squadrons for the experienced pilots it needed to fill its depleted ranks. Reluctantly, 121 Squadron relinquished to 71 Squadron Red McColpin—who once before had declined an assignment to 71—Don Geffene, Bert Stewart and Eddie Miluck. Transferred to 71 from 133 Squadron were Ross Scarborough, Gilmore Daniel and Harold Strickland. The arrival of this fresh talent heated up the rivalry in the scoring of enemy aircraft "kills" that had slackened with the permanent removal of Bill Dunn from the competition. Chesley Peterson shot down his first enemy plane three days after Daymond downed his fourth and accomplished his second kill the day before Daymond knocked down his fifth to become an ace.

On September 21, McColpin, flying one of his first Spitfire missions, shot down an Me 109E that was attacking RAF bombers as they left the Lille area. Then, on October 2, the squadron achieved one of its greatest combat triumphs of the war by shooting down five German planes without losing a single Spitfire. McColpin downed two of the five planes and shared credit for destruction of a third. Within an eleven-day period he became a leading contender for 71 Squadron honors.

Some of McColpin's friends told him jestingly that he was the beneficiary of extraordinary "beginner's luck." All England had been fogged in for several days at the end of September. Weather forecasts were so unfavorable that the senior pilots of 71 Squadron—the members of A Flight—were given a week's leave. That was why veterans such as Peterson and Daymond missed the October 2 engagement and why most of the participants—McColpin, Stanley Meares, Ross Scarborough, Newton Anderson, and Arthur F. Roscoe—were squadron novices.

McColpin describes the great day:

I was flying as alternate squadron leader, No. 2 to Stanley Meares, when I saw the Me 109Fs climbing to intercept us. I called out the bogies to Meares.

Being in the lead, he and I started accelerating first, diving for the enemy formation, and rapidly drew away from the remainder of the squadron. As a consequence, the initial engagement—two of us against 18 or 20 enemy—was a bit lean, to say the least.

While Meares was firing at the nearest 109 I overtook the same plane from below and fired a half-second burst from about 100 yards. It burst into flame. I broke away to port and found myself in position for an attack on another 109, so I gave him a burst. He pulled up and dived with smoke pouring out. I thought I saw a man bail out. The plane was seen to hit the ground. I saw another Me 109 below, dived on him, and followed him down to 3,000 feet where I gave him a one-second burst. He never pulled out, and he hit the deck as I pulled up.

Our first attack had scattered the Germans to the four winds. During the ensuing fight, wild and violent maneuvering was the order of the day on both sides. Due to the at times precarious position I found myself in during the dogfight, I was unable to follow the progress of the battle as a whole.

After things settled down I found myself quite alone, at tree top height heading for the English Channel and home. During the refueling at Manston I discovered that my camera was inoperative, and I thought there would be no confirmation this time. However, upon landing back at North Weald I discovered that the other pilots who hadn't been able to join the fight had already confirmed two and one-half kills for me and another two and a half for the others in the flight."

[Roscoe was unaware that he had downed one of the German planes until Jack Fessler and Humphrey Gilbert told him they saw the Messerschmitt burst into flames and crash.]

Gilbert and I and two other members of our flight had been detailed to remain at altitude to cover while the two remaining flights of the squadron attacked.

From our top position, looking down, we had a grandstand view, and since there was no enemy up at our altitude, we could afford to observe the battle below. Normally this was not the case, since one's eyes did not dwell on any one spot but were constantly roving about the sky looking out in all directions for the enemy.

Later that same month McColpin shot down two more Me 109s on a flight with Geffene and Scarborough, to bring his total to five. For the record, he explained that "I misunderstood the leader's instructions to return to base and lost the section in a rainstorm." Other pilots suspected that it was a bold rhubarb —an independent strafing mission which could have brought down the wrath of the squadron leader had it not turned out well.

"Five or six miles inland over France, 55 miles east of Dunkirk, I saw six Me 109s in two sections line astern at 500 feet," McColpin said in his personal combat report. "I pulled up behind them, and seemed to be unobserved. I fired a two-second burst with cannon and machine guns, and the rear man in the port section blew up. Firing a similar burst, I shot the rear man in the starboard section. He burst into flames. I saw both Me 109Es crash to the ground. I claim them destroyed from 75 yards range. I damaged a railroad engine on my return."

To his squadronmates McColpin became the "instant ace." Five kills in five weeks was a record.

Not long after his transfer from 121 Squadron to 71, Bert Stewart took part in a dogfight with five German fighters. His canopy was shot off, an explosive shell blasted a foot-square hole in his wing, and his plane was peppered with 130 bullet holes.

"Smoke was pouring into the cockpit," Stewart reports.

"What I didn't want was a forced landing far from home. I nursed the plane back to England where there were landing fields all over the southern sector, and glided in without breaking even a fingernail."

On another occasion, returning from a convoy patrol, Stewart forgot to lower his landing gear and the plane came in on its belly. In the mess that night a Free French officer asked if Stewart was the one who had bellied in.

When Stewart nodded, the Frenchman said, "I thought so. I could have given you a red light for a wave-off, but I had never seen a Spitfire land on its belly before." Stewart was so irate he slugged the Frenchman right there.

Harold Strickland recalls his own hair-raising return to North Weald, which had no control tower, runways or traffic controller. Landing aircraft had the right of way.

As I banked the Spitfire to decrease speed and approached into what I was sure was the right direction, with wheels and flaps down, I raised the nose. Somehow this combination of banking, turning and gliding put four other Spitfires, taxiing for takeoff far out on the upwind perimeter, right into my blind spot. There was a rise of the ground toward the center of the field. During the glide and three-point landing, the big long nose of my Spitfire obscured the four oncoming Spitfires taking off down-wind over the rise with wide-open throttle, in a loose— thank God—formation.

When I first saw them I was on my fast landing roll and they were on their takeoff roll. We were all on a collision course. I knew instinctively that with my high rolling speed I could not stop, change direction, or ground loop in either direction in time to prevent overturning or colliding with one or more of the oncoming planes. This was one of those split-second decisions —that the best chance for all of us would be for me to continue almost straight into the small gap between the two outer Spitfires on my left, in the hope that their gap would widen or that all four would be airborne when I arrived rolling in the opposite direction right through the left side of their formation.

The only pilot fully alert and on the ball was the leader's left-side wing man in the oncoming formation. Before I had seen them, and before his flight leader and two other pilots of his formation could do anything, that left-side wing man was executing a furious, unbelievable high-speed turn on the ground with throttle open while swerving away from the forthcoming disaster, probably screaming on his radio channel.

Somehow, in the remaining seconds, the three oncoming

Spitfires, still on their takeoff roll, executed a cool, controlled, slow and gradual separation of their formation, and I could see that heavenly gap immediately ahead widening. In that last fraction of a second, I passed directly between the two outer Spitfires with clearance of perhaps 20 feet on each wingtip.

Peterson recalls a similarly frightening experience at another base a bit later on:

Normally we were the only squadron using Martlesham Heath, since it was a green field with no runways. For a mission escorting bombers to Eindhoven, in Holland, Fighter Command sent in two wings of Spitfires—six squadrons—to use Martlesham as a forward base. We would be the reinforcing squadron for one wing. With seven Spitfire squadrons, it was a bit crowded.

The bombers were to fly on the deck, not more than 50 to 150 feet off the ground. As the first box of B-25s crossed over Martlesham, the Spitfires would start takeoff and join up, to accompany them as far into Holland as they could.

The Spits were able to take off from the grass field in squadrons—four flights of three planes each, in line abreast. The first 12 planes took off, and then the other squadrons, and all the while boxes of bombers were passing overhead, west to east, at 100 feet.

My squadron was the last to take off. The 12 of us were just barely airborne, probably 20 feet off the ground, heading north to south, when a straggling box of medium bombers came in on a direct head-on collision course 50 feet off the ground.

There was nothing they or we could do but continue straight ahead. I led my squadron directly underneath them. The bomber leader did pull up 10 or 15 feet, but we all had to stay below 100 feet so that German radar would not pick us up.

It was sort of hairy for two or three seconds as we passed underneath their prop wash, in such close proximity that we were between the bombers and the tree-tops. Everything turned out all right. We made a turn and joined up with the whole armada headed out over the Channel at 50 feet, and escorted the bombers as far as we could.

The youngest person to become an Eagle was Gilmore Cecil Daniel. When he enlisted at a Royal Canadian Air Force recruiting station in December, 1939, he presented a doctored birth certificate (obtained from his father) showing that he had been born on the Osage Indian Reservation in Oklahoma on November 30, 1921. He had a baby face framed in curly auburn hair. The smooth olive skin of his face was lightly freckled. He weighed only 140 pounds, was five feet eight inches tall, and looked much younger than eighteen.

Daniel's parents were Osage Indians with traces of Cherokee, Choteau, French and Irish blood. His mother's grandfather was Captain Choteau, a founder of the Oklahoma Indian Territory. A cousin, Sylvester Tinker, was chief of the Osage Nation. Sylvester's brother, Major General Clarence L. Tinker, was a World War II fighter and bomber pilot who commanded the U.S. Seventh Army Air Force and was killed in the Battle of Midway; Tinker Air Force Base near Oklahoma City was named for him.

Years after the war, Daniel tried to find out his real birth date. Reservation records had been poorly kept, he said, and only in recent years, after an Indian Agency search of many family records, was his true age substantiated. Those records showed that he was born November 30, 1925, and therefore was only thirteen when he graduated from Spartan Flying School, in Tulsa, and fourteen when he entered the RCAF. He served briefly in all three Eagle squadrons and in six other RAF squadrons as well.

In 242 Squadron Daniel's commanding officer was Douglas Bader, who had lost both legs in an accident in 1931 and yet had become a proficient fighter pilot. After Bader bailed out of his burning Spitfire and was placed by his German captors in a French hospital at St. Omer, his old squadron flew a most unusual mission: "We escorted Bader's legs to St. Omer."

Bader had boldly asked the Germans for a new set of legs to replace those lost when he bailed out, and they relayed the request by radio to London. The Luftwaffe offered to allow the British to send the legs to France in a plane marked with a white cross. RAF fighters would be permitted to escort the plane across the Channel, where German fighters would take over.

"The RAF told the Germans 'no deal,' " Daniel recalls. "It would have been a German propaganda stunt. Instead the RAF sent in a bomber flight escorted by almost 100 fighters, and dropped the legs over St. Omer in a box addressed to Bader. Afterward we went on and bombed a target—I think it was Ostend."

On October 13, 1941, flying as a pilot officer for 71 Squadron, Daniel was shot down while escorting Blenheim bombers to Bethune, France:

I had broken formation to attack three 109Fs. I shot the lead one up and he exploded, knocking the other two down also. I was so surprised and excited that I turned for England, forgetting to watch out for other enemy planes. I was soon being fired at by other 109Fs.

I don't know to this day why I was not killed, because the cockpit was a shambles. I looked over my left shoulder and saw a plane off my port wing shooting at me in a 90-degree deflection. There was an explosion in my starboard wing. I could see a big hole where my cannon ammo had been, so I started to dive at 28,000 feet.

Smoke was pouring from two holes in the gas tank in front of my legs. I knew it would be just seconds before fire broke out. I jettisoned my canopy, and when I pulled my Sutton harness pin I flew out, hitting the tail. I opened my chute immediately, not realizing how high above the earth I was.

The 109Fs kept buzzing me and even shot at me until I waved at them. Upon hitting the water I released my chute. Then I knew I had been hit by shell fragments. My leg hurt like hell.

The 109Fs went away, and then darkness came. I had a grandstand seat for the bombing of Calais that night. I was about five miles from Dover, so I wasn't worried about being picked up. But the next day, when Lysanders flew over me and I waved, they did not see me. Then I started to worry. I waited all day and saw many fighters and a Walrus flying-boat, but no one saw me.

Night set in again, and it was like the night before. The next day it started to rain. It was very cold when my face and hands were out of the water. My leg hurt and my wounds were very sore. Still I wasn't picked up.

Nighttime set in again. Hours later I could hear the roar of the surf and could distinguish land. Some time later I was thrown up on the beach. I crawled the best I could as soon as I felt ground. That was the last I knew until a very bright light was shined on me and I heard foreign voices.

Later in the evening I awoke in a bed with a German sitting beside me on a chair. He asked in English how I was and whether I would like something to eat and drink. He told me they had found me when they turned on floodlights to clear the beach and fire their big guns at Dover.

I had been in the water in my dinghy for 78 hours. The water had helped to sterilize my wounds and kept me from freezing, but I did have frostbite and a cracked or broken leg.

I was taken to St. Omer hospital and given very good care, and then was removed to a hospital at Lille. Later I was taken to Germany and put in Stalag Luft III, where I remained for over three years. When I was released from prison camp I had in my kit only a shirt and a pair of worn-out shoes. My other belongings were not returned.

The toll of losses—both combat- and noncombat-related—kept mounting. Curly-haired, red-headed Roger H. Atkinson was killed on October 15, 1941, only four days after joining 71 Squadron. His friend Denver Miner said, "Roger had a mischievous look in his eyes that set feminine hearts to fluttering. His looks betrayed the inner man. He had a very serious side, and to him the war was no lark."

One week after Atkinson's death Larry A. Chatterton, who had been in the squadron only twenty days, crashed near London under similar circumstances. It was assumed at first that both men had flown into barrage balloon cables.

After an investigation, however, RAF specialists found that both Spitfire II aircraft had had cracked wing spars for some time. These older-model Spits had been given hard usage and were near the end of their operational life cycle. The crash analysis teams attributed both fatal accidents to structural failures. All Spitfire IIs were immediately ordered grounded for inspection and repairs.

One amusing incident involved Oscar Coen, a North Dakota-born former schoolteacher, and W. J. "Lulu" Hollander. They returned from attacking a target in France with pictures proving that their marksmanship had been excellent. But Wing Commander Duke-Woolley took one look at the photographs and groaned, "My God! What have you done? You've blown up the only Benedictine factory left in France."

There was nothing amusing about Coen's rhubarb flight with Peterson on October 20, 1941, however. Every new man in the squadron flew on Peterson's wing until he was qualified, usually a month or longer.

According to Peterson, Coen "was a real crackerjack, and had pretty well 'graduated.' He was very keen and eager. Early that morning he said, 'Let's go,' so the two of us went out on a rhubarb. We found a freight train near Lille, moving toward St. Omer. I told him, 'I'll take the engine, you take the cars.' I fired away, and the next thing I saw was a ball of flame. It looked as though an ammunition car had blown up and debris had hit Oscar. I could see glycol coolant fumes streaming out from his plane.

" 'I'm hit—I'm hit,' Oscar called out. 'I'm going down; I got to get out.' And then, his last words, 'I'm out.' I could see that his parachute was open."

The sadness was heavy in the squadron that evening. The pilots thought Oscar was gone but told themselves, "Don't worry about him. He'll be back in a month." Sure enough, the Maquis helped him. He got out of France through the Pyrenees, was smuggled into Gibraltar, and flew back, rejoining the Eagles three days after Christmas.

By prearrangement his buddy, Mike McPharlin, was to inherit his boots. The first thing Coen said when he walked back into the mess was, "Mac, take off those damn boots."

The next Eagle to be knocked out of the war, eight days after Coen's disappearance by bail-out, was Jack Fessler.

Forced down in enemy territory, Fessler set fire to his plane to guarantee its destruction before hiding from German searchers using dogs. He later wrote this account:

> My last day as an Eagle: October 28, 1941. It was a dawn rhubarb over France with Wally Tribken as No. 2.
>
> I started a gentle dive at a large freight train engine in the marshalling yards at Boulogne, firing with cannon and machine guns.
>
> I continued the attack until I had to pull up to clear the engine. At that moment either the freight engine blew up, or I flew into it—I'll never know. I felt no impact, but my oil cooler and radiator cooling both had been damaged, and my engine was missing badly.
>
> I pulled up to about 2,000 feet, looked for a place to land, and set down in a plowed field just outside Boulogne. I used a post-fire to ignite my plane, then took off on foot. It was 6:15 A.M.
>
> Within 15 minutes search parties with dogs were after me. I kept to streams, using hedgerows for cover, and we played hide and seek until the searchers gave up in midafternoon. At one point I hid in a clump of bushes not 75 feet from men and dogs assembled at a crossroads intersection. Luckily I was downwind from them.
>
> I watched a farmhouse for the rest of the afternoon and evening. About 9 P.M. an automobile drove up and the occupants went into the house. At 11 o'clock I went to the back door and knocked. A farm woman in a long nightgown let me in, and the farmer appeared, in long johns. They invited me to sit in the kitchen, and the woman stirred up the fire and started warming some soup.

The farmer's daughter came into the kitchen, and then two French gendarmes pulling their pants on over long johns. One had his pistol in his belt. These police officers were the persons who had come in the car. They were billeted in the farm home.

We all discussed my situation. I had with me an English-French pocket dictionary and had also studied French in school. We could understand each other.

They fed me soup and offered me wine. "The Germans know you are in this area," one gendarme said. "Tomorrow they will be back with larger search parties. If your scent leads them to this house and they do not find you, they will know we helped you. They will cut all our throats, as a warning to other French people not to aid the enemy. We know they will do this because they have done it before."

I knew they were telling the truth. I wondered whether the gendarme with the pistol would fire at me if I were to run out the door into the night. At the same time, I wanted none of these people killed because of me. Therefore I allowed the gendarmes to take me with them and turn me over to the German authorities.

Thus began my three and one-half years as a prisoner of war.

———

Meanwhile, the Eagles in 121 Squadron were having navigational problems. Hal Marting, who kept a diary at the urging of a novelist sister, commented, "The weather here is pretty lousy for flying. When the radio quits, we are just out of luck, usually. Bailing out is the only smart thing to do."

A case in point was the experience of Reade Tilley while returning in inclement October weather from a dusk convoy patrol. His radio telephone went dead, and he was unable to get position information or approach instructions from Fighter Control. He dropped down into the overcast several times but could find no openings in the clouds. Low on fuel, he had to bail out.

Tilley happened to be wearing a parachute normally assigned to a considerably bulkier pilot. When the chute opened, the harness was so loose Tilley almost slipped out of it. In the darkness the pilot was unable to determine his height above the ground. Just as he had calculated that his altitude must be about one thousand feet, he hit the hard surface. Leg and back injuries were to keep him in the RAF Officers' hospital at Torquay, the Palm Beach of England, for two months.

Another instance of the hazard of communication loss was

related by Marting in a report of November 8, 1941, not long before his own transfer from 121 to 71:

"Eight of our pilots were taking some Hurricanes down south and got lost. Only one had a radio and it went bad. They could not find an airdrome before five had run out of gas. Three got to a drome, four made belly landings, and one bailed out. All the pilots are okay, but it was a damn poor show."

In a tragic incident a week later Malta Stepp and J. I. Brown shot down what they identified as a Ju 88. It turned out instead to be a Blenheim bomber. The British pilot bailed out, but the rear gunner went down with the plane. At a Court of Inquiry the bomber pilot said he did not know he had been fired upon until the port engine cut out and the plane was on fire.

No one could have called Richard F. Patterson an inexperienced pilot or a careless one. In fact, many of the Eagles considered him the best pilot in the squadrons with the possible exception of Red McColpin. Yet misadventures beset him.

Patterson, a Princeton University pole-vaulting star, had made a living for a time in the Miami area by playing golf. Patterson would hang around the golf course looking like an innocent bystander, while colleagues engaged well-heeled visiting players in a match and then invited Patterson in as a fourth. In addition to his prowess as a golfer, Patterson was an expert in backgammon, darts, snooker, craps and virtually any other competition that could be devised.

"Whatever the game, Pat would study it intently, figure the odds, and win every time," McColpin said. "That's why he was top dog in fighters. If he shot 100 bullets, there would be 100 holes in the target."

Red Campbell comments, "Pat was a highly polished precision flier, a real master pilot, extremely aggressive, hardheaded as hell, never averse to taking a chance to find the enemy."

Nevertheless, Patterson made a macabre joke of his recurrent misfortunes. He called himself "the only German ace in the RAF" because he had managed to destroy five British planes. The first was a Fleet trainer which he put flat on its back in the snow in Canada. Next, as an RCAF instructor, he struck a cable with his Harvard AT-6. The third accident was a collision with another plane during a practice dogfight. Both pilots bailed out.

"In the fourth accident, we were practicing dogfights at 30,000 feet when Pat's plane started streaming white smoke from a glycol leak," Campbell recalls. "I chased him on down, and he pulled out at about 10,000 feet over Kirton. As he started to jump he got caught in the aerial mast right behind the cockpit. He pulled himself off of it just in time, but broke an ankle when he came down in the parachute."

Incident number five occurred when Patterson prepared to take a newly delivered Hurricane up on a test flight. The engine quit on takeoff, and the plane veered in, damaging a parked aircraft.

Patterson failed to return from a low-level ship-strafing mission with Gene Watkins near Blankenberge, Belgium, December 7, 1941.

"I used to wonder," said Bert Stewart, "what it was in Pat's past life that caused him to be so sober. He was deeply serious—no wildness in him at all."

———

The pace-setting squadron, No. 71, lost its last English leader, Meares, and another highly regarded pilot, Californian Ross Scarborough, during a training flight on November 15, 1941. Instead of flying the usual position of the squadron leader at the head of White I, the middle four-plane section, Stanley Meares chose the Blue IV position at the right rear of the twelve-plane formation. From that position he could best observe all of his flights and sections.

Red Flight, on the left, was led by Sam Mauriello. Peterson occupied the White I slot as acting squadron leader. Newton Anderson led Blue Flight, followed in close line astern by Strickland, Scarborough and Meares.

The twelve Spitfires were in a tight squadron formation called *Balbo,* in which the planes of each flight flew especially close to their respective flight leaders, and the three flights close to each other. This formation made it possible for the planes to climb, change direction, and descend through thick clouds and rain almost as a single unit.

"Pete maneuvered the squadron into a simple widening out of the flights, a lateral separation where the three flights weave like a snake if desired for greater maneuverability," Strickland wrote later.

"In Blue Flight we had separated a reasonable distance from White Flight and were closing in gradually when the two Spitfires immediately behind me collided. Squadron Leader Meares' Spitfire burst into flames and fell into the clouds below. Neither pilot used his parachute. One of the wrecked planes struck a third Spitfire from another squadron.

"This was tragedy indeed. We had lost our highly admired, distinguished British squadron leader, a veteran of Dunkirk, the Year Alone, and the Battle of Britain, and we had lost our colleague Ross Scarborough, a very aggressive and skilled pilot who had destroyed four enemy aircraft. The squadron did not fly for two days but stood by on readiness. On the third day we attended the military funeral and the ceremonies of Last Post."

The loss of Meares made 71 an all-American squadron for the first time. Peterson became acting squadron leader, the burden of command falling upon him at the age of twenty-one.

Meares had been married for only two months. Shortly before his death, his mother had watched King George VI pin the Distinguished Flying Cross on his tunic. Squadron Leader Meares had accounted for three German planes.

───

In October, 1941, 71 Squadron reached the top in combat ratings. The Air Ministry announced that the American unit led all RAF squadrons that month with a total of nine enemy planes. McColpin accounted for four of the October kills.

In November, 71 led the RAF scoring once again. The Eagles at last had proved that they could fly with the best. King George pinned DFCs on Daymond, for becoming "the first ace" among the Eagles, and on McColpin and Peterson for their equally brilliant performances.

Meanwhile Bill Dunn, still crippled from the amputation of part of his right foot, still sure in his own heart that he had become the first American ace, went back to the United States. Before long he was teaching aerial gunnery to RCAF cadets in Canada and to U.S. pilots in Florida. Then, amazingly, he was back in combat in England with the 406th Fighter Group of the U. S. Ninth Air Force—flying in support of the D-Day invasion of Normandy, shooting down three more enemy planes, sinking a German troop ship in Brest harbor, destroying twelve enemy planes on the ground and 168 enemy vehicles. After finishing this combat tour in Europe, Dunn transferred to the Burma and then the China front, where he finished his war service as a lieutenant colonel.

In 1965 Dunn responded to an appeal by the Air Force Museum in Dayton, Ohio, for Eagle Squadron memorabilia by sending in an old uniform, some photographs and his RAF logbook. Colonel William F. Curry, director of the museum, noted the kills listed in the logbook and asked RAF Air Marshal Sir Patrick Dunn, no relative of the Eagle pilot, for a recheck of the official records. Sir Patrick and another authority, W. J. Taunton, of the RAF Historical Branch in London, both verified that Royal Air Force files showed that Bill Dunn had shot down five enemy planes and had shared credit for another kill with a second pilot while a member of 71 Squadron. These findings were published in the USAF *Airman Magazine* in August, 1967.

Bill Dunn was a chief warrant officer and the strike plans officer of the Seventh Air Force at Tan Son Nhut Air Base, Vietnam, when he received this letter, dated March 19, 1968, from Raymond F. Toliver, historian of the American Fighter Aces Association, the semiofficial judge of U. S. air victory claims:

> As you know, research into the victory credits system of World War II is a continuing process due to the many facets of the credits system employed at that time. The American Fighter Aces Association is happy to inform you that in a recently completed study in conjunction with the Royal Air Force, victory credits clearly indicate that you are America's first fighter ace of World War II. As a result of the above-mentioned research, the American Fighter Aces Association records are being changed to reflect this fact.

In the April, 1973, issue of *Air Force Magazine,* retired Air Force Colonel James R. Patterson wrote:

> A funny thing happened to Bill Dunn on his way to making U.S. Air Force history. When he transferred from the Royal Air Force to the U.S. Army Air Forces in 1943, somebody forgot to make a note of his records that he was America's first ace of World War II. The oversight remained uncorrected until 1967.

"I was certainly glad to have the matter settled," Dunn told friends later. "For a long time it was just my word—or if there was a reference to my score, it carried the qualification that I 'claimed' the distinction. I always felt that my honesty was being questioned."

Asked for his side of the story, Gus Daymond, an executive of an Anaheim, California, electronics company, declined comment. Daymond said he had "sold my life story to Warner Brothers in 1946, and they own the rights to my war time experiences in toto."

Chesley Peterson stands firmly behind Daymond's claims.

"For a couple of years I have known that Bill Dunn claimed to be the first Eagle ace," Peterson said in 1975. "This I don't believe. I believe Gus Daymond was the first of the Eagles to become an ace. The records were not of the best, but Gus and I were the first to be awarded DFCs. It is evident to me that for Gus to be given a DFC when he was just a section leader, it had to be awarded for being the first American Eagle to become an ace."

Bill Dunn has made his position clear: "I hope I don't sound bitter. It doesn't really make any difference now after these many years. I do believe, however, that both British and American historians have confirmed my victories—for a second time—and that should settle the matter once and for all."

Charles Sweeny (above), after he was made an honorary commander for his role in recruiting for the Eagle Squadrons. Eagles Harold H. "Strick" Strickland (above right) and Edwin Dale "Jessie" Taylor (right).

Three of the early Eagles, (left to right) Andy Mamedoff, Vernan "Shorty" Keogh and Gene Tobin, pose aboard a Hurricane.

Gilmore "Danny" Daniel, the youngest Eagle.

One of the favorite British members of the Eagle Squadrons, R. C. "Wilkie" Wilkinson.

Below, What the well dressed RAF pilots wore as displayed by Eagle Don McLeod (left) and Jack Mooney.

Barry Mahon, the day he scored his first two kills.

Oscar Coen ready for takeoff with his B Flight.

Don Young in the cockpit of his Spitfire VB, at Debden, November 1942.

Richard Lear "Dixie" Alexander in U.S. gear.

Vic Bono (left) toasts the groom and bride at Andy Mamedoff's wedding.

Rival aces, William R. Dunn (left) and Gregory "Gus" Daymond (seated in cockpit) with fellow ace, Chesley "Pete" Peterson.

Eagles being briefed for a mission, after their transfer to the USAAF. The tension was ever-present.

Luke Allen is helped with his chute before a 71 Squadron takeoff.

Grim pilots leave the briefing prior to the costly bomber escort mission to Abbeville, France, July 31, 1942. Among them are Eagles Spike Miley, at left with bicycle and just to the left of George Sperry, Coby King, walking through the doorway, and Dixie Alexander, with bike at right. Alexander describes part of what happened: "There were enemy aircraft coming down on us from everywhere, and it was at this time that four 190s bounced the lead element of Coby and Grant Eichar. Coby literally exploded on what was probably the first burst, and I doubt if he ever saw his attacker. The radio was a solid chatter of voices, with aircraft engaged everywhere. I had just time to observe Eichar being hit, and starting a slow spiral down, and smoking. Bill Baker in the meantime had gone on his back and started down after the last 190 in the group that had fired on Coby and Ike. . . . I saw him fire at the 190. . . . His pictures later confirmed it destroyed." George Harp was also shot down and Jessie Taylor severly injured. "The pub at Grave's End was not a very happy place that evening."

Eagle Squadron Spitfires lined up for takeoff on a mission to France.

Below left, a 121 Squadron Hurricane during the early months. Below, the graceful lines of the Spit belie its lethal superiority, as an Eagle patrols over the Channel.

Bill Dunn has painted his last action with the Eagles. This is his description of the critical moments: "The 109 was now in my range. With a burst of only three seconds I had him out of commission. A wisp of smoke from the engine turned almost instantly into a sheet of flame. The plane rolled over on its back. As it started down the tail section broke off. I had claimed my second victim of the day. I fired at another Me 109 and saw smoke come from it. Just as I started to press the gun button again my plane lurched sharply. I heard explosions. A ball of fire streamed through the cockpit, smashing into the instrument panel. There were two heavy blows against my right leg, and as my head snapped forward, I began to lose consciousness."

Two adversaries the Eagles confronted in their baptism of fire. The Messerschmitt 109E (above) and the Junkers 88, a versatile twin-engine bomber, this one shot down over England.

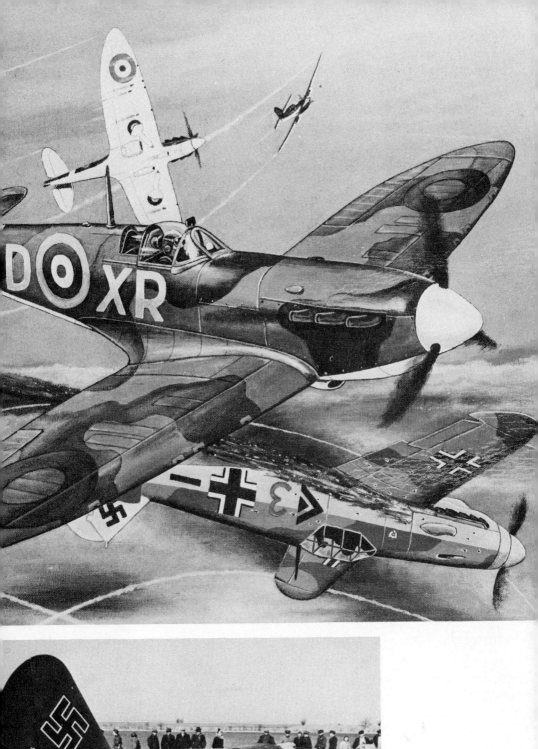

Jim Daley beats up the 121 Squadron field at Southend-on-Sea on his return from a mission.

At Biggin Hill, in May 1942, pilots of 133 Squadron anxiously await the return of their buddies: left to right, Eric Doorly, M. E. Jackson, Bill Baker, Jessie Taylor, Grant Eichar, Bill Arends.

After the battle, debriefing, Jim Daley (center) is questioned by Mike Duff, 121 Squadron intelligence officer, while (left to right) Wing Commander Peter Powell, R. F. Patterson (on wing), Squadron Leader Hugh Kennard, Leroy Skinner and Clarence "Whitey" Martin prepare to give their accounts of the mission.

The Spitfire of Squadron Leader Eric Thomas at the ready, with the pilot's parachute on the wing.

The funeral of an Eagle. The ceremony was marked by a slow march to the gravesite and a quick march back to the Station.

Eagle pilots taking their Spitfires off for Malta from the deck of the U.S.S. *Wasp,* after the carrier had slipped through the Straits of Gibraltar. **The ship's contribution was vital to Malta's defense.**

Hand flying: Vic Bono (left) and Art Roscoe, of 71 Squadron, on readiness and discussing tactics.

Into the USAAF. The Eagles stand rigidly to attention during their final review before transfering from the RAF to service under the American flag. Leading the reviewing officers is Sir Sholto Douglas, followed by Major General Carl A. "Toohey" Spaatz and Brigadier General Monk Hunter, of the U. S. Army Air Forces.

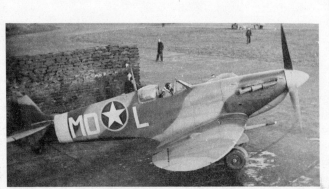

Carl "Spike" Miley's Spitfire VB with U. S. markings. The plane flew for 133 Squadron.

The first Americans of the Eagle Squadrons holding the British DFC to return to the United States: (left to right) Mac McColpin, Sam Mauriello, William J. Daley and Reade Tilley.

Among the returning, triumphant pilots of the Eighth Air Force: (left to right, top row) Captain Jack McClosky, Lieutenant Al Haynes, Lieutenant Dick Beaty, Captain Reade Tilley, Major Carroll McColpin, Major Jim Daley, Captain Sam Mauriello; (bottom row) Captain Harold Strickland, Lieutenant Fred Cullen Smith, Lieutenant John Innes Brown, Captain Michael McPharlin, Lieutenant B. A. Taylor.

Eagles regathered. In September 1976, the Eagle Squadron Association held its reunion in England, visiting some of the old bases. Among the American and British veterans who went to Biggin Hill were (left to right) R. J. Wood—an English groundcrewman, Sir Michael Duff, Dixie Alexander, P. T. Salkeld—a British intelligence officer, Bill Dunn, Danny Daniel, R. C. Wilkinson, Michael Miluck, Bert Stewart, James A. Gray, Chesley Peterson, F. D. Smith and Reade Tilley, president of the association.

6

THE TIME
OF
PEARL HARBOR

Squadron Leader Pete Peterson had retired early on the quiet December Sunday evening at North Weald. He was beginning to doze off when his roommate Robbie Robinson, 71 Squadron's intelligence officer, came storming in.

"My God, Pete, have you heard the news?" Robinson shouted.

"I've been in bed for an hour," Peterson replied. "What news?"

"Pearl Harbor has been attacked. Japanese bombers have set fire to ships and killed a lot of people. The United States is at war."

Peterson leaped out of bed.

"All the fellows are down in the bar. Everybody wants to volunteer for the Air Corps." With that, Robinson was gone.

That night, for the first time, the bar in the North Weald officers' mess remained open after hours. So did those for 121 Squadron at Kirton-in-Lindsey and for 133 Squadron in Northern Ireland. British pilots and other Allied fliers dropped by. Over drinks, the momentous events in the Pacific and in America had to be discussed.

By telephone the two Eagle squadrons in England made a rare agreement. Each squadron would appoint two representatives to meet in London the next day and proceed together to the American Embassy to offer their services to the U.S. flag. The hour was so late that the 121 Squadron emissaries, Shine Parker and Donald McLeod, could find no more buses or trains and had to hitchhike into the city.

The Embassy was a beehive of people scurrying around. Parker and McLeod were introduced to the Ambassador, John Winant, who assured them that their combat experience was badly needed by the Army Air Forces and that something would be done about their transfer soon.

An aide came in to say that a line was open to President Roosevelt in Washington. Mr. Winant relayed the Eagles' position to the president, and the men could hear Mr. Roosevelt talking: their services and experience would be much appreciated. Every effort would be made to bring the Eagles into the U.S. forces as soon as possible.

The wheels of government turn slowly. The transfer of the Eagle squadrons into the USAAF did not take place until September, 1942, nine months later.

At a 71 Squadron meeting, Peterson warned his pilots that any mass transfer into the U.S. air organization was certain to be delayed for a fairly long time. "Since what we really want to do is fight the Japanese," Peterson said, "why don't we go out there as an RAF squadron? Let's all go to Singapore."

The proposal won the squadron's instant and unanimous approval. Peterson took his plan to Fighter Command, directly to Air Chief Marshal Sholto Douglas. The fighter commander shook his head.

"Young man, I am not going to waste a squadron on Singapore," Douglas said. "That city will not last another six weeks."

The appraisal of the rate of the Japanese advance was off only slightly. Singapore's downfall was about two months away.

———

Orders arrived from 11 Group for 71 Squadron to return to Kirton-in-Lindsey. The squadron had had six months of forward duty at North Weald and, in accordance with RAF rotation policy, now would be posted to the relative quiet and rest of 10 or 12 Group for six months.

"I hit the ceiling," Squadron Leader Peterson recalls. "I went to 11 Group Headquarters at Uxbridge to see Air Marshal Leigh-Mallory, and told him, 'Nobody in 71 Squadron is willing to go up north. The men will quit first. They came here to fight. Nobody wants to go back to Kirton Lindsey.' "

Leigh-Mallory was completely unsympathetic. "Rotation —that is my policy," he said.

Peterson decided to go over Leigh-Mallory's head once again, straight to Sholto Douglas.

"I was only twenty-one and a squadron leader, and I had nothing to lose," Peterson said, thirty-five years later. "I had a bunch of guys that were hard to control. We had a good unit. We were the high squadron in the RAF in October and November. We had very few losses. We did not need a rest.

"Sholto Douglas was a most impressive man. He had pale blue eyes. If ever the phrase 'eyes of steel' described anyone, it applied to him.

"I stood straight, eyes ahead, and said, 'Sir, I know I shouldn't be here. I should not jump channels. But I just had a conference with Leigh-Mallory. He made a decision I am appealing. You cannot send 71 Squadron out of 11 Group. We are here to fight. That is all there is to it.' And I told him the whole story."

Douglas told Peterson he would see what he could do. Within a few days 71 Squadron was removed from North Weald as ordered, but not to Kirton-in-Lindsey. Instead, the Eagles went back to Martlesham Heath, the field from which they had been transferred only six months earlier. Thus, they remained in 11 Group, in the main combat zone.

"At Martlesham we were a free-lance squadron, ready to fly with any wing that was short," Peterson says. "Usually a wing consisted of three squadrons, and when it had the job of high cover for bombers it really needed to be reinforced with an additional squadron. Some of the really tough battles were fought by top cover. Whenever the North Weald wing drew the top cover assignment, we would reinforce them. The same with the wings at Tangmere, Hornchurch, Biggin Hill or Duxford. For six months we really had a good time.

"I don't think Leigh-Mallory ever forgave me, but he never mentioned it. More than two years later I worked for him as a colonel of the U.S. Air Forces when he headed the Allied Expeditionary Air Force, and I was with his Forward Headquarters on D-Day."

———

No sooner had 71 Squadron vacated the premises at North Weald in mid-December, 1941, than 121 Eagle Squadron moved in—from Kirton-in-Lindsey. The pilots of 121 were delighted at last to be a part of 11 Group. Their sightings of the enemy during seven months of flying out of Kirton had been infrequent and inconclusive. Sel Edner and Jack Mooney had damaged a Ju 88 in August. Ten days later Powell had been credited with probably destroying a Messerschmitt 109F. Most of the Kirton-based missions were flown without enemy contact.

The squadron attributed its good fortune, in the move close to London, to its intelligence officer, a tall, thin, black-haired Welshman who signed his daily reports as M. Assheton-Smith. The Americans knew him first as Mike Smith and then as Mike Duff. Only belatedly did most of them discover that he was Sir Michael Duff, and that when he was away on week-end leave the telephone number through which he could be reached was usually that of Buckingham Palace. His godmother was Queen Mary, a longtime close friend of his mother.

His connection with 121 Squadron began in the spring of 1941 when an old friend, Lord Sherwood, Secretary of State for Air, said to him, "You get on with Americans. How would you like to go to an Eagle squadron?" Duff replied that he would be delighted and immediately went to 121 to do intelligence work for Squadron Leader Powell.

Duff discovered quickly that the Eagles were unhappy with their inactive role. He told Lord Sherwood the pilots were bored at Kirton and asked to have them moved south. Sherwood spoke to Leigh-Mallory, and the move to North Weald followed.

Although he had been brought up on the large family estate at Bangor, Wales, Duff fit easily into squadron life. After every mission, regardless of the hour or the weather, he rode his bicycle out to each airplane to interview the pilots. He endeared himself to the Americans by loading as many of them as possible into his little car every time he drove into London. He had a warm and ready smile that offset his aristocratic appearance, and he was always ready with humorous anecdotes about British customs and traditions.

———

In Northern Ireland the 133 Squadron pilots had been speculating when the United States would enter the war. In an informal poll taken in November the majority estimated that by March of 1942 U.S. forces would join Britain and her allies in conflict with Nazi Germany. The guessing ended December 7, 1941.

Eric Thomas, the new squadron commander, quickly proved to be even more of an air disciplinarian than his predecessor, George Brown. His basic approach to fighter tactics was the development of teamwork. This meant constant practice, concentration on formation flying, rigid adherence to instructions—and more practice and more practice, day after day, usually in deplorably bad flying weather and with Hurricane IIB and Spitfire IIA aircraft that by no stretch of the imagination could be called first-line fighters.

Early in December the rumor swept through Eglinton that 133 Squadron would soon be returning to England to complete its training and to be equipped with new Spitfires. Then, with the coming of spring, 133 would be sent to an active post in 11 Group.

Rumor became fact when an RAF squadron arrived to take over the Hurricanes and convoy patrol duties of 133, leaving the Eagles time to practice flying Spitfires. The relieving squadron—notorious individualists famed as "the Bad Boys of the RAF" for their wild ways— had just returned from a summer in Russia checking out Soviet pilots on Hurricanes. Their arrival at Eglinton resulted in the biggest brawl Eglinton had yet seen.

The base commander, Dickie Bain, disturbed by the noise, arrived at the mess just in time to catch the highlight of a hotly contested football game involving all members of both squadrons. Angrily, he told the Americans that they soon would be sent back to England. The Eagles were so delighted with the base commander's inadvertent and premature disclosure of plans that they and their newfound friends from Russia began celebrating with renewed exuberance. Bain, incensed, ordered all of the pilots out of the mess. Irrepressible by this time, both squadrons moved the party to a Londonderry pub. Another party, at Yuletide, also careened out of control. When the supply of wood for the fireplace ran out, the Eagles chopped up the Christmas tree, and the whole mess caught on fire.

On the morning of December 31 all of 133 Squadron, less its aircraft and flying equipment, departed by train for Belfast with orders of posting to the RAF Station Kirton-in-Lindsey. On arriving in Belfast at 11 o'clock on New Year's Eve, the 120 enlisted men and officers found that the British transportation detachment had slipped a cog, and no arrangements to feed and house them had been made.

The Eagles waited in the snow for about an hour before being herded into an empty mess hall. After another long wait they were served canned bully beef, bread and hot tea.

"To make the best of it, we pretended that the cold meat was roast turkey, the bread was chocolate cake and apple pie, and the tea was champagne," George Sperry said. "We toasted and sang the New Year in. Our hosts stood and stared, convinced that we were off our rockers."

The squadron arrived at Kirton on January 2, 1942. Its "welcoming notice" that day was a grim warning from the base commander that no riotous actions of the type inflicted on the station by members of 71 and 121 squadrons would be tolerated.

────

The coolness of the RAF's reception of 133 Squadron at Kirton-in-Lindsey was understandable, and the station staff was justly apprehensive. Shine Parker noted that the conduct of each Eagle squadron at Kirton, or before coming there, had been progressively worse.

"As each squadron replaced another, it took months to live down what the preceding unit had done," Parker recounts. "In 121, we flooded the mess before leaving, causing most of the upper floor to fall in. We had a friendly little game of turning on all the faucets in the bathtubs and then snatching early-to-bed types out of a sound sleep and dropping them into the cold water. It was fun until someone forgot to turn off the taps."

Barry Mahon recalls that on the first night he reported to his squadron at Kirton "I stepped from the lorry into the officers' mess to be greeted by loud whooping and hollering from the upstairs area. All of a sudden in formation came the whole squadron on bicycles down the steps, only to prang horribly at the bottom in a mess of wheels, handlebars and blue uniforms."

Reade Tilley remembers a disastrous football game in the Kirton anteroom during what he called a particularly good bash. "A soda syphon was used as a football. Nobody had thought to remove the furniture. The old mess steward stood aghast at the wreckage. At the end of the game they threw everybody out into the blackout, and the leading elements crashed into the wing commander's car which had thoughtlessly been parked in front of the door."

At a farewell party for Lulu Hollander, R. D. McMinn and Thomas J. Andrews, several Eagles appropriated a bicycle that had been left by a British officer and demonstrated that it *was* possible for five men to ride the vehicle at the same time.

The owner came on the scene during the demonstration and joined in the jeers and cheers—until he found out it was his bicycle.

On a foggy December evening some of the Eagles decided, despite the lack of an invitation, to take part in joint training exercises of the British Army and the RAF for the rehearsal of defenses against an enemy invasion. Afterward the participating Eagles boasted that they had taken over a train and a railroad station and a number of weapons, and had seized forty Welsh guards. Other Eagles scoffed that most of the action had taken place in a pub, as a beer-drinking contest.

One thing the partying accomplished, in addition to amusement and relaxation, was the development of talent. Hollander was an accomplished pianist, and he and Deacon Hively —Howard D. Hively, of Ohio—worked up a series of sketches that proved vastly entertaining to the Eagles.

Hively's most elaborate act involved Stew Stewart, who used to wear a Scotch tam-o'-shanter and kilts off duty. The two men schemed to make everyone think they had had a falling-out. They carried this out for four or five days with things getting worse and worse, until it seemed that they were about to come to blows.

One evening at the bar in the officers' mess one of them made a disparaging remark. The other returned the slur. Before the pilots knew it, Stewart had stormed out and up the stairs to his room. Soon he came back down the stairway, shouting to himself. He opened the door brandishing a .45, leaving his audience aghast.

Stewart leveled the gun at Hively. There was a great blast, and Deac tumbled off his chair. Everyone took shelter. When the startled watchers returned, they found Stewart and Hively in hysterics, embracing each other.

Many months later Hively and Stewart reenacted their gun battle while the Eagles were assembled to await a Hollywood USO group that included actresses Martha Raye, Mitzi Mayfair and Carole Landis.

"Some of the other fellows—Stan Anderson, McMinn and Oscar Coen—were in on the plot," Stewart confessed. "Deac and I had traded our .45s with some Navy men for .38 revolvers. We took the lead out of the bullets and packed cotton in.

"Andy, Mac and Oscar spread the word that Stewart and Hively had had another bad quarrel and were out to kill each other. The chaplain went to the base CO to try and stop the fight before it could begin. Everyone was in the mess, an ante-room 55 or 60 feet long, waiting for the Hollywood crowd when Hively came in one door and I came in the other. The crowd fell back.

" 'Deacon,' I said, 'don't you think you ought to apologize for what you said about me?'

" 'Hell no,' he growled.

"I punched him on the shoulder, as we had rehearsed in my room. As he staggered back, I crouched behind a chair. We pulled out our guns and started shooting.

"There was instant panic. Some of the fellows jumped out of the windows. Others ducked to the floor. Lee Gover leaped on top of me to grab my gun hand. My gun barrel gave him a good cut on the forehead. We are good friends now, but I don't think he spoke to me for two years.

"Hively and I got up and started laughing. Some of the others didn't think it was funny. The movie stars? They got lost in the blackout and never did show up."

The customary pattern for the Eagles in England was to remain on flying duty for a week or ten days, and then have two or three days off. Usually the fliers would make a rush to the train as soon as time-off began, to get to London quickly. Most often they would check in at the Strand Palace or Regent Palace hotels or the Cumberland at Marble Arch. A few who preferred the quiet life or were particularly mindful of economy stayed at the modestly priced, friendly English Speaking Union or at the Overseas League.

A favorite gathering place was the Eagle Club at 28 Charing Cross Road, which was operated mainly for Americans in the British service. Volunteers from the various women's groups in London ran the club under the capable direction of a charming woman called Mrs. Dexter and a petite, vivacious blonde, Miss Brooks.

The Eagle Club was the only place in London where the Americans could get a hamburger and a Coke. Also always available were free cigarettes, donated by tobacco companies or obtained through the Red Cross. The Eagles could pick up their mail at the Club, and now and then they were interviewed by radio broadcasters such as Charles Collingwood and Edward R. Murrow.

Also popular with the Eagles, though strictly as a drinking spot and a place to meet friends and dates, was the Crackers Club at 14 Denman Street, just off Piccadilly Circus. Marie Cook, the Maltese woman who operated the Club, functioned as a sort of mother to the Eagles, listening to their troubles, offering them advice, and now and then slipping them taxi fare to their hotels when they had spent money too freely at the bar.

The bottle clubs favored by the Eagles included the Kit Kat, the Blue Pencil, the Spotlight, 21 Upstairs, and Murray's, on Beek Street. One relatively plush establishment of the bottle party type, the Embassy Club, was frequented by London society women. Although the Eagles found the prices steep for their pockets, they managed to stop by now and then. As for culture, the closest that most of the Eagles came to it was the Windmill Theater on Leicester Square, famed for its beautiful showgirls and nude burlesque.

In wartime London good food was hard to find. The American fliers favored Maxim's, a Chinese restaurant, especially after one of the Eagles convinced the owner that the RAF's American squadrons were closely associated with the AVG, the American Volunteer Group (also called the Flying Tigers), which was helping to save China from the Japanese. From that time on, any wearer of the Eagle Squadron patch would receive the best table in the house and the best food.

Some of the Eagles bought their RAF uniforms off the shelf at department stores. Others, such as Jim Moore, six-foot-two and almost an all-American basketball player, had to rely on tailors. Some of the London tailors—Geeves, Austin Reed, Moss Brothers, Hobson's—extended credit to American officers without question. For many years, in RAF service and afterward, the Eagles found it impossible to pay for a British decoration. If an Eagle bought his uniform at Hobson's, for example, any British or American decoration was sewn on without charge.

Among the American war correspondents in London, Collingwood, Murrow, Ray Daniel and Drew Middleton were familiar names, but Quentin Reynolds, of *Collier's*, was perhaps the best known to the Eagles. Reynolds and his photographer, Robert Capa, visited the squadrons and made friends, and thereafter many of the Eagles would visit Reynolds' suite at the Savoy or the Dorchester, where drinks were always available and where checks could be cashed.

"Every time one particular Eagle was in London he would go to the Savoy florist shop and buy a beautiful corsage for his girl friend and charge it to Quent," Barry Mahon recalls. "I'm sure that if Reynolds ever did discover the trick he would have said nothing about it. We were his boys. We could do no wrong."

Jessie Taylor remembers a nightclub tour with his squadron buddy, Moran Morris, and Reynolds' secretary, Betty Morais, during which Miss Morais picked up all the tabs. Reynolds wrote a feature story about Taylor's miniature dachshund, Herman the German, a sort of squadron mascot. Months later friends were still sending Taylor clippings of the article.

A letter from Charles Cook of 133 Squadron to his parents in Alhambra, California, depicted the day-to-day life of an Eagle:

> You only get one egg a month, a teaspoon of sugar a day, and no beef over the size of a quarter in one piece. We live mostly on fish and the internals of animals. We get considerable liver, kidney and hearts. Even the people with plenty of money can't get any better than that.
>
> We eat in the officers' mess, and are fed like kings compared to the rest of the population. I have never been in a colder or more damp place. We all have slight colds. If you have too bad a cold and happen to be on readiness and have to scramble in a hurry to get to 30,000 feet or above, your chances of getting home are not very good. Quite a few have "gone in" that way during the winter months here.
>
> The RAF pilots always call their planes "kites." Each pilot has his own kite and crew. The pilot is dependent upon the crew to see that his plane is in perfect shape. I'm able to get a few extra packages of cigarettes a week, and I give them to the crew. This brings very good results.
>
> I am looking forward to a two-week leave during which another pilot and I will be allowed to go on a British destroyer on active duty in the North Atlantic. The pilots take turns making that trip. I understand the officers and men on a destroyer are wonderful to you.
>
> The Royal Navy likes the Eagles. At one time or another most of the British navy men have been in the United States, and the people over there really treated them up to our usual American standards. They also know just how much the good old U.S.A. means to England as they see all the materials, airplanes and foodstuff being sent over to meet England's needs.
>
> The things we Eagle pilots miss very much are the American magazines such as *Life, Look, Click, American, Saturday Evening Post, Time* and *Collier's*. There is not much to do in the

long evenings. The magazines keep us posted on events there at home.

Charlie Cook, like the other Eagles, did manage to find diversion. A trim, bubbly little WAAF, Edna Maude Hutchinson, recalls, "They made me echelon to that crazy American squadron, 133, and here came this big fellow on a bicycle, all smiles, one day. He had his hat on sideways, like Napoleon, with the visor down over one ear, and said to me and my friend Moya Mills, 'Hello, girls. Come on in. We have some oranges from California!' "

One of Edna Maude's jobs was to refuel planes from an enormous tanker truck. Cook watched in fascination as the slip of a girl wheeled her Fordson tractor around, maneuvering the four-ton petrol "bowser" into position. He was charmed at the grace and dexterity with which she descended into the grease pits to lubricate the vehicles.

"We don't really know what we're doing down here," Edna Maude would grin up at him. "These oil smudges on our faces—they tell us they're good for our complexion." Then Charles would boost her up on his bicycle handlebars and give her a ride home, little dreaming that after the war she would come to California to marry him and later present him with two sons destined also to serve in military uniform overseas.

Selden Edner, of Fergus Falls, Minnesota, was the first member of 121 Squadron to escort his English sweetheart to the altar. Bert Stewart named his Spitfire "Elaine" for his fiancée, Elaine Howells, an Australian correspondent in London for the newly launched *Sydney Daily Mirror.* More than a quarter of a century later, in another war on the opposite side of the earth, their second son, Rod, was to name both of the U.S. Army Birddog spotter aircraft he flew in Vietnam after his mother. Rod Stewart won the Silver Star and the Distinguished Flying Cross.

John Guilbert DuFour married the WAAF commander at Ford Air Base in somewhat unusual circumstances. DuFour had gone to Canada shortly after Britain and Germany went to war, and had tried to join the RCAF but had been rejected. Later he returned to Canada and joined the Seaforth Highlanders. For fear that he might be turned down because of records showing the RCAF's refusal, he signed up under the name of James Crowley and as a Canadian citizen.

At Camp Borden in Canada, he applied for a transfer into

the RAF as a fighter pilot, was accepted and sent to 71 Eagle Squadron. He retained the name of Crowley and became known as Gentleman Jim to the Eagles.

"I kept the name of Crowley because I knew that doing otherwise would cause a lot of trouble and provoke a bunch of red tape activity," DuFour explained later. "Then I became engaged. I wouldn't dream of getting married under an assumed name, so I had a lawyer in Ipswich change my name back."

Accordingly, the name James Crowley disappeared from the daily listing of missions flown and was replaced by that of John DuFour. Under either surname, the Eagles continued to refer to him as Gentleman Jim. Thirty-four years later, through inadvertence, the name of Jim Crowley still appeared on the roster of the Eagle Squadron Association, on a list of 157 deceased Eagles.

The most celebrated of the Anglo-American romances during this time was that of Pete Peterson, the tall, quiet young man from Utah who had skyrocketed into the post of the first American to lead an RAF squadron into combat, and Audrey Boyes, a beautiful actress and dancer from Capetown, South Africa, who had studied with the Russian Ballet, had distinguished herself in motion pictures, and was then appearing with Raymond Massey in Robert E. Sherwood's Pulitzer prize-winning play *Idiot's Delight.*

The catalyst for this seemingly unlikely combination and hugely enjoying his role of Dan Cupid, was Robbie Robinson, who had introduced his squadron leader to the young lady. "Pete had been persuaded to make a broadcast to the United States over the BBC," Robinson, later Lord Martonmere, recalls. "He found this more terrifying than fighting the Germans. To soothe him afterwards I took him out with Audrey and her friend, Zoe Gail."

Robinson entertained Eagle Squadron members at his London mansion as frequently as working schedules would permit. Peterson and Miss Boyes were regular guests. They became engaged at Robinson's birthday dinner party for Gus Daymond on Thanksgiving night in 1941. Their wedding took place at St. Margarets, Westminster, the same church in which Robinson had been married.

Members of the British peerage owning large country estates frequently invited Eagle pilots out for weekends of shooting, elegant parties or restful quiet. Some of the Americans who

were from modest homes found themselves a bit overawed by
the luxury and the sense of history.

Vernon Parker and his roommate, William L. C. "Casey"
Jones, of Baltimore, Maryland, enjoyed the unique experience
of fourteen days in neutral Eire as guests of Lord Charles
Cavendish and his lady, the former American dancer Adele
Astaire, at their Lismore castle. Eire had closed its northern
border to Americans serving with the British, but Sir Michael
Duff had helped with special arrangements for this one visit.

"While we absorbed the art of becoming fighter pilots we
got to know and understand our British cousins," George
Sperry observed. "We could not buy a drink in the pubs. Theater tickets, dinner invitations and well-stacked females were for
free. Several thousand miles from our homes, feeling a rather
questionable future over enemy-held France, we indulged in
unbridled celebrations and uninhibited acts that gave others the
impression that we thought we owned the whole of England.

"We saw so many of our friends die that we developed a
defense against any betrayal of emotion and refused to senti-
mentalize friendship and parting and death. To many, therefore, we seemed to be without loyalty or deep feeling. We
trained for air warfare in England during a time of great tension
and war nerves, when liquor, carousing and wenching provided
a means of escape from grim realities."

Religion among the Eagles? Dixie Alexander recounts,
shaking his head, "First of all, these were young people, most
of them lacking a great sense of responsibility. They were soldiers of fortune. They were there for many reasons, but the
primary ones had to be love of flying, adventure and glamor.

"Some just wanted to avoid an infantry draft or for various
reasons were not acceptable to the USAAF. Unlike the Euro-
peans who flew with the RAF, few of the Americans had a deep
feeling of hatred for the Germans. There had been no physical
contact; for many it was a continuation of World War I and a
case of natural adversaries. We were the good guys, they were
the bad. We were all fatalistic to some degree, and this can be
a substitute for religion in itself. We all sort of believed we
would probably 'buy it,' one way or another, before the end—
but never today, never tomorrow. It was a reckless kind of false
courage, bordering a bit on the suicidal. The German pilots had
it, along with their love for the Fatherland and their belief in
their cause.

"A lot of us were loners. Certainly these were all headstrong young men, capable of making decisions on their own. I am sure that many like myself prayed quietly by themselves —gave thanks and approached it in their own way and, although not ashamed, preferred to have it go unnoticed by the others."

Britain went to great lengths to assure that the Americans who gave up their lives in wartime England would never be forgotten. Of seventy American and four British Eagle Squadron members killed in action or while on active service, twenty were buried in Brookwood cemetery near London. Others were laid to rest in the American cemetery at Cambridge and elsewhere. At St. George's Chapel of Remembrance at Biggin Hill, the fallen Eagles are memorialized on a killed-in-action Roll of Honour. Years later, surviving Eagles returned to Biggin to present the Chapel with a silver chalice inscribed, "To those who came with us and now remain forever."

The names of the Eagle dead also are recorded in London at St. Clement Dane, the Royal Air Force Church in the Strand, a handsome structure bright with the colors of red, blue and gold, its floor inlaid with the crests of all the squadrons that served in the war. Each hassock was lovingly sewn in petit-point by friends or relatives. The Eagles who worshipped there were told many times, "This is your church as long as you are in London." Still another memorial, to those who have no known graves, is at Runnymede, high on a hill overlooking the flat country around Heathrow Airport. Sprinklings of Flanders poppies among the white stones are offerings from families that still remember. Jet planes thunder across this quiet dignity, as though in tribute.

Another living monument is the famous poem *High Flight* by Pilot Officer John Gillespie Magee, Jr. (Half a dozen Eagles and wives of Eagles requested that it be included in this story of the Eagle Squadrons, even though the poem has appeared in many books and magazines.) Magee, born in Shanghai, went from Yale University into the Royal Canadian Air Force in 1940. He sent a copy of his poem to his parents a few months before his death in a Spitfire December 11, 1941.

> Oh! I have slipped the bonds of earth
> And danced the skies on laughter-silvered wings;
> Sunward I've climbed, and joined the tumbling mirth
> Of sun-split clouds—and done a hundred things
> You have not dreamed of—wheeled and soared and swung

High in the sunlit silence. Hov'ring there
I've chased the shouting wind along, and flung
My eager craft through footless halls of air.
Up, up the long delirious, burning blue,
I've topped the windswept heights with easy grace
Where never lark, or even eagle flew—
And, while with silent lifting mind I've trod
The high untrespassed sanctity of space,
Put out my hand and touched the face of God.

7

TAXES, TEXANS AND NIGHT FIGHTERS

The Eagles were outraged at their British hosts. The gall, the insolence, the insult of it all. Here it was, the tail end of 1941 —some of the Eagles had been in England for more than a year by this time—and notice had come that the American volunteers were to pay British income taxes! And pay them on RAF salaries that were miserable: fourteen shillings sixpence a day —about three dollars—including flight pay for pilot officers; twelve shillings for officers on ground duty. There were yelps of defiance and bitter jokes about the British having failed to learn the lesson of the Boston Tea Party. Was this any kind of gratitude for Americans who were fighting and risking their lives for a brother nation?

In Northern Ireland, the members of 133 Squadron were more or less out of touch at the time. Furthermore, the two squadrons in England had always remained aloof from each other, except for their cooperative presentation to U.S. Ambassador Winant following the Pearl Harbor attack. This time, however, the pilots of 71 and 121 Squadrons agreed that the emergency called for a united protest.

"We went jointly to the RAF and told them we simply could not live on the money we were getting and pay taxes on it, too," Red Campbell says. "We told them that since they gave us no recourse, we were seriously considering resigning en masse. The RAF Air Marshal called a special meeting. We pointed out to him that an English officer on leave could go to his home, but Americans on their days off had to go to expensive hotels and restaurants. This, we said, was clear discrimination, unfair to the American volunteers."

The air marshal told the Eagles they had made a convincing argument. Shortly thereafter, the American pilots were informed that they were exempt from British income taxes on their military pay which meant a saving of almost half their income.

A majority of the Eagles, or at least the noisiest group among them, was from Texas. Some of the brasher representatives of the Lone Star state called upon the Air Ministry with a proposal that a fourth Eagle Squadron be established exclusively for Texas pilots; they were not surprised, however, by the blunt response, "Hell, no. No more bloody American squadrons!"

A more serious proposal, in view of the fact that in RAF arithmetic three squadrons equalled one wing, was that the Eagle Squadrons be melded into one all-American wing.

"The idea made sense, because everything was being done in wing formation at the time," maintains Pete Peterson, an unofficial spokesman for the Eagles. "The Poles had an RAF wing—why not the Americans? We had conversations with Fighter Command, 11 Group, and some friends in the Air Ministry. Charles Sweeny, acting in a liaison role, was pushing the proposal. If Pearl Harbor had not come along and changed everything, we would have had an American wing in the Royal Air Force. It was in the mill."

———

RAF reports from Ireland late in 1941 about the unruly conduct of 133 Squadron's pilots infuriated Air Chief Marshal Douglas at Fighter Command and Air Marshal Leigh-Mallory at 11 Group. Leigh-Mallory summoned Mac McColpin, 71 Squadron's newest ace, a recent recipient of the DFC and a former member of 121 Squadron, and told him, "You are being posted to 133 Squadron as B Flight commander. The boss [Sholto Douglas] is furious at them. Before they left Eglinton they stacked furniture in the mess and set fire to it, broke into the liquor locker, and did all kinds of mischief. You are going to Kirton to straighten them out and make a fighter team out of them."

McColpin was to succeed Ed Bateman, who had developed sinus trouble and was being posted to Training Command. The transfer meant for McColpin the same kind of double promotion, from Pilot Officer through flying officer to Flight Lieutenant, that had been granted to Peterson.

McColpin assumed his new duties January 23, 1942. Seasoned by experience with the two older American squadrons, he already knew the Eagles' side of the 133 Squadron story. They had received what they deemed to be shabby treatment —had been moved from base to base, given lip service on personnel and aircraft, and sent to Ireland a long way from the war they had come over to fight. At Kirton they had been given old war-weary VA model Spitfires, battered from long service in Operational Training Units, with canopies so dirty they were almost opaque.

McColpin realized that "in combat, a spot on the canopy looks just like an enemy aircraft at high altitude. No wonder morale and spirits were low."

The newly commissioned flight lieutenant acted with characteristic directness. Immediately upon his arrival at Kirton at 8 P.M. he went to Dispersal, asked for the best aircraft in B Flight, took it into the air for one circuit of the field, and landed. Then he inspected all of the other B Flight Spitfires—and promptly grounded the lot. He called out all the airmen and started an intensive maintenance program that also involved the pilots of that Flight. When the B Flight chief sergeant refused to obey the orders, McColpin promptly ordered him into confinement.

"It was rough treatment, but it worked," McColpin recalled many years later. "The Flight was on its way to great things. By the time Squadron Leader Thomas returned three days later, A Flight was pushing to get aircraft as good to fly as those in B Flight. Thereafter, 133 Squadron never slackened off from that competitive spirit between Flights. It was a great bunch of fellows—and the sergeant and I became very good friends."

Not all the Eagles disparaged the Spit VAs assigned to them. George Sperry said that in comparison to the Hurricanes and the Spitfire IIAs they had been flying, "although slightly disappointed that we had not yet received the 20 mm. cannon VB models, we quickly found our aircraft with the more powerful engines to be truly wonderful to fly."

Richard Alexander said of his first Spitfire, "It still remains the most enjoyable aircraft I have ever flown." He had been warned that the VA model had a good bit of fabric and floated for miles, and his first circuit resulted in three passes at the field before he could get down. He found that the plane stalled off at 62 miles an hour, cruised at about 240 at plus 4 boost pressure or 32 inches of mercury at 2400 RPM, had a top speed of about 320, and was rated at about 23,000 feet. "Later there were VBs, Cs, then 9s, 8s, 11s, 14s, and after that I don't know what. They were all lovely aircraft and gave a person a true feeling of flying. I don't believe there was an aircraft in the war that could match those last four models in air-to-air combat."

The first real taste of combat for 133 Squadron came on the heels of a snow-and-sleet storm that paralyzed the Kirton-on-Lindsey base on February 1, 1942. The station commander ordered every able-bodied man and woman, including all the pilots, out to shovel snow. Three days later two runways had been cleared—just in time.

Early on the morning of February 5 a four-Spitfire patrol was launched from the newly reopened field and stationed over a convoy of ships approaching Hull. Although the cloud ceiling was down to about eight hundred feet and visibility out over the water was near zero, the patrol sighted a Ju 88 bomber and radioed an alarm. The alerted squadron was able to maintain a standing patrol of eight Spitfires over the ships throughout the daylight hours, while relays of Ju 88s and Dornier 217s tried to destroy the convoy.

During one sortie that lasted an hour and twenty minutes and included "a more or less uninterrupted series of combats with one or more Do 217s, lasting about 15 minutes," McColpin silenced the port gun's return fire from one enemy aircraft and shot off a large piece of the engine nacelle of that plane or one identical to it. He returned to base with all his guns empty.

Flight Lieutenant Hugh Anthony Stephen Johnston and Pilot Officer M. E. Jackson battled several Do 217s, and the escort patrol at the tail of the convoy confirmed that a Do 217 had crashed into the sea. On piecing together the time involved, that plane was credited one-half to Johnston and Jackson and half to a pilot from a Hurricane squadron.

"Best of all, no ships in the convoy were sunk or damaged," said George Sperry, one of the participants in the fighting. "We had fought off the enemy in the worst type of weather, had operated as a team, had sustained no losses—and most of us had fired our guns at the enemy for the first time."

Fighter Command Chief Douglas read to the assembled Eagles a telegram from King George congratulating 133 Squadron on its outstanding performance. Douglas also announced that 133 would be re-equipped immediately with new Mark VB Spitfires and would be moved south into 11 Group when the weather improved in the spring.

If there were gains, there were also losses.

One of the most highly regarded pilots in 133 Squadron was Hugh Card Brown, of Glendale, California, a great-grandson of Brigham Young, the great Mormon leader. Pilot Officer Brown and Flight Sgt. Carter Woodruff Harp, of Columbus, Georgia, ran into difficulty on a weather-checking flight on March 16, 1942. Harp called his companion on the radio telephone to say that he was returning to base because of zero visibility. There was no reply. No trace ever was found of Brown or his Spitfire.

On April 15, Sam F. Whedon, of Beverly Hills, California, collided with another plane at 7,000 feet and had to bail out. Other pilots, circling, saw his parachute open and observed Whedon waving, to show that he was all right. Later it was learned that he was caught by wind gusts as he landed. Tumbling backward, he struck his head on a rock and was fatally injured.

On April 26, McColpin, the former 71 Squadron ace, shot down his first plane as a 133 Squadron member—a Focke-Wulf 190. It was also 133's first confirmed victory and the first downing of the recently introduced 190 which was to win a reputation as the best conventional German fighter plane of the war. The 190 with its air-cooled radial engine could usually take more punishment than aircraft with liquid-cooled engines that quickly overheated or froze if they lost their cooling fluid. The Germans used the Fw 190 for bombing, rocket firing, and strafing as well as for fighter-interceptor duty.

The very next day two Texans, W. H. Baker and Robert L. Pewitt, were each credited with probably destroying an Fw 190 while escorting Douglas Boston bombers to Ostende.

The Luftwaffe had been hitting English cities hard at night with high-flying bombers such as the Me 110, the Ju 88, and the Do 17. RAF Blenheims and the old Boulton-Paul Defiants were ineffective against this menace. In response, Fighter Command inaugurated night training for selected pilots. Dick Alexander recalls, "Spitfires and Hurricane squadrons now became operational on moonlit nights for interception purposes. Each squadron would have at least twelve moonlight operational pilots and at least five who were designated dark night. Having always liked the Link trainer and instruments, I soon became one of the latter.

"Flying a Spitfire on a moonlit night was a glorious experience, but on a dark night under combat conditions it could be disastrous. Gyros tumbled easily, and one needed complete confidence in the old needle, ball and air-speed indicator, plus his ability to fly therewith. There was the added hazard of being temporarily blinded after firing the guns. Then, too, the Jerry fired back and had the nasty habit of leading you half-blinded into objects such as towers, wires, chimneys or other barriers."

One night, Alexander was ordered up, presumably on a local flight to intercept the customary nocturnal Ju 88 reconnaissance plane. The cloud layer was solid at 8,000 feet, but on top there was "a fleecy new wonderful world."

"I was told to climb to Angels 24 and was given various headings to fly," Alexander recounts. "I had been airborne with no incident for about 30 minutes when suddenly the whole sky seemed to explode.

"A pilot who is bracketed in heavy flak and who knows that every bit of it is directed solely at him is forced into swift decisions. I immediately rolled over on to my back and lost 6,000 feet of altitude, while changing my direction.

"Once clear of the barrage and again in peaceful skies, I called Control and asked them to alert the ack-ack boys as to my presence. They acknowledged and asked me to return to Angels 18—18,000 feet. Again I was given a vector, and all was serene. Then, suddenly, Fourth of July at the Kankakee Fairgrounds! Once more, everything was happening. I went through my swift get-well-lost routine again. This time I stormed a bit to the controller when things had settled down. He gave me a heading back to base.

"Assisted down through the cloud, I landed without mishap and was told to report to Operations. I had fully intended to anyway, and I gave a rather vivid report of the flak, the gunners, and communications in general. After hearing me out and letting me unwind, the controller told me that communications were actually impossible. I had been sitting directly over Boulogne the first time and then later over Calais. Intelligence wanted to know exactly what antiaircraft strength the Jerries had at those two locations. They told me I had described it admirably, and then they thanked me and dismissed me. They had certainly found their answer—and so had I."

The numerous solo interceptor missions in darkness became known to the 133 Squadron pilots at Kirton as fighter night flights. The first night mission for 133 in squadron strength, as contrasted with Spitfire individual night fighting, took place on April 28 as the Luftwaffe engaged in one of its so-called Baedeker raids against clearly nonmilitary targets, such as cathedrals and universities in the guidebook cities of Hull, Lincoln and York.

Clusters of incendiary bombs had set York ablaze. The Spitfire pilots set out after some of the enemy bombers and drove them away. Eric Doorly, of Garden City, New York, was lucky to come out of the engagement alive:

> We stacked up at 2,000-foot intervals, starting at 6,000 feet. Around York we could see the bomb blasts, tracers from cannon fire, and the mass of flames across the city. It was obvious from the tracers that the enemy aircraft were coming in well below us. I dropped down and pulled in behind a Dornier 217 that was just beginning his run. The tail gunner and I exchanged fire all the way down as I closed to about 50 yards. The tail gun fire stopped and I suddenly became aware of trees going by. I pulled up involuntarily and that was the last I saw of the Dornier.
>
> As I climbed, the glycol indicator pegged, and I assumed that the tail gunner had hit my radiator. I called Kirton Ops for a vector home and turned on it without much thought. At about 2,500 feet the engine seized, and I simultaneously realized that I had been given an outgoing vector. I made a 180-degree turn, and could see the funnel lights three or four miles away—too far to reach.
>
> At 1,000 feet I started getting out, with the Spit trimmed for 120 miles an hour. I had one foot on the wing and one in the cockpit, and my chute jammed in the side flap opening. I finally jerked it free, sat down and pulled the cord. The chute popped; I made one swing and landed standing up in a plowed field. The plane landed half a mile away. I walked to it the next morning. It was intact except for a broken propeller and a damaged radiator—a pretty good landing all by itself.
>
> I had come down near Church Fenton. As soon as I got out of my parachute I made my way to a farmhouse. The farmer was suspicious of my odd American accent until Ops sent a man out to pick me up.

———

At North Weald, 121 Squadron acquired a new commanding officer in mid-January, 1942. Peter Powell was promoted to command the wing at Hornchurch, and Hugh Kennard became 121 Squadron leader.

An incident only a week earlier had demonstrated anew Kennard's intelligent and alert response to emergencies as well as his ability to command. He had planned to lead the squadron on a mission, but immediately after take off the unit lost sight of the ground. Sensing at once the potential for disaster, Kennard decided to cancel the flight. He called for a vector back to base and directed that Operations begin shooting flares to guide the returning pilots.

"You cannot abort the mission without authority from the wing commander," the controller replied.

"I don't care about the wing commander," Kennard retorted sharply. "I want a vector and flares immediately."

Kennard knew that if he lost contct with the ground completely, there soon would be Spitfires crashing all over England. He led the squadron back on semi-instruments, turned it near the ground until he found the airfield, and supervised the landings. All of the pilots but one returned safely.

On another occasion the pilots of 121 Squadron sighted a green patch in the sea two miles west of Boulogne. Closer inspection revealed a man in the green water. The squadron dropped close to the surface and found that the pilot was without a dinghy. He was floating in a life preserver and waving vigorously.

Kennard ordered four pilots to circle the area while he and the rest of the squadron climbed to seventeen thousand feet to search for rescue boats. The fliers found four boats, all heading in the wrong direction.

Waggling their wing tips and circling the boats, the pilots finally induced the vessels to take a course that would lead them toward the green spot. Low on fuel, the Spitfires had to turn for home base while the boats were still 300 to 400 yards from the man in the water.

Kennard stayed on for a last look around but was unable to see the man in distress. Apparently the unfortunate fellow had drifted out of the green patch. Later, however, the squadron learned that the rescue boats had found the man and brought him ashore. Five of the Spitfires were so low on fuel they had to land at intermediate fields. The squadron leader acknowledged that while there also had been a considerable risk in venturing so close to the French coast, the risk was warranted under the circumstances.

Under Kennard's direction, 121 at last attained maturity. In an encounter near Calais on March 23, Jack Mooney, a smiling Irishman from Long Island City, New York, shot down an Fw 190, and Reade Tilley was credited with probably destroying another. In three clashes within a twelve-day span in April the squadron shot down four more enemy planes and damaged four, with Leroy Skinner scoring in each battle. In the first engagement Skinner destroyed one enemy plane, and Kennard, Tommy Allen, and Barry Mahon damaged their opponents. Three days later Skinner and Sel Edner each destroyed an Fw 190, and Allen damaged one. On April 24 Skinner and William J. "Jim" Daley shared credit for shooting down a Junkers Ju 52 transport.

As always, there were penalties. Four days after the Ju 52 battle Skinner became a war prisoner and a squadronmate, C. O. Bodding, was killed in a bail-out at low altitude. On a strafing mission over France, Casey Jones, who was to have been married within a fortnight, was last seen losing altitude, his plane streaming glycol fumes. At the 121 mess that night the pilots painted a locomotive on the anteroom in tribute to their missing colleague nicknamed for the legendary engineer who had "mounted to the cabin with his orders in his hand." However, the station commander took a dim view, and the squadron had to split the tab and pay to get the mural painted over. Things brightened a month later, when the men learned that Casey was a German prisoner.

On the night of February 11, 1942, three of Germany's most powerful warships, the heavy cruiser *Prinz Eugen* and the battle cruisers *Scharnhorst* and *Gneisenau,* took advantage of rain and fog to make a dramatic, historic escape from Brest harbor where they had been trapped by British ships and planes for almost a year. For almost twelve hours the three ten-thousand-ton pocket battleships avoided detection as they moved eastward toward the sanctuary of the North Sea. In the English Channel they were joined by a German naval escort and, from early dawn onward, by an umbrella of Nazi planes which had been invisible in the thick cloud cover. They had sailed some 360 miles and were only three or four hours away from the relative safety of Ostend when, at 10:30 A.M. February 12, an RAF patrol sighted them off Le Touquet, approaching the narrow neck of the Channel at Calais.

In England most of the airfields were snow-covered and fogbound, the runways muddy and unserviceable. The two

Eagle Squadrons in 11 Group barely managed to get into action. As Assheton-Smith, intelligence officer, wrote laconically in the 121 Squadron Operations Record Book, "It is believed that no great damage, if any, was done to the three ships." According to an Eagle pilot:

The Germans had picked an absolutely perfect day for the operation. They had waited a month for it. The clouds were dense and low, and most of our airfields were socked in.

The German ships were discovered by Group Captain Victor Beamish, station commander at RAF Kenley.

Vic was flying a morning reconnaissance with a wing man. They were stooging around above and in the clouds when, through just a little break in the clouds, he looked down toward Dunkirk and Le Touquet and saw a battleship. They kept radio silence, and reported the battleships when they landed at their base. The Germans had 50 to 75 planes over the escaping flotilla at all times. They knew where it was. We didn't.

I was sitting on the ground at Martlesham Heath screaming at Sector Control because it was time to get off. Finally at 11 A.M. I took the squadron of 12 planes out and headed for the Channel. Sector Control didn't know where the ships were. They thought they might be in the Ostend area. I remember coming out of dense clouds, getting as low as I could, and seeing what I thought was a big ship. I pulled up and immediately lost sight of my wing man.

We were right in the middle of something. The next thing I knew there were Me 109s all around the place, coming at me. I never got a shot at them. My wing man saw an airplane 50 feet above me and thought it was me. It was an Me 109. There were seven different layers of clouds, and the Germans would come down through the layers and take cracks at us.

At North Weald, 121 Squadron stood down because of the weather. It was supposedly impossible to get into the air, but Squadron Leader Kennard and some of his pilots got off. I heard him say, "Tuck in, tuck in, boys. Everybody tuck in."

I flew between two flak ships while trying to establish where the ocean was and whether this was a convoy. We tried to block the area so our slow, cumbersome Swordfish torpedo planes could get in. The single-engine Swordfish had a top speed of 139 miles an hour, and when loaded with a 1,600-pound torpedo it cruised at only 85. It had an open cockpit and a three-man crew—a pilot, an observer, and a gunner handling the machine gun in the rear cockpit. The Swordfish were sitting ducks.

They were protected by 10 fighters, but they didn't have a

chance. All six Swordfish were shot down almost before they could launch their torpedoes. Five of the 18 crew members were rescued from the Channel.

Kennard got so low the German ships were afraid to fire lest they hit each other. Four flak ships were grouped right together. I thought: What the hell are we trying to do? I knew we were not sent there to shoot battleships, but we were not finding airplanes to shoot down.

The British lost 71 of the 398 planes they sent out. Not a single bomb reached a target. Of the British planes lost, perhaps 50 hit the cliffs of Dover, which were invisible in the fog, or flew into the water in zero visibility.

More losses and hazards dogged the Eagles. A freak accident on March 27 came close to wiping out two of the 71 Squadron pilots, Michael G. "Wee Mac" McPharlin and Bob Sprague. A plane from another squadron lost its brakes on landing, crashed into McPharlin's taxiing plane, caught fire, and then hurtled into Sprague's aircraft. The pilot of the runaway plane was killed.

An April 12 mission claimed Ben Freeman Mays, a former Wharton, Texas, oilfield worker and a four-letter athlete at Southwestern University. "Oscar Coen led Blue Flight, followed by Bill O'Reagan, myself and Ben Mays," recounts Strick Strickland. "As we approached the target area, the Haze-brouck marshalling yards, I noticed that Ben was more than 50 yards astern. I called for him to close up, and when I rechecked he was narrowing the gap.

"At about this time the two other wings with us were attacked by Me 109s and Fw 190s diving out of the sun and firing from long range. When I checked Ben again, he was gone. Somewhere well within a fraction of a second he was hit. Sprague saw smoke and a Spitfire going down. The BBC reported later that 370 RAF bombers had been over targets on the mainland and that two enemy had been destroyed and eleven Spitfires were missing."

On April 27, in the fiercest battle thus far for 71 Squadron the team shot down five 190s and damaged or probably destroyed several others, for the loss of one pilot, John F. Flynn. Coen and McPharlin fired simultaneously at an enemy plane, sending it earthward, and immediately shot down a second German craft. A few minutes later, heading homeward, they destroyed a third Focke-Wulf which had been pursuing a Spitfire.

Peterson, leading the bomber escort mission, shot down two planes and damaged a third. Art Roscoe probably destroyed one. O'Reagan's Spitfire was disabled over the Dunkirk area, but he managed to glide it back across the Channel to a safe landing.

8

IN
THE EAST

In England's damp and chilly climate, John A. Campbell suffered from a serious sinus condition that grounded him for two weeks. He began to consider the possibility of a transfer to a drier, warmer locale.

"Also, things were slow in England then, in late autumn of 1941, with regard to fighter activity," he remembers. "I wanted to go where the action was. We were not getting much of it in 121. Powell wanted me to stay with the squadron and kept telling me to wait. But I put in for the Middle East. Once you were in an Eagle squadron it was hard to get out."

Campbell transferred to the 258 New Zealand Squadron which, with two other squadrons, was to proceed through the Middle East to the Russian Eastern Front to replace the RAF wing that had been there as a token force.

Two other former Eagles were in 258 Squadron when Campbell arrived. Don Geffene, of Los Angeles, had served in 121 with Campbell for three months and had joined the New Zealanders after a month in 71. Art Donahue, the fourth pilot to join 71 Squadron and the first to quit it less than a month later, had wearied of endless RAF patrols over the English Channel and reconnaisance over northern France.

They left England on November 3, 1941—Campbell's

twentieth birthday. At the time they knew their destination only as Egypt. They were equipped with cannon-firing Hurricane IICs and had been loaded with another Hurricane squadron aboard a seaplane tender, HMS *Athene.*

At Gibraltar half the wing—one full squadron and half of another—were loaded on to two carriers, the *Ark Royal* and the *Argus.* They were taken into the Mediterranean and flew off to Malta, where they stayed.

On the way back the *Ark Royal* was torpedoed and sunk within sight of the Rock. The Royal Navy decided against risking the *Argus* any more in the Mediterranean, so the Americans sat on Gibraltar for seven weeks and were there when the Japanese attacked Pearl Harbor.

During the long wait at Gibraltar the Americans whiled away hours at clubs and cafes. "I remember Donahue standing at the bar, drinking beer, with one hand tucked into his tunic," Campbell says. "Some people thought it was a war-hero pose, but it wasn't. He had to hold his hand that way because of his Battle of Britain injuries. Art was an idealist—one of the few real ones in the squadron. He had high principles. His former flight commander once told me Art had tried to resign his commission so he could be a sergeant pilot. Donahue felt he should be no more privileged than any other fighter pilot in the squadron. He was not trying to shirk responsibility. He would gladly have been the squadron leader as a sergeant pilot. I guess he just didn't conform.

"Christmas of 1941 was a bad time for Art. It was the first chance he had for a lot of time to think about what the war meant to the parents of fighter pilots on both sides. He said he felt like weeping for the mothers of the German airmen he had killed.

"Art wrote a series of articles about air combat for a magazine—I think it was the *Saturday Evening Post.* Someone suggested he do a book. I was with him when he bought a typewriter."

Donahue wrote *Tally-Ho! Yankee In a Spitfire,* describing his flying career up to mid-April, 1941. He made no mention in the book of the period in October, 1940, that he spent with 71 Eagle Squadron. He confided to Campbell, however, that he had considered the Eagles "a motley crew that would never amount to anything."

While the three Americans were at Gibraltar they were delighted at the arrival of Oscar Coen of 71 Squadron, who had been missing since a strafing mission over France on October 20, 1941. Coen had walked from France to Portugal and had found so many escapees waiting in Lisbon for release that he walked on through Spain with an English squadron leader who had been hiding in France since the Dunkirk evacuation. After his stay on Gibraltar, Coen went back to England and rejoined 71 Squadron.

At Gibraltar the pilots of 258 Squadron flew daily low-level patrols along the Spanish coast with their long-range Hurricanes, hunting for Focke-Wulf Condors believed operating out of Cadiz against Atlantic shipping. On one of the patrol missions Geffene's engine failed, forcing him to land in Spanish Tangiers.

"I created an international incident by using my cannon to destroy his plane on the ground in neutral territory before the Spaniards could bring their German friends over to look at it," Campbell recalls.

"Don was interned, of course, but not for long. Somehow, in his smooth and charming manner, he obtained the cooperation of the governor general's daughter. We were told later that presumably through her arrangements a *New York Herald Tribune* correspondent, Al Raymond, visited Don in Tangiers and handed him a gun and maps.

"Don escaped—not too difficult a matter for him. He tried to rejoin the squadron but did not make contact with it until he reached Colombo, Ceylon. We heard later that he was shot down and killed on Easter Sunday, 1942, when the Japanese raided Colombo and sank the battleship *Warspite.*"

The *Athene* ferried 258 Squadron to Takoradi, Gold Coast, where wings were refitted to the Hurricanes. The squadron flew across Africa to Khartoum, Anglo-Egyptian Sudan.

"Somebody decided they could use us in Singapore, so they loaded us aboard the aircraft carrier *Indomitable,*" Campbell recalls. "They took away our cannon-firing Hurricanes to use in the Northern Desert and gave us machine gun-equipped Hurricane IIBs. The *Indomitable* took us from Port Sudan to a point near Christmas Island—not the American island in the Pacific south of Hawaii but British Christmas, 300 miles south of Java.

"We flew off the carrier to Batavia, where we unbolted our long-range fuel tanks. Installing these tanks had meant disabling a pair of guns. We would not need the extra range in this part of the world, and removal of the tanks left the Hurricane exterior clean enough to enable it to fight. From Java we proceeded by way of Sumatra to Singapore, where all hell had broken loose."

By the time 258 Squadron reached Singapore on January 29, 1942, the Japanese had taken Hong Kong, Wake Island and Manila and were sweeping down through the Philippines, Borneo and Malaya. British forces were withdrawing from Singapore. The Hurricanes were called on for defense against increasingly severe Japanese bomber attacks.

On one mission Donahue flew into a strange shower of white objects. He said they looked like snowballs streaking past, and he thought they might be a new kind of tracer bullet. He learned later that they were propaganda leaflets dropped by the bombers. The leaflets, entitled "News Reports from Lisbon," said that President Roosevelt had proposed that Singapore be declared a neutral zone and that Japan was considering the suggestion.

"This was a heck of a war, a case of too little too late," Campbell says. "No ground support nor proper maintenance, but we did put up a hell of a fight. Having no maintenance, we did our own. We lost some of our planes, banged some up on landings. The largest squadron formation we ever were able to put up was seven, in our first major combat on February 1, 1942. The Japanese had two squadrons of 27 bombers each, and three squadrons of fighters."

In the February 1 air battle Campbell destroyed a Zero and damaged a bomber and another fighter. Donahue shot down his first Zero. Three of the RAF fighters were lost.

The Japanese landed on Singapore island February 7 and began their final conquest of the city. The Hurricanes fought on from Palembang, Sumatra. Campbell shot down a Zero that crashed on the airport perimeter there. Donahue was cited for destroying several enemy planes and for attacking Japanese troops landing in the Singapore area.

Singapore surrendered on February 15, ending a campaign in which the Allies lost 9,000 killed and 130,000 captured; but the pilots remaining elsewhere in Malaya, in Sumatra and in Java had their orders: the enemy advance toward Australia must be slowed by forcing the Japanese to land on every island in their path.

"Churchill had said that the RAF would fight to the last aircraft and then take to the hills and fight to the last man," Campbell recalls. "That was us!"

While on a patrol, Donahue was warned by radio not to land at Palembang but to fly to another airdrome to the southeast. More than two hundred Japanese parachutists had been dropped around Palembang. From the alternate airfield Donahue telephoned his Palembang hotel and talked to his roommate, Red Campbell. The Japanese were not yet in the city, Red said, but the airport was surrounded. The current plan was to escape up river by motorboat.

"Red," said Donahue, "is there any way you could bring with you the little writing case inside my traveling bag? It has all my valuables."

"I'll try," Campbell replied. "I'll bring both bags."

Donahue said later that Campbell somehow got the bags to Java where he handed them over to a crew leaving for India.

"They reached me more than two months later," Donahue reported to friends. "I was especially happy because most of the films I had taken in Singapore were there. I have never seen or heard of good old Red since."

Primarily because of Donahue's gloomy report, Campbell was listed officially as missing and presumed dead. The pilots managed to get out of Palembang with their planes, however, and fought on from Java. "That's where we ran out of luck and airplanes," Campbell says. All that remained of 605, the sole surviving RAF squadron, was four planes and six pilots.

"On February 28 we four Hurricanes were ordered to tallyho on two Japanese bomber formations plus 30 fighters. We never got to the first bombers. We got caught below them and then started to climb to get above, to catch the second group coming in. Nine fighters chasing their own tails were coming up to us. We had just made the decision to dive through them to get at the bombers when six fighters streaked down from out of the sun and the whole thing became a general dogfight.

"A Zero took on the Hurricane ahead of me, and I went after that one. This guy was kind of dumb. He'd do things like half rolls and a couple of slow rolls in front of me. Finally I nailed him. He went up in a real steep climb. The wing came away, and I watched him go spinning down. The next thing I knew there was stuff all over my plane, shooting up between my legs. I went into a dive, and when I started to pull out of it, half of the right wing broke away.

"In my flying I never closed the cockpit canopy completely. I had a thing about it—about trying to get out and finding myself locked in. And now the track was damaged, so I couldn't get it open or shut. I couldn't believe this was happening to me. It was more like something remote, away from me. I was scared at first, then angry at myself. I could see the ground coming up. I told myself that when I hit the ground it probably wouldn't really hurt because it would be over so fast. I stood up on the seat, braced my back against the canopy, and gave a big shove. Out I shot, high above Java. It was almost as though the canopy had exploded. As my friend Eric Doorly said to me long years later, a quart of adrenalin can do a lot for you."

As Campbell drifted down in his parachute, an airplane came toward him slowly. Red steeled himself, fearing he was about to be machine gunned. The plane proved to be another Hurricane. It turned, then went down like a falling leaf, its pilot probably already dead.

Campbell landed in a rice paddy. He had twisted a leg badly and for a while thought he had broken his back. He had chunks of 20 mm. shrapnel in one leg and was bleeding from deep cuts where he had come in contact with the canopy. One side of his left arm felt paralyzed. There was no flotation gear, no Mae West, in his parachute kit, and he had lost his knife and gun.

Natives who had watched him come down found him in the jungle. At first, they seemed belligerent. Although the pilot had lost his gun when the parachute opened, he was wearing a cartridge belt, and he had placed a stick inside his shirt to give the semblance of a weapon. Whenever a native looked menacing, Campbell would take a bullet out of the cartridge belt and look at it.

The Javanese gave him food. Chinese from another village, passing by in a boat, took him down the river to a Dutch officer in a patrol craft. The officer had found the wreckage of the other Hurricane and the remains of its pilot, a New Zealander named Harry Dobbin, and had gathered up a part of Dobbin's gear.

On his return to Batavia, Campbell learned that only two Hurricanes remained, along with one New Zealand pilot and two sergeant pilots. The Japanese had landed close by that morning, March 1, 1942, and were moving upon the city.

"The Dutch, upon whom we depended for ground support, would not fight," Campbell says. "They never fought a major battle. Instead, they stole the two Lockheed Lodestars that were supposed to be our transportation and used them to fly their wives and children out. They surrendered the island and declared Batavia an open city. Those of us who were left took to the hills and made like guerrillas for the next three weeks. In one town, not yet taken over by the Japanese, we went to the Dutch officer in command, seeking help. Instead, the lieutenant in charge ordered us to turn in our arms, saying, 'We have surrendered, and you must too. We will help you get to a concentration camp. We have been ordered to do this.' We started to back out. He ordered us to stay and pointed a gun at us. Some among us who had weapons fired, and we ran to our truck. One of our men was killed.

"The British army men with us started raiding for food, and we were picked up on the south coast of Java by a Japanese patrol. One of our men started to run and was shot dead. The rest of us surrendered. It was March 20. If we had stayed in hiding much longer, we probably would have died anyway of dysentery or malaria."

Campbell remained a Japanese prisoner in Java for three and one-half years until September 14, 1945—the only Eagle pilot to have that dubious distinction.

Art Donahue and a few other pilots, finding Sumatra's airfields no longer tenable, also started flying out of Batavia. There they learned of the February 28 mission from which Campbell failed to return. In April Donahue led an air search for Japanese barges moving up a river. The barges threw up antiaircraft fire, and Donahue told the other pilots to hold off "while I put down that flak."

On his first pass over the flotilla Donahue was hit in the leg by a 20 mm. shell. He stuffed a glove into the wound to slow the flow of blood and then used up the rest of his ammunition flying back over the barges. The action was to win him the RAF's Distinguished Flying Cross.

Donahue received emergency treatment at a Dutch hospital in Bandoeng and then went by hospital ship to Ceylon for further care. While recuperating he wrote his second book, *Last Flight from Singapore.*

Recovering once again from critical battle wounds, Donahue returned to England and resumed combat with his old unit, this time as squadron leader. On an early-morning weather reconnaissance over the coast of France, an enemy plane followed him but failed to catch up with him, radar observers reported.

Suspecting that a German night fighter had mistaken him

for a bomber, Donahue returned to the same area the next day, September 11, 1942, and flew along slowly enough to permit a pursuing plane to come close. The trap succeeded. Donahue made a quick 180-degree turn on the German plane and shot it down. His own plane was damaged, however. Donahue reported by radio that he had destroyed a Junkers 88, that his engine was overheating, and that he was ditching in the Channel. Weather conditions were severe; air-sea rescue units were unable to find him.

9

THE
MALTA
CAMPAIGN

Malta—4,000 enemy air raids in 400 days. Malta, where every fighter pilot figured himself a fugitive from death. Losses —one fighter pilot each day.

—Denver Miner, 133 Squadron

In the dreary early part of 1942 the RAF began readily granting transfers out of England to Spitfire pilots who volunteered for duty in Malta. The 122-square-mile British crown colony south of Sicily had long been under enemy attack. It needed help desperately.

The Eagles from 71 and 121 Squadrons electing Mediterranean service included Leo Nomis ("I was of Sioux Indian descent so it was inevitable that in the RAF I would be typed as an Indian"), Art Roscoe, John J. Lynch, Reade Tilley, Douglas "Tiger" Booth, Don McLeod, Jim Peck, Fred Scudday, Bruce Downs, and Richard McHan.

At 133, Squadron Leader Thomas resisted more strongly than did the other unit commanders the actions that would deprive him of his best men. He flatly refused the transfer requests of Jessie Taylor and Moran Morris, Oklahoma buddies since high school days, on the basis that they were first-line pilots who could not be spared. Thomas reluctantly acceded to the postings of F/Lt. Johnny Johnston and of Hiram Putnam.

In a paper written many years later, Leo Nomis reminisced:

They should have awarded a medal for the mere arriving at Malta. I have never been to another place with such a visible atmosphere of doom, violence and toughness about it at first sight. Coming out from England as we did, the filth, flies, diseases and near starvation absolutely fascinated us, the more so because the interception missions—which were boundless—were not in the least deterred by these handicaps.

The air war seemed more deadly there, the 109s more sinister than the 190s of northern France. Perhaps again it was the atmosphere and the conditions.

A lot of the Eagles, some of whom were seemingly clueless in England, ran up their scores and got their gongs in Malta. Not speaking for myself, because I was involved in more farces than victories, but for Eagles such as Roscoe, Lynch, Tilley, Peck and so many others. Malta either made or broke them.

In 71 Squadron Art Roscoe was my ground companion and John Lynch was usually my air companion. We were in different squadrons in Malta, but Lynch, who was out there later than those of us of the summer of 1942, ran up a mighty score. Roscoe, who went out with me in July of that year, was involved in an absolute epic in his final episode there.

The Jerries were employing both the Hermann Goering and Kesselring groups of 109s out there at that time. Both groups had all-yellow cowlings and spinners on their aircraft, and both were renowned for their slyness and ability to hit what they were aiming at.

During one of the increasingly huge dogfights of October, Roscoe managed to get himself in the reflector sight of one of those dangerous chaps. In the flick of an eye the rude fellow actually put four cannon rounds directly through Art's cockpit, the miracle being that only one hit Art—going completely through his upper body at the shoulder without killing him. The other rounds smashed everything in the cockpit and set the engine alight.

To say that Art was shocked and concerned would be an understatement. While he was dazedly pondering his predicament, the 109 boldly flew alongside to view his handiwork and no doubt to inspect the bloody hulk in the Spitfire cockpit.

Roscoe was still flying straight and level. By then the Spit was beginning to blaze a bit more respectably from the engine. Art tried to bail out but found himself so weak from shock and loss of blood he could not even get the safety harness off.

He sank back and looked over at the 109, whose superior speed was carrying him close by Art's port wingtip. The German pilot, as Art later related, was positively overcome with morbid curiosity.

Then, in one of those rare moments or pieces of moments in which we can hardly recall later how or why we acted, Roscoe kicked his rudder, swerved to the left and, pushing his cannon button, shot the 109 down. This while his cowling was shooting flames and he had the dreadful fear that he was dying.

The action continued as though it were taken from a Hollywood movie. Unable to bail out and with the Spit on fire, Art somehow managed to get back to Takali, where he crash landed. When the plane hit the ground it flipped over, pinning him in the wreckage.

That would have been the end of Art, except that a ground crewman rushed into the blaze and pulled him out. The man later received the George Cross for his heroic act. Long hospitalization followed for Art, and finally a return to duty. I consider this a classic example of what some pilots did and endured in those days.

In Malta we used tropical Spits—that is, we flew without cockpit canopies. The largest of the three fighter bases on the island was Luqa. Our base, Takali, was a two-squadron airfield. The other base, Halfar, struggled through with one squadron, the mighty No. 185. Everyone was so keyed up and crazy out there that I was fearful most of the time of being shot down by some keen oaf from Luqa or Halfar.

The RAF had flown Hurricanes into Malta off the carrier *Furious* as early as August, 1941. The pilots in that contingent included Howard M. Coffin, who had served briefly in 121 Squadron, and three other Americans who had trained with the Eagles but had been assigned to other squadrons: E. E. "Pete" Steele, Edwin E. Streets, Jr., and Don A. Tedford. Coffin wrote a book, *Malta Story,* published in 1943, about the grim early days of constant enemy air attacks and dedicated it to Steele, Streets, and Tedford, all killed at Malta. Among other non-Eagle Americans in the Malta defense was Lance Wade, a Texan who shot down twenty-five enemy aircraft to become the leading American ace in the British forces.

In early March, 1942, the small British carriers *Argus* and *Eagle* delivered to Malta fifteen Spitfires, the first fighters arriving there that were adequately armed for combat against the Me 109F. The Spits promptly shot down one attacking Me 109 and probably destroyed others. Predictably, the Luftwaffe intensified its assault.

The RAF launched more Spitfires for Malta reinforcements on March 23. Among the pilots were Jim Peck and Don McLeod, formerly of 121 Eagle Squadron. Before leaving England, McLeod had acquired the distinction of being the only person to have been shot down while flying a Link trainer—a unique accomplishment because the device is used only on the ground. McLeod was in the trainer in a small shack when a German plane strafed the field and shot the trainer off its pedestal.

The day after Peck flew to Malta he shot down a Ju 88. The following day he and McLeod each shot down two Me 109s.

According to McLeod, by April 2 the RAF forces in Malta still had not been reinforced. "We only had about half a dozen planes to meet the scores of bombers and fighters the Italians and Germans were sending over.

"Four of us went up to meet 24 Me 109s escorting bombers on a daylight attack. I thought I was all right until I saw stuff flying around me like a horizontal hailstorm. Then I knew I was in for it. I said to myself, 'So this is how it feels to die.' My Spitfire was shot up so badly that the right aileron was sticking up vertically, and the elevators were disabled. The only thing to do was to hold the plane in a 200-mile-an-hour glide.

"I was at 21,000 feet when the attack started. I saw the machine being torn apart as Jerry after Jerry attacked. I kept looking over my right shoulder. I'd see two of them coming at me. Then I'd skid some and they would miss. Then I'd skid again. I felt something burn my left arm and leg, and saw blood. But it didn't hurt. I skidded again. That was all I could do. The radio was shot out from in front of me. I couldn't talk to anyone, so I decided to get out of there."

McLeod bailed out five to eight hundred feet from the ground. When the parachute opened, the straps struck his chin and snapped his body so hard that his thyroid cartilage was fractured. He came down off the coast and was picked up by a ship. Despite his broken neck and the cannon shell fragments in his left arm and leg, McLeod was back flying again within two months.

As the campaign against Malta intensified, Winston Churchill appealed to President Roosevelt for help in the form of the U.S. aircraft carrier *Wasp,* then in the Atlantic. If the

Wasp could sneak into the Mediterranean at night, he said, it could launch Spitfire reinforcements near Sardinia for a four-hundred-mile flight to Malta. Roosevelt concurred.

The big American carrier took aboard fifty-four Spitfire VCs at Glasgow, raced south around the Iberian peninsula, and slipped through the Strait of Gibraltar in darkness. Early on the morning of April 20, off Algiers, forty-seven Spitfires lifted off the flight deck. Among the pilots were two former Eagles of 121 Squadron, Reade Tilley and Tiger Booth.

"This must certainly have been the first time Spitfires ever took off from an American carrier," Tilley maintains. "Everybody would have preferred a more leisurely and less hazardous way of reaching Malta with Spitfires, but there wasn't any.

"The main worry was that the *Wasp* might get sunk before the launch point was reached. The thought of the great air battles yet to be fought at Malta provided us with a lot of incentive and encouragement to aim down the deck, open the throttle, and start praying.

"All 47 of us landed at Malta, which was pretty good considering the fact that Me 109s picked up the last flight of the group, just before they reached the coast. Nobody had enough petrol to do more than run some 109s out of the pattern."

The next day more than three hundred German and Italian bombers gave Malta's airfields a working over. Only seventeen Spitfires remained serviceable that night. By the third day all the Spits that had not been destroyed on the ground or in the air were out of commission.

About sixty more Spitfires were flown into Malta on May 9 from the *Wasp* and the British carriers.

"One Spit's belly tank did not feed, and the pilot landed back on the *Wasp,* confounding all the experts," Tilley says. "Even the Admiralty took note of the landing without an arrester hook. This experience accelerated development of the Seafire, the carrier version of the Spit."

Tilley led another flight of Spitfires into Malta in June, from the *Eagle,* for his second deck launching of the land-based fighter. This particular mission was spiced by the fact that the Spitfires were assembled on the dock and loaded directly onto the carrier. Thus, the initial test flight began with a sea launch and a seven-hundred-mile flight over unfriendly territory. The situation at Malta was desperate and the time factor critical. The Spits were needed to cover a ship convoy due in less than a week.

A Floridian whose erect posture makes him look even more than six-feet four-inches tall, Tilley loved fast automobiles and had planned to become a professional racing driver. In Malta he was to become an ace: seven enemy aircraft destroyed, three probably destroyed, and at least five damaged. He and Peck were to become the first Americans in the Malta campaign to receive the RAF's Distinguished Flying Cross. A 1968 book, William C. Anderson's *The Two-Ton Albatross,* said of him:

> Colonel Tilley, who resembled an out-of-training Green Bay Packer fullback, was a warm, gregarious, soft-spoken southerner. . . . A very colorful and highly controversial figure, he was the architect of the Strategic Air Command's information program during the heyday of General Curtis E. LeMay. A highly skilled and dedicated man, he could charm the wings off a butterfly, or chew the transmission out of an erring subordinate, with equal aplomb. He was irascible, blood-thirsty, vindictive, insidious, unyielding, magnanimous, determined, calculating, and hard-headed. You couldn't help but like him.

An article in *Collier's* Magazine said that quick thinking by Tilley and a British pilot on a return to Malta broke up a formation of fifty Messerschmitts. The Spitfire pilots had had only seconds to decide what to do.

"If they went up, down, sideways or turned back, they were lost," the magazine said. "So they did the only thing that gave them a chance. They flew straight into the Nazi formation and put the German fighters at a disadvantage.

"If the Germans fired at the RAF planes they would hit their own also. In a flash it was all over. The Spitfires were clear, heading for their home base, and outdistancing the enemy planes. Two of the Me's burst into flames and crashed into the sea."

Tilley's citation for the DFC, awarded for great gallantry at a time when he had been credited only with destroying four enemy aircraft, said that "on three occasions by making feint attacks after having expended all his ammunition he has successfully driven off many fighters which attempted to machine gun our aircraft as they landed."

Booth, regarded by his colleagues as a typical Brooklynite, won the nickname "Tiger" because, although normally mild mannered, he could be something of a terror when his anger was aroused. One evening at Malta when two native policemen annoyed him, he threw them both into the harbor.

Jim Peck recalls the day he saw Booth flying from a cloud on the tail of a Ju 88 with another Junkers right behind him: "While Tiger was firing at the Junkers in front, the one behind gave a long burst. His Spitfire sort of disintegrated in the explosion.

"Doug said he never remembered getting out of the cockpit. He must have been knocked out. He came to, falling through the air, and pulled the ripcord. Then he passed out again. He was unconscious when he landed."

Although Booth received no decorations in the RAF, the USAAF later awarded him the DFC and the Air Medal with three oak leaf clusters. "The DFC and Air Medal were awarded on standard citations," Booth explains. "They did not refer to anything specific; they were given for remaining alive. The U.S. Eighth Air Force gave an Air Medal for 10 completed missions and a DFC for 50. All you had to do to get them was survive."

Jim Peck and Don McLeod, inseparable friends since their first days in the Eagle squadrons, were a Mutt-and-Jeff pair on Malta—Peck small in stature, quick, dark-haired with snapping black eyes, gifted with a tremendous sense of humor; McLeod, a former Boston cop, huge, stocky, well over six-feet tall, and Irish as Paddy's pig.

"These two buddies used to have a lot of fun playing little games," Tilley says. "Jimmy would walk into a bar, pick out a medium-sized gent, and try to start a fight with him. When Jimmy had the fellow irritated almost to the point of being ready to flatten him, Mac would come up and say, 'What do you mean, picking on my little friend? You're not going to hit that little guy, are you?' Mac was good at double talk.

" 'I'm not picking a fight with him, he's picking one with me,' the victim would say. Then he'd take another look at the big Irishman and move down to the other end of the bar. Jimmy and Mac would start laughing, and then they would explain their act to the guy and buy him a drink."

McLeod was shot down a second time during the Malta campaign. He inflated his dinghy and was rescued by ship once again. Peck, on the other hand, boasted that he survived forty-five air battles without so much as a bullet through his plane.

"I never even got a scratch on a plane until one morning at Malta I took off and the communications system turned out to be faulty," Peck told reporters after the Malta campaign had ended. "I could get ground commands but I couldn't talk back.

"I was told to come in, and I hit a shell crater. It didn't

do the plane any good, but I wasn't hurt. In all the fighting I haven't received so much as a scratch."

Peck attributed his good fortune to an inexpensive wristwatch which he never removed except when taking a shower. He said the first owner of the watch was Larry Chatterton, of 71 Squadron, who was killed in a crash. The second owner was Jim Coxetter of 133, also killed in a flying accident. "I kind of figure lightning won't strike three times in a row," Peck said. "Anyhow, I have been lucky."

Peck pointed also to the occasion when Flight Lieutenant Johnston of 133 was about to land at Malta and a bomb exploded on the field fifty feet below him. "The explosion wrecked his controls but pointed the plane upwards, and he rose to about 800 feet," Peck said. "Then he took to his parachute and landed safely. He came away with only a sprained ankle.

"Johnny blamed that on the fact that he didn't have his little white elephant charm in his pocket. We fliers aren't exactly superstitious, but. . . . In Johnny's case, he did have a crackup later even with the elephant along. As for me, I never fly without this lucky wristwatch."

Peck went from Malta to North Africa and got in on the heaviest action there, destroying or damaging three more enemy planes. In a single day's action, twenty-three German aircraft were shot down, and Peck received a decoration from Major General James Doolittle, commander of the Twelfth Air Force, for his part in the combat.

Despite Jim Peck's confidence, lightning did strike a third time. Jessie Taylor recalled that in 1944 the Lockheed P-38— a fast fighter named "Lightning"—was just becoming operational with Peck's squadron in England.

"He had one, and he came over to visit us and let us fly it," Taylor said. "On his way back to his base, one engine quit. The plane augered in, and Jimmy was killed."

10

BEST DAYS, WORST DAYS

In the first week of May, 1942, two of the Eagle squadrons moved into two of the best-known air bases in England, 71 to Debden and 133 to Biggin Hill. With 121 ensconced at North Weald, all three Eagle units at last were in the forefront of the air war, carrying out key responsibilities in full partnership with other RAF squadrons.

"A wonderful runway and beautiful accommodations," said the 71 Squadron logbook about Debden after the transfer from Martlesham Heath. The pilots of 133 Squadron were even more excited over their release from Kirton-in-Lindsey. At last they were a part of the highly active 11 Group.

At this stage of the war the Luftwaffe was beginning to feel its losses so painfully that it had to discontinue for the most part its sustained bombing assaults on England's cities and airdromes. A rapid increase in British and American aircraft production and the arrival of ample fuel supplies from the United States enabled the RAF to move into stronger, more frequent offensive operations. Fighter sweeps and bomber-escort circus missions over German-occupied France, as well as low-level rhubarb raids with RAF interceptors shooting up ground targets, forced reluctant German fighters into aerial engagements.

Also in May the RAF began using fighters for attacks on

German shipping. Bombers had been effective, but now cannon and machine guns would be applied against enemy vessels as well.

Describing the first raid of this kind by 121 Squadron on May 20, Barry Mahon recounted: "We lined up astern and made passes one after another at an armed trawler. The trawler returned our fire until our bullets and shells wiped out the resistance. Those of us coming in last were able to blow a gaping hole in the side with our cannon, and the ship sank."

Three days earlier Jim Daley and Sel Edner each had shot down an enemy plane. On May 27 Daley blew up a 1,000-ton minesweeper and shot down his third enemy aircraft, putting him well on the way to becoming one of the war's great aces. In the same engagement Sgt. Pilot Fred Vance damaged two enemy planes. Barry Mahon, Gene Fetrow, and Sgt. Pilot William Kelly jointly destroyed a 2,000-ton minesweeper in spite of accurate fire from a protecting German destroyer.

Blond, crew-cut Tommy Allen, who had recently been promoted to flight lieutenant to succeed Wilkie Wilkinson and who had been given command of a Hurricane squadron at Manston, was lost during an attack on two ships off Walcheren Island, The Netherlands, on May 31. Don Young, on his first combat mission with 121, saw Allen's Spitfire with the Confederate flag painted on its side firing at one of the German flak ships in a broadside, wave-height attack. About two hundred yards from the target the Spitfire struck the water, broke free, and pulled up over the ship and out of Young's field of vision.

Allen called out by radio, "I hit the drink but will try to make it home. My engine is shaking badly." Moments later he said, "I'm going in at a hundred miles an hour." Those were his last words. No one saw him go in.

"That flak ship off Holland had nothing but guns on her," said Joe Durham later. "It took a lot of courage to attack one of those things. It was like a destroyer going after a battleship."

By the end of May, the RAF was powerful enough for the first time to hurl a 1,000-bomber night attack against the enemy. The target was Cologne.

The British had to throw in every type of aircraft available —even old Ansons that carried a 200-pound bomb on a wing panel—in order to reach the 1,000-plane total. Actually, 1,052 RAF bombers took part. It was a costly effort: forty-four aircraft were lost.

"But the bombing was a great morale builder," Pete Peterson recalls. "From over Belgium you could see the smoke rising above Cologne. It was the turning point of the air war. Now we could see that we could really do it—hit the enemy where it hurt."

The following day the RAF followed up the bomber strike with a sweep over enemy territory by 100 fighters. The Germans, thoroughly aroused by the Cologne raid, responded strongly by attacking the RAF fighters in force.

Eight Hurricanes bombed Bruges, Belgium, on June 1, with the entire Debden wing flying top cover. Fifty Fw 190s attacked. Peterson shot down one and damaged another; Eugene M. Potter probably destroyed one; and Daymond and Sprague each damaged one. One Eagle, George Teicheira, was lost. The following day a teammate, Frank Zavakos, flying a search-and-rescue mission, crashed into the sea after his engine failed, and was killed. Later in the month Newton Anderson, a former Chicago newspaper reporter who had been transferred from 71 to the command of 222 Squadron and had thereby become the first American to lead an all-British unit into battle, was shot down and killed while leading an entire 36-plane RAF wing, escorting bombers attacking Hazebrouck.

Over at Biggin Hill, 133 Squadron was involved repeatedly in missions to France that encountered spirited Luftwaffe resistance. On May 17, Red McColpin and Moran Morris battled enemy planes northwest of Le Treport. McColpin shot down one Me 109F and probably destroyed another. Two days later, in fierce battling over the Fecamp-Le Treport area, Carter Harp shot down two Fw 190s, and Moran Morris and George Sperry each accounted for an Me 109. The Eagles counted about forty enemy planes in the area and were jumped by some fifteen of them as the squadron started for home.

"The fight was pretty hot—heaviest opposition we'd had in weeks," Harp told reporters. Davis Florance failed to return from the mission. Robert Pewitt almost made it back to base, but ten miles south of England's Beachy Head promontory was seen going down with two enemy planes after him. Rescued from the water that evening, he died of head injuries before he could be taken to a hospital.

Jessie Taylor, mourning the death of his roommate, Bob Pewitt, shot down a Focke-Wulf 190 during a sweep from Dieppe to Fecamp on May 31. Taylor's oldest friend, Moran Morris, was lost on that mission, as was William Kenneth Ford, a new member of the squadron.

In the days that followed, Squadron Leader Thomas and K. K. Kimbro probably destroyed one Fw 190 and damaged two more in the Abbeville area. Fletcher Hancock was last seen in a dogfight over the French coast at Cayeux. Bill Arends was shot down on a sweep to Hardelot and St. Omer.

McColpin, one of the hottest of the Eagle pilots, departed 133 Squadron on June 4 for ten weeks in the United States. He had been placed on a ten-man British army-navy-air force team to assist U.S. fund-raisers for five weeks on their first War Bond tour. Four weeks of home leave would follow.

Meanwhile, 133 had acquired an interesting, highly experienced new member, Flight Lieutenant Donald James Mathew Blakeslee, of Fairport, Ohio. Blakeslee had joined the RCAF in July, 1940. In May, 1941, he was posted to RAF 401 Squadron. By the time he was sent to 133 as a flight commander he had destroyed an Me 109, probably damaged two Fw 190s, damaged four other enemy fighters, and had been decorated with the DFC.

On June 3, his first day of action with 133, he took part in a bomber-escort mission in the morning and led the squadron on another bomber-support operation after lunch. He topped off the day's chores by going out on a late afternoon convoy patrol. Blakeslee flew sorties daily for the next five days and again acted as squadron leader on another bomber-escort assignment.

Dixie Alexander remembers a curious and unsettling experience on a return from a sweep over France. "I came across the cliffs of Calais by myself at full throttle, longing for the cliffs of Dover. A short distance out at sea I observed what I took to be a couple of birds flying past my starboard wing. This had no great effect on me; we were constantly coming into contact with birds over England. Once before I had one lodge in my air scoop, damaging the propeller. A moment after the sighting, however, I realized that I had not passed these birds—the birds had passed me, going in the same direction. I remember reflecting on this for only a second or two, inasmuch as getting home safely was the prime objective. Later, in the mess, I gave it some thought."

Alexander forgot about the incident until a week later when almost the same thing happened again. "I began to wonder. I was confident that there was nothing wrong with my eyes. I was positive I had seen something. While I wanted badly to talk about this with someone, I feared I would be ridiculed for the idea of birds flying faster than my plane."

Several weeks later the swift-bird sighting occurred again. This time Alexander consulted F. J. S. Chapman, the squadron medical officer. Dr. Chapman referred him to Squadron Leader Thomas.

"Thomas, who had a beautiful sense of humor, tugged on his horrible, rarely lit pipe and looked up at me through half-closed eyes. Finally he told me that what I had seen was not new. It had been experienced by many. The Jerries, with their big 16-inch guns on the coast near Calais, sometimes used practice firings to take an odd shot at aircraft returning to England. The difference in speed between a Spitfire racing home at 400 miles an hour and a 16-inch shell with low muzzle velocity, traveling in the same direction, was slight enough that a round was clearly visible. Those were my big birds!"

At the start of June, 1942, 121 transferred from North Weald to Southend-on-Sea, a one-squadron station strategically located thirty-five miles east of London. Like most of the RAF bases except Debden, Southend had only grass runways. The officers, quartered in a large country mansion about two miles from the station, used bicycles or a van for transportation. There was a great deal of activity. Pilots were frequently called upon for three missions a day. When the weather was too bad for formation flying, they went out in pairs on low-level hunts. One of the most enthusiastic seekers of action was Jack Mooney, who was due for leave and was planning to get married on July 4.

"Jack Mooney was a very unusual guy, a soft-voiced, friendly fellow who had a way of chuckling as he talked," according to his close friend, Reade Tilley. "He was completely without fear, and had an altogether ruthless approach to the Germans. He had a habit, whenever he had ammunition left after a mission, of going down low and taking a few squirts at the antiaircraft guns on the French coast. This meant that he usually got back after everyone else had landed.

"Once he returned with a seagull in his airscoop and almost didn't make it. Another time I thought I was the last man in the squadron coming in from the French coast, and when I saw a fighter behind me I figured at first that it was a Messerschmitt. But here it was Jack Mooney, coming up alongside and waving, nodding and smiling—having scared the hell out of me. Jack scored quite a few victories and probably was one of the better, more aggressive pilots."

Mooney and Mahon had double triumphs on a hotly contested sweep over St. Omer on June 9; each shot down two Fw 190s. Mahon's gun camera film showed that he had followed his last victim in a complete slow roll while the Fw took evasive action, but Mahon had no recollection of such a maneuver, showing the power of concentration necessary in such a dogfight.

A week later Mooney and Sel Edner attacked and halted a freight train on the main line between Bruges and Ostend. During the strike Edner lost sight of Mooney. Edner's radio calls went unanswered. A fire burned fiercely beside the stalled train, and it was evident that Mooney's plane had struck the train at that point. The RAF promoted Jim Daley, a new recipient of the DFC, to flight lieutenant and named him to succeed Mooney as B Flight commander.

At Debden the posting of Jack Robinson out of the RAF to the U.S. Eighth Air Force Headquarters, newly established in London at 20 Grosvenor Square, marked a milestone for 71 Squadron. Robbie had been the squadron's intelligence officer from the beginning and in that crucial role had won the respect and friendship of his American charges.

In mid-1942 it was an open secret that the RAF soon would hand its three Eagle squadrons over to the U.S. Army Air Forces that were taking shape in England. The USAAF needed a highly experienced officer to brief the Headquarters air staff in England on daily operations, and Robinson was the logical choice. When he joined Eighth Air Force Headquarters, the staff consisted of five officers and three enlisted men. It was soon to grow, under the command first of General Carl "Toohey" Spaatz and later of General Ira Eaker, into a force capable of hurling up to two thousand bombers and two thousand fighters against the enemy.

At that meeting Group Captain Ramsbotham Isherwood announced that an Overseas Wing had been formed out of 71 and two other squadrons and placed under his command. Its mission would be to fly with and help the Soviet air forces. The wing was to be equipped with Spitfire IXs, the newest and finest in the fighter line. Already the aircraft were en route by ship convoy to Murmansk.

The departure for the Far North was to take place within a week to ten days. Meanwhile, the men were to be made ready to go overseas—have their shots, get their belongings packed.

Peterson fondly recalls: "We were all elated about it and eager to go. A celebration was in order, we decided. In the bar everybody was gung-ho, ready for anything. Things got wilder and wilder. The wing commander, a marvelous guy named Rook, was a motorcycle nut and had a big motorbike. A loud argument broke out over the relative merits of British and American bikes.

"The permanent mess at Debden was in a beautiful building with a main hallway about 80 feet long. There were swinging glass double doors at each end. Rook made a bet that he could ride his bike through the hall at 60 miles an hour.

"We all pooh-poohed the idea and egged him on. We found long planks and laid them up over the steps of the entryways. We opened all the glass doors and placed blocks in front of them, so that he could get a running start, go up over the planks, down the hall and out the other end. We would clock him to make sure he was going 60 miles an hour. He came roaring at a good 60 mph past the first set of doors. Unfortunately, the vibration loosened the blocks holding the second set, and they closed just as he got to them. He smashed through them and out the other side. Luckily, he was not hurt much.

"We thought this was a great celebration, especially for a wing commander to do this. Almost as good as a Fourth of July party, which we now decided we ought to have. There was a large fireplace in the lounge, ideal for setting off firecrackers, only we couldn't find any fireworks. But the control tower had foot-long Roman candles used in England when dense fog came in—fog a couple of hundred feet thick—to show pilots where the airdrome was. These would make excellent firecrackers.

"We brought an armload in, put one in the fireplace, lit it, and rushed out to see the result. It shot up the chimney and on up 200 or 300 feet in a great burst of flame. We had to do it again. The second one got halfway up, backfired in a shower of soot and flame, and ended up in the middle of the lounge. This called for a fire brigade with buckets of water and lots of fire-extinguisher foam.

"We put out the fire, but we had ruined the carpet and a lot of furniture. The station commander, a real fine guy, surveyed the damage the next morning and fined us all enough to pay for the repairs."

There was a formal farewell dinner for the Overseas Wing at the Debden officers' mess, followed by two days of hasty packing for a tour of rigorous duty near the world's largest city north of the Arctic Circle. Then, to the bewilderment of almost everyone, the transfer was cancelled. The 71 Squadron team would remain at Debden but would soon prepare for the removal of all three Eagle units from the RAF and their merger into the USAAF. No formal reason for the cancellation was announced, but the unofficial explanation was that the ship carrying the beautiful new Spitfires to Murmansk had been sunk. The Russian fliers would have to fight on without reinforcements.

At this juncture, with much of the world embroiled in furious fighting on the ground and in the air, all of the Eagles in London were invited to the premiere of a new motion picture, *Eagle Squadron*. The cast included Robert Stack, Diana Barrymore, Jon Hall, Eddie Albert, Nigel Bruce, Leif Erikson and John Loder.

The film opened with a commentary by Quentin Reynolds, the favorite war correspondent of the American pilots. Reynolds said in the film's introduction that the young men portrayed in the film had refused to be "stabbed in the back" and had quit jobs and college classrooms in the United States to join the RAF. "I lived with them, saw them fight, saw them die," Reynolds said.

Singled out for special mention among "these few to whom so many owe so much" were Squadron Leader Peterson, McColpin, Bill Geiger, Forrest Dowling, Gus Daymond, Gene Tobin, Tommy McGerty, Vic Bono and Newt Anderson. There were realistic shots of squadron activity, and then the film veered off onto a preposterous fictional line.

The Eagles, aware that they were special guests, endured the picture as long as they could. Then, overcome with embarrassment, some of them walked out.

"We couldn't all leave," said Jim Gray. "There were important British people in the audience. To storm out en masse would have been to insult our hosts."

"That movie upset everybody, and Squadron Leader Peterson in particular," said Geiger. "We had been told that it would be a documentary, like the *March of Time* of those days. It came to all of us as a great shock when it turned out to be very third-rate. We all felt that we had been doublecrossed. Pete was so bitter about it that he never responded to any requests for information or publicity about the Eagles from that day forward. This may have been one of the reasons why the Eagle squadrons never became quite as well known as the Flying

Tigers and the AVG, out in the China-Burma-India Theater, although we certainly did as much for the war effort as they did."

Years later Peterson explained why material glorifying the Eagles or presenting them in a false light was repugnant to him.

"Just about once a week, on the average, I'd get a call that some writer or cameraman wanted to come out and do a story about us, maybe get us a spread in *Life* or some other magazine. But we had to live with the other RAF outfits. To them, we were just another unit, no more deserving of attention than anyone else.

"I wouldn't even let Quentin Reynolds come out to the base, although he was a favorite with a lot of the fellows because he'd been so open-handed with them. The pilots could meet him at the Savoy if they wished, but I did not want any 71 Squadron publicity.

"Eventually it worked out well. Since we didn't ask for or want any favors or special consideration—since we did our jobs and tried to stay out of the limelight—we became solidly entrenched with the people in the RAF. We were accepted by them as just another squadron."

By coincidence, 121 Squadron chalked up its highest score —seven enemy aircraft destroyed—and 133 suffered one of its most devastating setbacks on the same day, July 31, 1942, as they escorted separate formations of bombers returning from attacks on Abbeville airdrome.

A new pilot in 121, Norman Young, failed to return from the mission, and the squadron commander, Ken Kennard, was badly shot up, barely making it back to England. In 133 Squadron the count was three pilots killed and one gravely injured— all of them combat leaders of great experience—for three enemy planes shot down and another probably destroyed. Two more of 133 Squadron's new pilots had been killed in training accidents during the preceding week.

Don Young (no relative of Norman Young) describes the 121 sortie:

"We arrived over Berck sur Mer at the appointed time for rendezvous with the Boston bombers returning from their Abbeville raid. As we swung in behind and above the Bostons, we suddenly were bounced by a number of Fw 190s and Me 109s. Our squadron was broken up by wild evasive action, and

I found myself alone over the Channel at 15,000 feet, headed toward England.

"I saw a 190 spinning down from above, followed by a parachute, and then another 109 going down in flames. A lone Spitfire swung in. From the letters I knew it was flown by Norman Young, who was on his first combat mission. I waggled my wings, a signal for him to join me. An Fw 190 appeared below me, headed in the opposite direction. I dived at it, and the 190 went into a steep descent toward the water. I applied emergency boost, and by the time the 190 had leveled on the deck I had closed to 600 yards. I fired a long burst, and then another during which my cannon ran out of ammunition. Tracers began whipping by my right wing. A hard turn to the left and I was headed for England."

Don Young lost sight of his fellow Spitfire pilot. German fighters pursued him a good part of the way across the channel, knowing that he was almost out of machine gun ammunition, but he managed to elude them. He was unable to sight Norman Young again.

Squadron Leader Kennard recalled the memorable flight some thirty-five years later in an interview in the London office he occupied as managing director of Invicta International, one of Britain's leading independent airlines:

"Sergeant Bill Kelly, my wing man, and I were at 25,000 feet when Wing Commander Scott-Malden called from very high above and said, 'You have an attack—do something about it.' I thought the man must be mad.

"Then there was an explosion and blood all over my arm. The throttle control and all the instruments went out. Oil and glycol were streaming all over the place. To my horror a 190 shot past me, and then two more with him. I had no throttle control or prop control, but the engine kept going. I pulled up 500 feet with two of the enemy planes behind me and told myself, 'This is it.' But Scott-Malden saw what was happening. He shot down the two, and the third one ran.

"I had 16 miles to go to the English coast, and I knew I had to make it, because I couldn't get out. When I reached the coast I was down to 100 feet.

"I had no power, no oil, no glycol and no control. I landed very fast. The port wing started to fold, and then I was upside down. Upside down and buried in the plane, unable to get out. I was still conscious. I heard crackling sounds, and thought that any moment now I'd be on fire. But I had remembered to turn off the fuel tank. Anyway, the engine had been knocked out, so there were no flames.

"The plane had buried itself in the ground in an inverted position. After about 20 minutes I heard voices. Some boys appeared, and they ran and got several farm laborers who started digging with spades and pickaxes. I called out to them to be careful not to hack into me. Then they made a little hole and I could see daylight. I worked my arm and hand through, and someone reached down and grabbed my hand. 'Just pull,' I said. They pulled me out through that tiny hole."

Kennard had come down near New Romney, close to his family home. He had a cannon shell in his backside and other injuries. Denys Laing, squadron physician, ordered him to a hospital. Kennard remonstrated.

"You have to have rest, and we have to get that stuff out of you," Laing insisted.

An ambulance took the wounded man to a hospital, but Kennard remained obdurate. In the receiving room he declared that he was allergic to anesthetics, said he would not be operated upon, and demanded an X-ray. He ordered the attending medical men to put him through by telephone to his squadron and asked for Jim Daley.

"Jim," the irate squadron commander yelled into the telephone, "the bloody medics are trying to get me into this hospital by force. You bring the fellows over and get me out."

What followed was one of the most bizarre scenes of fighter pilots in revolt ever experienced by the Eagles. Within ten minutes of Kennard's call for help, the men of 121 Squadron came storming in, brandishing guns. "You can't do this to our CO," they shouted to the startled medical team. "He wants to come back to the squadron."

For a few tense moments it was a band of angry Americans —armed and seemingly prepared to use their weapons if need be—and their greatly admired English leader against a stubbornly determined team of British medical men. Kennard finally agreed to remain in the hospital if he could have a private room with three beds so that Daley and his buddy, Roy Skinner, could stay and keep watch.

"I was afraid the medics might spike my food or tea, trying to knock me out so that they could operate," Kennard explained later. "I was afraid that if they cut into me they might damage nerves in my arms or legs and do real harm. So I had

Daley and Skinner taste everything I ate or drank before I would touch it.

"The next morning they let me go back to the airdrome. As it was, I gradually recovered without a further stay in the hospital."

In the final scoring of the squadron's encounter with the German fighters, Barry Mahon and Sel Edner were credited with shooting down two planes each, and Kennard, Kelly and Frank R. Boyles, of Mount Vernon, New York, with one each.

In the 133 Squadron air battle led by Tommy Thomas, Woody Harp, the Georgian; Coburn Clark King, of Hollywood, California; and Grant Eugene "Ike" Eichar, of Elgin, Illinois, were killed. Jessie Taylor narrowly escaped death but was badly wounded.

King and Taylor had been flying in combat for ten months, Harp for nine, and Eichar for five. In addition to the casualties among its most experienced pilots, within the five preceding days the squadron had lost new arrivals Ben Perry DeHaven and Gilbert Omens in fatal flying accidents.

Coby King, a thirty-year-old native of Oregon, had been flying since he was eighteen. He had been an instructor with the RCAF in Canada and had ferried Lockheed bombers to England before becoming an RAF combat pilot.

Woody Harp had been a barnstormer, a wing-walker and stunt pilot, and probably had had more flying time than any other member of the squadron. Occasionally he performed daredevil feats learned during his flying-circus days.

Dale Taylor—Jessie, to his brother pilots—at 155 pounds and a height of five feet seven and one-half inches fit neatly into the compact cockpit of the Spitfire. A superb athlete like many of his fellow Eagles, he had played on football, basketball, baseball, swimming, tennis and track teams in high school and college. His brown hair and bright blue eyes spoke of his mother's German ancestry. Raised in the Chickasaw District of southeastern Oklahoma where his father, a Choctaw Indian, was a sheriff for twenty-five years and his uncle was an Indian peace officer, Taylor developed keen eyesight and superior marksmanship.

Taylor was also something of a philosopher and lyricist. "One of my pleasures," he wrote, "was cruising at around 20,000 feet, looking upon scenery that at high altitude was magnificent. Giant masses of white cumulus clouds, like misty mountains and valleys—in that setting, it was always playtime.

"Diving through shadows and rainbows, through valleys a mile deep, and then up into rolls, loops, Cuban eights, spins and tight turns, you were absolutely alone—a free spirit—and time stood still."

As for the ever present spectre of death: "We all knew that some of the men we worked, played and lived with would be killed. We just did not dwell on the possibility. In my own little world I was almost out of touch with everything except flying, the air war, and day-to-day existence. The only way to lift the curtain on tomorrow was to wait for it."

Taylor, describing the fateful mission of July 31, 1942, said the bomb run on Abbeville by twelve Bostons had been successful and the results were good. "Just as we were leaving the target," he said, "we were bounced by about 30 Fw 190s and Me 109s. Going after an Fw 190, I committed the cardinal sin. I let one that I did not see get behind and under me. Harp called to warn me, but it was too late; I had already been hit. The 190 put a bullet through my foot and another across my forehead, temporarily blinding me. It was too late for Harp, my roommate, too. No one ever heard from him again."

Taylor and the other senior pilots had teased new members of the squadron about the "big, fat and fiendishly hungry" sharks that inhabited the waters over which they flew and had warned them not to become shark bait. Now, dazed and wounded in his damaged Spitfire, the image that had been lightly invoked for the benefit of the new pilots returned to haunt him.

"While I was flying, unable to see, I had a vision of a shark, cruising along down below," Taylor recalls. "An alarm rang in my mind, loud and clear, and suddenly I could see again. I felt that God had come down and given me back the use of one eye that had been closed by concussion. My terrible fear turned to anger.

"I could see three Jerries circling me. I fired at them, and before my ammunition was gone, two of the Fw 190s were down among the sharks, and an Me 109 was heading for the French coast with one wing down and flying sideways, almost sure to auger in after making landfall. I headed for England with a hole through my foot, a boot filled with blood, and one eye closed—nursing a sick engine. A Spitfire joined up with me. It was Jack Jackson. On a previous mission Jack had called out an enemy plane just in time for me to get out of its line of fire. I held up my bloody hands so that Jack could see them. My ammunition was gone, but I knew that Jackson would take care of any more Jerries that showed up.

"That was my last operational flight for the RAF—my last Eagle mission. My little Spitfire was riddled with 107 bullet holes."

Taylor quickly learned, as Bill Dunn had discovered eleven months earlier, that in the RAF out of action, like out of sight, was—so to speak—out of mind. Squadron Leader Thomas telephoned Taylor at the emergency hospital to say, "Jessie, your camera film was terrific. It shows you shot down two Jerries and damaged another."

Usually a particularly courageous act of this kind—a wounded pilot continuing to attack and destroy the enemy in spite of pain and stress—was recognized with a DFC or some other high award. But no one came to question Taylor or to obtain the facts of the combat. Thomas was busy packing up, having just received word of his promotion to wing commander flying at Biggin Hill. The July 31 mission had been his last with 133; preoccupied, he assumed that others would interview the man in the hospital. Taylor was removed to the RAF Officers' Hospital at Torquay. Eric Doorly flew down there with his clothing and other personal belongings. Aside from that brief visit, Taylor had no further contact with the Eagles before being sent back to the United States to recuperate. The war had moved on. Taylor had been overlooked, and no RAF award awaited him.

Taylor was not unduly disturbed by this, however. He had always held that the most vital members of a fighter squadron were not necessarily the pilots with the most dramatic encounters:

"There must be leaders and followers. Among the most interesting pilots were those rotated from day to day to make up a squadron. Of the twelve pilots in a full squadron flight, perhaps eight would be unsung, but they were the ones that insured a mission's success. They were the interior linemen, absolutely essential to the squadron's goal. In a cooperative effort, loyalty, faith, and discipline were required of all. These unpublicized individuals were good formation fliers, always available, dependable, always doing exactly what they were programmed to do. In a wide-open dogfight they pulled their own weight every time."

Strangely, Taylor came close to being killed while recuperating at Torquay. Ambulatory patients were allowed to leave the premises. Taylor and a roommate, a Free French pilot with one arm shot off, went to see a war movie about a Polish pilot. One scene showed aircraft attacking ground targets.

"By coincidence we walked out of the theater just as two German fighters came directly overhead and strafed the street," Taylor said. "We dived through an open doorway and landed in a huge trough of fish. Wet and smelly, we caught the bus back to the hospital. There we were horrified to see that the building had taken a direct bomb hit. The wing we had been in was demolished, and 119 persons had been killed. We had just been watching Poland under make-believe attack—and now we were back in the real world of enemy airplanes spreading havoc in England."

How could a rough-and-ready Eagle come to be known as Jessie? Fred Scudday and Taylor once had to confess to Dickie Bain, station commander at Eglinton, that they had broken into the officers' mess the night before and had helped themselves to the liquor supply. "Where do you come from, Taylor?" Bain asked. "Oklahoma." "Who do you think you are, Jesse James?" That did it. Taylor's squadron mates delightedly adopted the sobriquet as a substitute for Edwin Dale. They ignored the noun's gender in spelling Jessie with an i, which meant that on occasion Taylor had to deny that his new name was a derivation of Jessica.

11

JUBILEE

Eric Hugh Thomas had been an extremely popular leader of 133 Squadron. His pilots sang his praise as the architect of the squadron's rise to eminence in RAF performance categories. They cheered his advancement in early August to wing commander, even as they mourned his departure from 133. And they cheered again at the announcement of his successor as squadron leader: Flight Lieutenant Don Blakeslee. For the first time 133 Squadron would, like 71 Squadron, have an American commander.

Athletic in build, ruggedly handsome—"strictly a collar-ad type," one Eagle described him—Blakeslee, at times, was cool and aloof and, at other times, quite charming. "He's a hard man to get to know," an admirer said, "but he's probably the best leader and one of the finest pilots around. He's respected by everyone who has flown with him." Blakeslee had demonstrated, even in his short time with the squadron, that he was ruthless, aggressive, relatively fearless, and would never miss an opportunity to fight the enemy in the air.

With Hugh Kennard out of action because of injuries received in the July 31 bomber-escort mission, 121 Squadron also acquired a new commander, British Flight Lieutenant W. Dudley Williams, a holder of the DFC. Williams, who flew his first mission with the Americans on August 3, would lead 121 for the few weeks remaining before its transfer to the U.S. flag.

In mid-August, 71 Squadron, still under the command of Pete Peterson, flew once again from Debden to Gravesend, not far from the 121 Squadron station of Southend, while 133 moved from Biggin Hill to Lympne near the English south coast, as both units had done six weeks previously. The three locations were sealed off. Again, telephone calls were prohibited; no one was to leave base. The Eagle squadrons were poised for their first joint mission, a highly secret one. Operation Jubilee—which had been scheduled and then cancelled in July— was on again.

Early on the morning of August 19 British naval vessels would carry seven thousand commando troops of the Second Canadian Division and a U.S. Rangers unit—the first Canadian or American army forces to see action in Europe—and some British and French units across the English Channel to France. The way would first be cleared by shore and air bombardment. The troops would seize "Jubilee and vicinity," an eleven-mile-long coastal strip centered around Dieppe, and hold it long enough to destroy German installations in the area. Then, their mission accomplished, they would be taken back across the Channel before nightfall.

The purpose was to shake up the Germans and to test their defense capability against the Allied invasions already on the planning charts. The RAF's assignment was to maintain an air umbrella over the ships and beachhead to repulse any Luftwaffe resistance and to silence enemy groundfire. The umbrella would be raised throughout the day by seventy-six squadrons, including the three Eagle units and forty-five other Spitfire squadrons.

What followed was the most furious fighting that had yet developed on or above the French shoreline. Figures made public the following day indicated that 404 Allied officers and 3,890 enlisted men had been killed, wounded or captured, including more than 3,000 Canadians. The Germans conceded the loss of forty-eight planes, of which twenty were fighters. The RAF lost 108 aircraft, most of them Spitfires.

The three twelve-plane Eagle squadrons made four sorties of about an hour and forty minutes each, the first ones taking off in darkness as early as 4:50 A.M. and the last ones returning to base as late as 6:40 P.M. Altogether the Eagles shot down ten enemy planes, probably destroyed five more, and damaged twelve, for the loss of one pilot killed. Of five Eagle pilots forced to bail out, four were rescued. The fifth became a German prisoner.

For the pilots of 71 Squadron, the shock of the day was the sight of Squadron Leader Peterson—the seemingly invincible Pete—bailing out of his burning plane. Peterson had damaged one enemy aircraft, as had Strickland and Stan Anderson, and was on his third sortie when he intercepted a Ju 88 on a bomb run against Allied ships. Attacking from astern, Peterson set the bomber on fire but took hits from the rear gunner. Peterson pressed on, ignoring the enemy blasts, until smoke and flames forced him to take to his parachute. Wing Commander Raymond Myles Beacham Duke-Woolley, who flew all four sorties with 71 Squadron, saw the Ju 88 hit the water and watched as Peterson drifted down. On the same sortie Mike McPharlin and Oscar Coen damaged and probably destroyed another Ju 88. McPharlin also had to bail out. British vessels quickly rescued both men. For his daring leadership, Peterson received the only DSO to be awarded to an Eagle pilot.

For 121 Squadron, the first sortie of the day was the costly one. A large force of Fw 190s attacked as soon as the RAF planes reached their patrol line. Sel Edner shot down one enemy plane, Gilbert Halsey and Leon Blanding probably destroyed one each, and F. D. "Snuffy" Smith damaged one. Edner nursed his badly damaged plane home. Three pilots— Barry Mahon, Jim Taylor and Gene Fetrow—failed to return. On the next flight an enemy shell tore a large hole in Daley's Spitfire. The engine cut out, and Daley was preparing to jump when the engine restarted. He resumed his patrol and returned to base with the squadron later. On the final 121 sortie, Julian Osborne's engine caught fire, forcing him to bail out over England from a height of about five hundred feet. He landed safely and waved to show the other pilots that he was all right.

Blanding reported that somehow another Spitfire had attacked Jim Taylor during the first sortie, whipping into him very fast and striking head on. "There was a big bang a hundred yards out," Blanding said. Neither pilot survived.

The squadron learned later that Fetrow had bailed out of his damaged plane and had been picked up unhurt by one of the British naval vessels.

Wing Commander David Scott-Malden said in a *Liberty Magazine* article that Jim Daley came to him after the mission, weeping over the loss of Mahon. "I saw him get it," Daley sobbed. "He didn't have a chance."

Mahon had already been cited for a DFC, but it was not to become effective until August 20, the day after Operation Jubilee. In spite of Daley's despair, Barry Mahon was to live to tell about his last day with 121 Squadron. His narrative:

The air above Dieppe was thick with enemy and Allied aircraft. We went in as high cover. A flight of Focke-Wulfs came in below me, ready to dive on the boats. I called for my flight to follow, and I made an attack and shot down the wing man.

I saw another flight of Fws, came in behind the No. 2 man and fired at him. My deflection shooting was not as accurate as it should have been.

The Fw started smoking, and several pieces flew off the cowling. Just as he burst into flames, I ran out of ammunition. Then I broke a rule I had established for myself in the beginning of my combat experience—never break off combat until the enemy either breaks away himself or is shot down. I pulled away from the attack in a chandelle—a steep climb—in order to gain altitude for the flight back to England to rearm.

With his No. 2 man on fire, the leader of the section undoubtedly would have broken off combat and gone into a steep dive or continued on to France, if I had stayed in the fight. He had no way of knowing I was out of ammunition.

I got a funny feeling and looked out. There was a yellow-nosed spinner about 200 feet below me and climbing. The Fw had a better climbing ability than the Spitfire.

He started firing, and I could tell by his inability to get his nose higher that he could not get the right deflection to hit me. Shooting planes is sort of like shooting ducks. You must aim ahead of the moving target in order to hit it.

Eventually I was at such a steep angle that I stalled out and fell through his line of fire. The noise was terrifying—like a thousand shot-puts all being thrown on a galvanized tin roof over your head. The gun panels ripped off my left wing. The engine exploded, and oil covered the cockpit. Shells exploded on my right wing.

Blinded by the oil, I had rolled over on my back. I jettisoned the canopy, released my seat belt, and being upside down, fell from the cockpit. I had the presence of mind to pull my ripcord, and my parachute opened about 600 or 700 feet above the water.

We had been schooled to release our parachutes before we went under the water, so that there would be no danger of the chute coming down on top and drowning us. The parachute opened only in time to swing once or twice. I twisted my quick release when I thought I was a few feet off the water. Unfortunately, I misjudged and probably was still 40 or 50 feet high when I let go. It seemed as though I went almost to the bottom of the Channel. My Mae West provided enough buoyancy to bring me quickly to the surface.

I found my dinghy still attached to the parachute, and inflated it. The whole sequence had taken less than two and a half minutes. I lay on my back in the dinghy and watched the tremendous air battle, probably the greatest air show the world had yet seen. There must have been 80 or 90 German planes and an equal number of British aircraft in a five-miles-square cube of the sky.

The sights that morning and part of the afternoon were unbelievable. There would be a Spit being chased by a German being chased by a Spit being chased by a German, and the first three would be blown up, leaving the remaining one victorious until he turned into the guns of another opponent.

As a matter of fact, after the adrenaline level of my blood went down I found the spectacle fascinating—a giant Fourth of July display, only much more ominous. The spent bullets were falling like hailstones, so hot they made a sizzling noise as they struck the water.

Gradually I drifted to the Jubilee shore, confident I would be rescued by the evacuating troops. To my dismay there was no evacuation then under way. All the troops had been captured, and the losses had been tremendous.

Upon reaching land, I was taken up on the beach and led through a minefield to where the Germans were loading prisoners on trucks. It appeared that I was the only pilot among 2,000 or 3,000 Canadians and Allied soldiers.

One German officer spoke English. I asked him where the trucks were taking us, and he pointed to a road. I pulled a map from my jacket and showed him that road, marked with a red circle. "Our afternoon mission was to come back and strafe this area and this road," I told him.

The German paid no attention to me. When the trucks had moved down the road half an hour, sure enough, a squadron of Spitfires came over and started to strafe. We jumped from the trucks and hid in ditches, so I never got a good glimpse of the identification letters to find out whether this was my squadron. Whoever it was did a good job. About one-fourth of the Canadians were killed or wounded on the first pass.

After the Spitfires had gone the German officer came and asked for my maps. For the rest of the journey the remaining trucks were routed through tree-lined back roads, and there was no more strafing.

We were loaded into boxcars and taken to a prison camp

outside of Paris. After a day or two I was turned over to the Luftwaffe and moved to an Fw base. As their first American prisoner, I created a sensation. One pilot after another tried to buy me drinks, trade wings, or just practice English on me. An intelligence officer tried to question me, but the fliers refused to let me go.

The German pilots took me out to the airfield and showed me Fws, and let me sit in one. I asked if I could try it out. Taking me seriously, they explained that they could not risk a chance that I might fly back to England.

That evening a couple of the pilots took me to Paris and left me in a truck, under guard, while they toured the cabarets. They said they were afraid of the SS officers in Paris, but they kept coming back out to give me glasses of champagne.

I was beginning to wonder why we fought the Germans at all. They all seemed like very nice fellows—until they turned me over to the SS, the Gestapo troops, an entirely different type of men. The SS took me to Frankfurt and then to an interrogation camp at the Stalag Luft just outside of the city.

———

The most successful of the Eagle teams in Operation Jubilee was 133 Squadron, and the star performer of the day was its dynamic new acting commander, Blakeslee. By the time of the Commando raid, Blakeslee had flown thirty-three missions with 133 and had led twelve of them since his early-June entry into the squadron. On August 18, the day before Operation Jubilee, he led a fighter sweep and shot down an Fw 190.

Blakeslee was the only one of the Eagle squadron commanders to lead his team on all four sorties of Operation Jubilee. The Spitfires of 133 took off on the first sortie of August 19 at 7:20 A.M. with orders to orbit Dieppe at seven thousand feet. The German fighters attacked immediately. Blakeslee shot down an Fw 190, as did Flight Sergeant Dixie Alexander. Pilot Officer William H. Baker probably destroyed another.

"We had just made a turn with Blakeslee leading when four 190s carrying bombs approached from the north," Alexander recounts. "They were at about 1,000 feet and flew directly below us, heading for the ships in the harbor. Blakeslee immediately called them out, and we broke down and after them. I was flying Red Four to Eric Doorly. During the descent Eric's acceleration was taking him away from me, and he was in hot pursuit of the others in the group.

"Suddenly I saw two more 190s to the left and slightly below me. I closed on them and fired one burst at long range.

One of the 190s immediately jettisoned his bomb and flew inland. The other proceeded toward the shipping. I was able to close to within about 300 or 400 yards, and by then was well lined up. I gave him two more bursts, and we both passed directly over the entire convoy at about 300 feet.

"The 190 dropped his bomb. I had no idea where it hit. I was still firing and observed strikes on his port wing and fuselage. Suddenly his left wing disappeared, and he went directly into the water. I do not know whether my cannon bursts did the work, or if he was hit by gunfire from the British Navy.

"I flew on south and made a turn back over Dieppe, gaining altitude and looking for someone to tie into. Upon clearing the north edge of the city I saw three Ju 88s headed for the harbor, moving very fast. I tried to get into position, fired one full deflection burst at the hindmost 88, and then came around to line up. I was about 600 yards astern and losing ground. I fired one more burst and was out of ammunition. I headed back for Lympne."

The twelve planes of the first sortie landed safely at Lympne at about 8:20 A.M. Blakeslee led 133 up again at 10:15 A.M. on orders to fly top cover over Dieppe at twelve thousand feet.

Again the fighting began almost as soon as the Spitfires reached the beachhead area. Blakeslee and Donald Gentile destroyed two Fw 190s and a Ju 88. Gordon Brettell, Dick Beaty, Bill Baker, Eric Doorly and Dick Gudmundsen shared in damaging four 190s and three Dornier 217s.

On the third sortie, at midday, Alexander destroyed a 217, Jim Nelson probably destroyed another, and Blakeslee damaged an Fw 190. Alexander was flying Nelson's wing. They attacked six Do 217s just as they were dropping bombs on the convoy. Alexander singled one out, closed to about three hundred yards, and fired bursts until his cannons were exhausted. There was good return fire at the beginning, but he probably killed the gunner. By that time, Alexander and Nelson were south of Dieppe and over land. Alexander had observed numerous hits on the 217. Its port engine was smoking. He continued to fire short bursts of .303 ammunition. The Dornier made a gentle turn, dropped down, and crash-landed in a field two or three miles south of the town. Alexander fired one burst at the aircraft and crew as they scrambled for cover.

The evacuation of troops from the beachhead was under way by this time. The pilots returning to base reported that the

German planes were dive-bombing and that a destroyer and another vessel had received direct hits.

Blakeslee led 133 Squadron up on its fourth patrol of the day shortly before 8 P.M. The orders were to patrol the convoys returning from Dieppe, which now were ten miles southeast of Eastbourne. This time there was little air action. According to Alexander, "Things were uneventful until suddenly we were bounced by a lone 190. He had singled out Yellow Four, who was my wing man, Bob Smith. I called 'Break Yellow Section' in good time, and was able to come around and continue down after him, with Bob bringing up my rear. I fired short bursts at him from about 8,000 feet of altitude all the way down to 2,000. We were going full bore then, and he was at least 1,000 feet ahead of me.

"I blacked out, somehow missed hitting the water, and was all by myself at about 3,000 feet when I regained my vision. I started looking for the squadron, or someone to latch onto, and was surprised to see many squadrons consisting of only eight aircraft each, and a like number of sections of four flying about by themselves.

"It then occurred to me that I had completely forgotten to use our squadron call sign when calling the break. This meant that I had caused the yellow section of every squadron on the frequency to take evasive action. I remember vividly 36 sections of four aircraft each—the yellow sections of each squadron—scurrying about over Dieppe, trying to locate and attach themselves to the eight other members—the other two sections—of their squadron. They would fly into position, read the letters, and upon finding that they were not those of their squadron, peel off and search some more. All this accomplished by a guy named Dixie Alexander, who yelled 'Break Yellow Section' when his No. 4 was under attack."

A dramatic account of the day's operation was given by Leroy Gover who flew three sorties with the English 66 Squadron:

We went in at 5:45 A.M. and right on the deck. The flak was just solid. There were hundreds of planes screaming through the sky, dozens of dogfights going on, planes on fire, men in dinghies. I saw nine or ten Spitfires shooting hell out of a Do 217. We lost four Hurricanes and two Spits as we crossed the beach. Enemy gunfire was unbelievable.

At 11 A.M. there were only six Spitfires available in our squadron and we were sent back to hit the gun positions. By this time Dieppe was a real mess. The Germans were sending Dornier 217s to bomb the landing craft that were trying to take the men off the beach. Focke-Wulf 190s and Messerschmitts were everywhere. We lost another Spitfire on this mission.

There were only three Spits airworthy for the third mission. We were to take in four Bostons to lay a smoke screen along the beach for the withdrawal of the very hard-pressed commandos. We flew the mission at sea level, and when the Bostons hit the beach they turned 90 degrees to the right to lay their smoke. Two Bostons were shot down immediately.

We strafed the gun positions and followed the remaining two Bostons. As they turned to head for home, another Boston was shot into the sea.

Six Fw 190s came down on us. As we were right on the deck, there was no place to go. My wing man and roommate, Vic Nissen, a South African Air Force pilot, was hit hard from astern and crashed into the sea.

On the way back to England I counted 14 men in dinghies within one mile of shore, all waving and every one of them paddling away from France with no chance whatever. The landing craft that were leaving the beach had only four or five men per boat. The beach was covered with dead commandos.

The RAF claimed 185 enemy aircraft shot down, and the Germans had claims of about the same number of RAF planes destroyed. It was certainly the most hectic day of my life.

That evening I had the only Spitfire in the squadron that was still airworthy, and I was put on night alert. The commanding officer came and told me that I had been transferred to 133 Eagle squadron a week earlier. He had taken it upon himself to hold me over because he knew that the raid on Dieppe was coming up and that I would want to be in on it.

That made sense. If I had gone to 133 Squadron I would have had very little chance of flying on the raid, because they already had a full complement of pilots at that time.

Years later at the Pentagon in Washington, Gover and Oscar Coen watched a screening of captured German war films. "There was a shot of a Spitfire with the letters *LZK* coming in low and being fired at," Gover said. "I shuddered. That was my plane—*LZK*. Strangely, I hadn't worried at the time, over Dieppe, even though at the finish I was the only pilot in the squadron still flying."

Not all the Jubilee participants had positive results to report. "I led Blue section and didn't get a squirt at all," said Charles Cook. "Poor show. I could have claimed a Do 17, but with 87 fighters after it, there was no use getting in line."

Bob Smith lamented, "I had the only chance of my career for a double, zooming up in a vertical climb under a pair of Fw 190s, one tucked in next to the other. I fired a long burst from my cannons, saw a few strikes, stalled and spun out. As they say, eat your heart out."

Paul Ellington of Lafayette, Louisiana, who had joined 121 Squadron two days before, summed it up. "I stood around in shocked amazement at all the comings and goings, the tired and shot-up birds, and so on. The old hands earned their salt that day."

E. L. "Dusty" Miller, of 133 Squadron, had chosen August 20 as the day for him to take an English bride and thus was on leave from Biggin Hill at the time of Jubilee. Among the telegrams of congratulations after the wedding was a message ordering him back to base *immediately.*

Some observers contended that while the Dieppe landing was a costly one for the British, valuable lessons were learned that saved lives later in Normandy. From the viewpoint of one participating unit, however, this was the appraisal of Operation Jubilee in the 133 Squadron Operations Record Book:

"A great ending to a good day's work. Subject to reassessment, the Squadron score at the end of the day stood at six destroyed, two probables and eight damaged—for no losses!"

———

In August, three days after the commando venture at Dieppe, 133 Squadron was detached from Biggin Hill for nine days of gunnery practice with its new Mark IX Spitfires at Martlesham Heath, the station that twice had served as home base for 71 Squadron. Out of Martlesham one morning came news that startled the Americans and most of the other RAF fighter pilots as well: Don Blakeslee had been "busted."

Blakeslee, the new CO of 133, the man expected soon to lead that squadron to greater achievements in the U.S. Air Forces, one of the half-dozen most renowned pilots among the American Eagle volunteers. It was incredible.

Blakeslee had been reduced in rank from squadron leader to flying officer; in American terms this meant from major to first lieutenant. He had been banished from the 11 Group combat area and had been sent to purgatory. He would still fly a Spitfire but only to tow a target trailing far behind. Inexperienced pilots, fresh from the States, would be shooting at the target, learning how to fire at an enemy—and hoping not to hit the tow plane.

The offense? Entertaining female company in quarters after hours. Rules were rules; RAF discipline was tough. But wasn't this a bit severe, sympathetic fellow Eagles asked. The man's gallantry in action, his bravery, loyalty and skill were beyond question. Were college-dorm type restrictions important enough to warrant depriving 133 Squadron of its leader, one of its very best pilots? The message of the RAF High Command was clear: Certain after-hours antics would not be tolerated. Some of the more boisterous and unruly individuals among the Eagles suddenly improved their behavior.

Blakeslee's removal meant for 133 at least a temporary return to an Englishman's command. British Flight Lieutenant Edward Gordon Brettell, who had joined the squadron less than a month previously as a flight commander, took over as acting squadron leader.

Shortly thereafter, Mac McColpin returned from the ticker-tape welcomes and speech-making circuits of a bond drive in the United States and became 133's squadron leader. An American, this time an ace with the unique background of having served in combat in all three Eagle Squadrons, was again in charge. McColpin was to go on to ring up a total score of twelve enemy planes destroyed in 280 combat missions in thirty-six months of combat duty, and would become the first Eagle to achieve brigadier general and major general rank in the USAAF. As a major general he would command the U. S. Fourth Air Force. He would wear the American as well as the British DFC and would receive twenty-one decorations from four different countries.

On its return in September to Biggin Hill—Biggin on the Bump, the pilots called it—133 proudly introduced the Spitfire IX into combat. They were one of only three squadrons in the RAF to be equipped with this greatly advanced aircraft.

An identifiable characteristic of the 133 Squadron, particularly after the Dieppe triumphs, was justifiable pride. "Biggin Hill was the number one fighter base in England," explained Don Nee. "The Biggin Hill Wing was the first and only fighter wing to get the new Spitfire.

"We were in the hottest spot in England, there between the south coast and London. We had the best planes. We did a lot of night flying. We had dawn readiness—71 Squadron didn't. We would scramble in darkness. We considered ourselves the best without question. One-Three-Three was number one among the Eagles."

At about this time 71 Squadron lost a couple of promising pilots. William Douglas Taylor—the second Bill Taylor in 71 —was hit while strafing a German flak ship off the Belgian coast and had to bail out. His companion, Stanley Anderson, saw him get into his dinghy and wave a flag. Weather closed in; air-sea rescue craft were unable to find him. The following day a search plane caught a glimpse of him through the clouds. Then he was gone.

Joe Helgason, a Seattle car-racing enthusiast, was killed in a practice attack on airdrome gun positions. A month previously he had shared credit with John J. Lynch for shooting down an Fw 190. On another mission Helgason's alert reports by radio telephone concerning two fighter pilots who had parachuted into the water resulted not only in their rescue but also in that of a bomber crew shot down a day earlier.

Pete Peterson, having survived his own bail-out during Operation Jubilee, was released as 71 Squadron leader to go to Headquarters in London and then to the Wright-Patterson Test Center in Ohio to complete operational tests on American fighter aircraft. Meanwhile, preparations were under way for the orderly transfer of the Eagles from British to U.S. control. Inevitably there was confusion, even over the name of the U.S. organization the Eagles were to join. Although the U.S. Army Air Corps had changed its name in June, 1941, to the U.S. Army Air Forces, both designations remained in use, interchangeably for the most part. The commissions of some officers were with USAAC; others were with USAAF. The overlapping was not to end until 1947 with the establishment of a separate U.S. Air Force.

The formal transfer of the Eagle squadrons from the RAF to the USAAF was scheduled to take place at Debden on September 29, 1942. Together the three units, redesignated Squadrons 334, 335 and 336, would form the Fourth Fighter Group of the U. S. Eighth Air Force. For a couple of months this pursuit group, headed by Colonel Edward W. Anderson, would represent the entire fighter strength of the Eighth Air Force.

Squadron members were sworn into U.S. service a few at a time, day by day, in London. Every pilot had to be qualified before a special USAAF Board. Its members included Major General Carl A. Spaatz, commander-in-chief of U.S. Army Air Forces in Great Britain, and Brigadier General Frank O'D. "Monk" Hunter, head of the Eighth Air Force Fighter Com-

Each Eagle was asked a few questions, including what he thought his rank should be on transfer, and was given a chance to defend his position. McColpin boldly declared that he should be made a brigadier general but readily settled for the rank of major.

Although the Eagles remained with the RAF on detached service throughout September, for the whole of that month they were on the U.S. payroll. Most of the officers transferred to the corresponding U.S. rank which meant that their salaries were almost tripled. Noncommissioned personnel received second lieutenant commissions. Fittings in London tailoring shops for U.S. uniforms began in early September. The first group of Eagles was commissioned into the USAAF on September 15.

Some of the pilots were surprised at the casual nature of the changeover. "I don't know what I expected, but it was a strange anticlimax," said George Middleton.

"We just fooled around in the city for a week or more, drinking beer and trying to figure out how much our pay would come to in English pounds—and spending it too, in paper poker games, because it seemed to be about three times our RAF stipend. We continued wearing our RAF uniforms because no American ones were available at that time. Besides, most of us didn't have the money for new outfits."

At Headquarters, Pete Peterson, the senior squadron commander, submitted to General Spaatz his recommendations for appointments in the Fourth Fighter Group. On the list was the name of Don Blakeslee, proposed to command one of the new squadrons as a major.

General Hunter asked for the story on Blakeslee's difficulties. He was told that the elderly group captain commanding the Martlesham station, an ace of World War I, had been making an inspection. Just as he passed Blakeslee's quarters, he saw a WAAF jump out through a window.

The station commander, who had a strong distrust of fighter pilots—justly so, some had to admit—banged on the door. As he did so, another WAAF emerged from the window.

Hunter, a former cavalry officer and a longtime bachelor, roared, "Did you say two women? And you suggest that he become a major? Hell, I'll make him a colonel."

In view of Blakeslee's recent RAF demotion, he could not be promoted quite that rapidly. He transferred as a first lieutenant but was promoted to captain the next day and to major a month later. Peterson subsequently became a colonel, commanding the Fourth Fighter Group; when he went on to another assignment, Blakeslee succeeded him as colonel.

Although semiofficial lists of World War II aces credited Blakeslee with 12 1/2 enemy aircraft destroyed, his colleagues said the total must have been far greater. "Don never bothered to claim anything about which there might be a question," one friend said. Blakeslee did, however, become one of the highest decorated of American pilots. In addition to his DFC and Distinguished Service Cross with oak leaf cluster from the RAF and the French Croix de Guerre with palm, his American awards included the DFC with four oak leaf clusters—the first DFC conferred personally by General Dwight D. Eisenhower —and the Air Medal with five oak leaf clusters. "Don Blakeslee was the greatest fighter leader that the war produced, bar none," Peterson has declared.

————

And then there were the B-17s, the four-engine Boeing heavy bombers that the Eighth Air Force was beginning to station in England—the long-range Flying Fortresses.

"All B-17 missions in those days were of the public-relations type," says McColpin. "The poor Fortress guys were inexperienced, they carried only token numbers of bombs, they were sent to nonessential targets to gain experience, and they were commanded by inexperienced colonels and generals. The whole outfits were like babes in the woods. But the U.S. and Britain needed the publicity as partners in European warfare. I was told by the RAF to 'guard those B-17s with your lives.' The missions were a laugh. The bombers shot at us, their escort, whenever we came within range—within sight, that is. Then that night we would hear their great claims of destroyed enemy fighters—which were us—with never a German in view."

The Germans on occasion had used captured Allied fighter planes for surprise attacks on Allied formations. This tended to make B-17 crews trigger-happy. Typical of the confused missions early in the B-17 support area were those flown by 71 and 121 squadrons on August 21, two days after Operation Jubilee, as guards for Forts raiding Rotterdam. The Spitfires of 71 Squadron were ordered aloft, then immediately were recalled to Debden, refueled, and retained on readiness for almost an hour, only to be "scrambled" again. A simultaneous assignment for the entire North Weald fighter wing, including 121 Squadron, to meet the B-17s eighty miles at sea came to nothing because, the 121 daily report said, "There was a complete mixup."

On other B-17 escort missions that same week Wing Commander Duke-Woolley, flying with 71 Squadron, and Squadron Leader Daymond each destroyed an enemy plane, and Sergeant Anthony J. Seaman was credited with a probable. Sergeant Pilot Jack Elwood Evans failed to return and was listed missing. Dick Beaty, flying an older Spit VB of 133, had to bail out after damaging an enemy plane but was back in action after two days of hospitalization.

All went smoothly on a 71 Squadron B-17 escort mission September 5, but the following day 133 Squadron had to fight off Fw 190s attacking the B-17s—which again had been off schedule—near Meaulte. Eric Doorly and Dick D. Gudmundsen were shot down. Doorly survived, but Gudmundsen was not so fortunate. On the return flight, near the French coast, some B-17 gunners thought they were being attacked, and opened fire on the Spitfires. The fighters dived to sea level and returned to base alone.

"My wing man, Gudmundsen, and I were in the rear portion of the squadron at 28,000 feet when the 190s came in from above and behind," Doorly recalls.

"There was not much choice but to pull up and swing into them. I fired three bursts at one of them, going down, and then the cannon jammed, so I pulled up to rejoin the squadron. As soon as my climb was established, I checked to the rear for Guddy. I saw the right wing of an aircraft close behind, and assumed he was OK.

"The rearward vision out of the Spit's slab-sided canopy is pretty bad. The airplane behind me turned out to be an Fw 190 which immediately opened fire. The cannon shells poured over my shoulder into my instrument panel and engine. Instantly the canopy was covered with oil.

"The Spit went into a high speed outside loop that jammed me against the canopy up to the middle of my back. I could reach the stick with my foot. There was no reaction, so I assumed the tail was gone. At the bottom of the loop the Spit leveled out and stalled. I tried to get out but couldn't get the canopy open. Back into another outside loop I went.

"On the second stall I got the canopy open, dropped out and pulled the cord at what must have been over 20,000 feet. I was wearing a borrowed chute and had been too lazy to adjust the harness. I paid for that mistake with two sore ones for about a week.

"The 190 flew by about 100 yards away and started to

circle. Those four cannons looked awfully big, and I gave him a 'Heil Hitler' just in case. He continued to circle. I figured he was transmitting an RF fix on me. By the time I got lower I could see trucks coming out to the village toward which I was descending. It was close to dusk. Three trucks were following roads that went in the direction of my drift vector."

It took Doorly about fifteen minutes to reach the ground. He landed in a field in farm country, discarded his parachute, and made for trees that were growing in fairly wide rows. Since it was autumn, leaves were thick on the ground.

"I ran about 1,000 yards and dug under the leaves," Doorly said. "In the growing darkness I could hear trucks arrive and soldiers stomping around. I don't know why they did not see the leaves rustling over me. Maybe the wind blowing all the leaves hid the motion around me.

"I waited until about midnight and then started crawling until I kept getting into manure. Then, without any plan, I wandered around and finally crawled into some hay in a barn and went to sleep.

"I had lost my escape kit with my parachute and had nothing in the way of food or escape supplies. But some of the people in the area risked their lives to hide me and helped me eventually to get to Spain."

Again on September 7, the thirty-six B-17s assigned to attack Rotterdam were off schedule. This time they kept the Spitfires orbiting the rendezvous point for twenty minutes. As they approached the target, the B-17s broke formation, split into pairs, dropped their bombs helterskelter, and fled for home. Panic-stricken gunners fired on Spitfires that were trying to protect them. A few 190s were sighted near the Dutch coast. Bill Baker of 133 Squadron maneuvered into an ideal position behind one and riddled it with bullets. Although the Eagles did not see it crash, they said it certainly must have. In 71 Squadron, Deacon Hively's oxygen line broke. He sat in the cockpit unconscious and semiconscious for twenty minutes, reviving only at 3,000 feet over Ipswich.

Nuisance attacks by German bombers were a constant threat, as Don Young of 121 Squadron was reminded after taking off from Southend to visit friends Lee Gover, George Middleton and Mick Lambert of 133, at Biggin Hill. He heard a section of 121 Squadron being scrambled on an alert.

Climbing through 16,000 feet over the Thames river he spotted a Ju 88 about 3,000 feet above, being pursued by two

Spitfires. He started an all-out climb to get in on the action. The 88 soon did a 190 turn back toward the Channel. This enabled the Spitfires to cut the corner and move into firing range.

As the lead Spitfire opened fire, the 88 began weaving and went into a dive. The lead Spitfire drew smoke from the 88's left engine and then moved over, allowing the other Spit to open up. With this, the 88's left engine began streaming flames, and the Spitfires moved away. The 88 appeared to go out of control in a diving turn to the right. Young closed in and was able to get in a burst before it crashed into the Channel.

On the day that Robert G. Patterson of San Francisco joined 121, he and another newcomer, Frank J. Smolinsky, were sent up to become familiar with the local flying area. They decided instead to cross the Channel to enemy-held territory.

They flew at wave-top level to avoid radar pickup by the Germans. Approaching the coast near Ostend, Patterson told Smolinsky to skid out and keep his wings level so that the RAF markings would not be visible.

"A whole group of Germans were right in my ring-sight," Patterson said. "They were sitting outside their gunposts, enjoying the sun, and they must have thought we were friendly Me 109s.

"I used the cannons and six machine guns on them. I don't believe many survived. We didn't get much return fire until coming out of enemy territory. Then their tracers were quite visible going across the cockpit."

As Patterson and Smolinsky landed, they were met by their flight leader, Jimmy Daley. Daley asked how the local familiarization flight had gone. The two novices excitedly related their venture into enemy territory. "We think we got every one of those Germans," Patterson said.

Daley told them that they had been tracked by radar and advised them to stay out of the way of Squadron Leader Williams as much as possible. "That was an unauthorized mission," Daley said. Turning to Patterson, he added, "You were flying the CO's plane, and it looks like you got it shot up a bit. He'll be pretty teed off at you."

Daley thereupon confided that he had been informed that Williams was soon to be sent elsewhere, in view of 121's imminent transfer to U.S. service. "They're making me the squadron leader," Daley added. "I'll do my best to cover up for you."

Later Williams and Daley studied the gun camera film for the mission and found that the two freshman pilots had indeed punished the enemy. Patterson and Smolinsky were back in good standing once more.

There was to be only one more casualty in 121 before the squadron went under the American flag. John T. Slater's plane was hit while he and Bill Kelly were attacking a flak ship off Flushing. The Spitfire crashed into the sea as Slater attempted to bail out.

Six days after Slater's death Jim Daley led the last of the Eagle squadron combat missions. It was a squadron-strength shipping reconnaissance—a joint effort of 71 and 121 Squadrons—on September 27, 1942.

A Flight from 121 Squadron consisted of Daley, Pilot Officers Cadman Padgett, Bill Kelly and James R. Happel, and Sergeants Bob Patterson and Leon Blanding.

B Flight from 71 Squadron was led by Flight Lieutenant Bob Sprague. The other members were Pilot Officers James C. Harrington, Stanley M. Anderson and James A. Clark, and Sergeants Vernon A. Boehle and Tony Seaman. Clark, incidentally, was the nephew of John Winant, the U.S. ambassador to Great Britain.

The composite squadron shot up three armed trawlers and left them dead in the water. An explosion ripped one of the vessels amidships. It was a final blast at the Nazis by the still young, but aging, American Eagle Squadron volunteers. But it didn't quite make up for another, far grimmer, mission of the previous day, the mission the Eagles still refer to simply and bitterly as Morlaix.

12

MORLAIX

Mac McColpin, the twenty-seven-year-old newly appointed leader of 133 Squadron, was worried, deeply worried. An operations order called for 133 and two other Biggin Hill-based squadrons to escort B-17s on a mission to Morlaix about September 7. Stormy weather forced postponement of the mission day after day. There was no way of knowing when it might be flown, and not much time remained for further RAF flights. The three Eagle squadrons were to be assimilated into the USAAF on the next to the last day of September.

McColpin sent his pilots to London, two or three at a time, to go through the process of transferring into the USAAF. He was careful to keep enough squadron members on hand to fly the mission to Morlaix, should it be put into effect.

Fighter Command ordered 133 Squadron to Great Sampford, a satellite of Debden, on September 23 in readiness for USAAF consolidation of all three of the American units at Debden a month later. "When we moved to Great Sampford I remained the only pilot in the squadron who had not transferred to U.S. service," McColpin recalled many years later. "The weather and the type of mission planned worried me so much that I had refused to transfer until the flight either had been scrubbed or completed.

"On September 25 I received a call from General Monk Hunter ordering me to go to London and transfer. I refused on the basis that I was still in the RAF and was not required to take USAAF orders.

"I explained that I was worried about the impending mission because it would be at maximum range, almost certainly in adverse weather, into an area protected by the Luftwaffe's highly experienced Abbeville fighters—and it would consist of escorting B-17s, always an 'iffy' do, to say the least.

"Within an hour I received a personal call from Sholto Douglas at RAF Fighter Command ordering me to proceed to London and transfer. After a check with the meteorological office and their assurance that the weather would prevent the mission for another day or two, I went to town and transferred to the U.S. Army Air Forces."

Since McColpin's trip into London would leave 133 Squadron for a few hours under the command of Flight Lieutenant Brettell, McColpin had a long, serious talk with the Englishman before leaving the base.

"I tried to impress on Gordon the need for discretion as to the weather, the area, and the escort aspects of the mission," McColpin said. "Brettell was a good planner, impetuous to a fault, but a great guy. He lacked leadership experience."

It was understood among the Eagles that the RAF had sent Brettell to 133 to tighten up internal discipline. Some members of the squadron said they resented the fact that an English officer had been brought in and elevated to leadership over American pilots of greater combat experience.

"The fact that Brettell was only a flight lieutenant, the equivalent of U.S. Army captain, made it difficult for him to work with a unit that was strictly American," comments Dick Alexander. "There was some tension, and certainly a lack of cooperation in some quarters. On this particular occasion Brettell had a position which was, to say the least, insecure."

After breakfast on the morning of September 26, in McColpin's absence and with Brettell in charge, 133 was ordered to fly two hundred miles west from Great Sampford to Bolt Head, on the plain of Devon, to prepare for a bomber-escort mission. George Middleton recalls it as a cold, rainy, windy morning at Sampford, uncomfortable for the mile-long bicycle ride from quarters to messhall:

"As I was riding along in the rain with my head down as far as I could get it and still stay on the taxi-way, I thought I heard the chap next to me talking. I moved a little closer and discovered it was Don Gentile praying out loud. That shook me. I'd known these fellows for six or eight months. If any prayers at all went out, they were smuggled upstairs without doubting the Lord's hearing.

"The flight for the 200 miles south and west to Bolt Head, with a 200- or 300-foot ceiling in pouring rain most of the way, was about as hairy as some missions I'd been on, what with dodging barrage balloons and church steeples and wondering if the acting squadron leader, Brettell, knew where we were. I swear he was lost most of the way, but he'd never admit it. We broke out at last and the sun was shining and it was a beautiful day on the south coast."

Bob Smith was taken aback at the location of the Bolt Head drome. "The approach end of the runway was situated at the top of a sheer limestone cliff. Fortunately, by that time the pilots had had enough oxygen and exertion to dilute the effects of the previous night's dissipation. None landed short."

The Eagles scoff at suggestions that topping-off of fuel tanks at Bolt Head may have been careless and haphazard. Bob Smith and George Sperry, among others, observed conscientious work by ground crews.

After lunch at Bolt Head, Brian Kingcombe, the RAF wing commander, presided over a briefing for the crews. The bombers, eighteen B-17s of the 97th Bombardment Group, were to attack a Focke-Wulf aircraft maintenance plant and the adjoining railroad yards in Morlaix. Their secondary target would be submarine pens at Brest, thirty miles to the west.

Two RCAF Spitfire squadrons, 401 and 412, would provide escort along with 133. The Spit IXs were fitted with small *papier-maché* belly tanks with extra fuel for the long flight. The tanks would be jettisoned on a time-elapsed basis on climb-out. The mission would be led not by Kingcombe but by Wing Commander Keith Hobson. Any bombers unable to attack their targets would jettison their explosives. Aircraft were not allowed to return to base with a bomb load.

Although all pilots were expected to attend the briefing conducted before each mission, some of the Eagles of 133 had become overconfident on recent flights. "We were late," said M. E. Jackson, who was to lead one of the squadron's trio of four-plane sections. "Nobody went to the briefing except the acting squadron leader."

"We didn't go to the briefing because there was no point

to it," said Charlie Cook. "We had been doing this kind of flying for a year. Every one of us had flown 50 or 60 missions.

"It was a real quick thing, a hurry-up do. That mission wasn't supposed to get underway until the next day. If we had known what we were getting into—well, we would have been thinking ahead."

Actually, one other pilot did accompany Brettell, the acting squadron commander, to the briefing. George Sperry described it as "rather casual." The wing was to take off at 4 P.M., meet the B-17s at 25,000 feet over the Channel, and accompany them to the target. "After the bombers laid their eggs we were to proceed back to our home bases. Sounded like a pretty simple mission."

Bob Smith agreed. The distance between takeoff point and target was less than 150 miles. "It all seemed very elementary. Simply fly south, pick up a bunch of B-17s on their bombing mission, escort them back to the friendly shores of England, and buzz off home again. It sounded like a piece of cake. If we'd known what was in store for us, we would have resigned and joined the WAAFs on the spot!"

Perhaps because of last-minute haste, the weather briefing was incomplete and in error. Bob Smith said, long after the war:

"The big hooker was the metro briefing. Some clown masquerading as a weather officer forecast a 35-knot head wind at 28,000 feet, our mission altitude. Instead, we had a 100-knot tail wind—a 135-knot bloody streaking catastrophe.

"We never found out if it was stupidity or carelessness or whatever—or even who was really responsible. Whoever the thick-headed incompetent son of a bitch was, he can take credit for 12 Spitfires, brand new, destroyed; five good fighter pilots down the tubes; and assorted types of grief for the rest of us. He should have gotten the Iron Cross and a pension from the Third Reich."

(The actual count, aside from the twelve Spit IXs lost, was worse than Smith's estimate. Four pilots were killed outright; of six taken prisoner by the Germans, one was executed for taking part in a mass escape.)

———

There were two last-minute changes in the starting lineup. On his way to his plane Dusty Miller was informed that he and Don Gentile would be "spare" this trip and would fly the next mission.

"My roommate, Gene Neville, was allocated my Spitfire,"

Miller recounts. "I reluctantly removed my parachute and helmet from the cockpit. I didn't realize then how lucky I was."

George Sperry had experienced carburetor trouble on a flight two days earlier and had flown his plane to Bolt Head, as No. 13 in the squadron, to check out the engine. Since it ran perfectly, Sperry informed Gentile at Bolt Head that he, rather than Gentile, would fly the mission as No. 2 to Brettell.

"Wouldn't you know," comments Middleton. "Gentile, the spare pilot who had come along to replace anyone who developed mechanical problems, the one who had been doing the praying—he wouldn't have to go on the mission after all. Considering the next few hours, I'd say he got a top priority answer from on high."

After the poorly attended briefing, the pilots wandered out to their aircraft. Bob Smith realized that he had forgotten his escape kit, a packet that contained money, maps and compasses. "Why worry?" was the way he later described his attitude. "No flak. Remote chance of enemy fighters. Just out and back, and off to the local pub. Not even a butterfly in the stomach.

"Too lazy to go back to Operations. No money, maps or marbles—and not a hell of a lot of common sense."

At the readiness line there was a long wait for the signal to rendezvous with the bombers. "Nobody knew just when the B-17s would be overhead, or when they would take off from their home base, for that matter," said Middleton.

"The cider we had for lunch had more authority than we realized, and most of us went sound asleep under our airplane wings. Finally the call to scramble came, and all hell broke loose.

"Usually about one in 10 of these airplanes would start on its own battery—but then you had to get the prime just right and the throttle just so, and the battery itself had to be a stout one. Consequently, when 'scramble' was sounded, the ground crew went ape.

"Three battery carts—the auxiliary power units for starting—were all we had on this sketchy mission, and the poor guys had to spread them around to start 10 or 11 planes. It was an unforgettable scene—those riggers and fitters pushing carts at full gallop between spinning propellers and in the blowing dust, sweat pouring off of them, expressions of fanatical determination on their faces, and pilots screaming for help from all directions. It was like a Dodge-Em game gone amok."

In the lead Spitfire, Brettell taxied out toward the takeoff point, only to hear and feel his right tire blow out. By means of hand signals he arranged a quick trade with Sperry, who had been following close behind. There was a delay of only about a minute. Then Brettell and the rest of the squadron were taxiing the length of the field and taking off to catch up with the other two squadrons. The ground crew managed to change the wheel on what had been the lead plane within four minutes, so swiftly that Sperry was able to catch up with the other pilots midway across the English Channel.

Since all of the American members of 133 except for Squadron Leader McColpin had completed their transfers to the USAAF, they had assumed their U.S. military titles, although RAF records for this final mission still identified them by their British designations. Flight Lieutenant Brettell, leading Red Section, was followed by First Lieutenant Sperry and Second Lieutenants Beaty and Neville.

Captain M. E. Jackson led Blue Section, which included Second Lieutenant Robert E. Smith, First Lieutenant Cook and Second Lieutenant Middleton.

Yellow Section, led by First Lieutenant William H. Baker, contained three second lieutenants—Dennis David Smith, Len Ryerson, and Gil G. Wright.

Just before takeoff, Jackson had instructed Cook to change radio communications from C channel, normally used for a homing vector, to B channel, usually reserved as an emergency link, and then to pass the same instructions on to Middleton, directly behind him.

"Middleton's foot slipped off his rudder pedal while taxiing and he just about cut off the back end of my plane," Cook said. "I never did get to his plane to tell him about the radio channel change. I felt real bad about this, because on the whole flight Middleton never heard a word on his radio telephone."

In a postwar interview Middleton added: "I didn't know what was going on because my radio didn't work from the start. I would have turned back right then except I had done just that on the last mission, and the crew chief was beginning to look a little askance. Besides, there were only 12 of us. I figured I could see everything going on anyway."

Shortly after takeoff, the Spitfires were on top of a solid overcast. Thereafter, at cruising altitude throughout the mission, all sight of the surface was blotted out. Fifteen minutes after the planes left the English coast, radar coverage ended, and radio communications were lost.

When the three squadrons of Spitfires reached the planned rendezvous point, the bombers were nowhere to be seen. The fighters circled the area, unaware that the B-17s had arrived there twenty minutes early and had continued south. Finally the Spitfires flew southward too, with the wing commander insistently calling for position information and getting no reply. Fighter and bomber pilots alike were unaware that they were being whisked along by tail winds of 100 to 115 miles an hour.

The bombers, far ahead of the Spits, unwittingly had crossed the 75-mile-wide cloud-blanketed Brest peninsula and, far south of their assigned target, were racing across the Bay of Biscay toward Spain. The lead navigator for the B-17s later estimated that the bombers had reached the base of the Pyrenees on the Spanish border before turning back. But turn back they finally did, meeting the Spitfires which also immediately swung north toward home.

Two of the fighter pilots had turned back earlier. When Neville's Spitfire developed engine trouble fifty minutes after takeoff, Brettell ordered Beaty to escort the crippled plane back to base. After flying northward for half an hour they started letting down through the clouds on the assumption that by now they were over England. Instead, they were over France and its deadly array of German antiaircraft guns. Neville was shot down and killed near Guingamp, forty miles east of Morlaix. Beaty flew on until he was out of fuel, still with no land in sight beneath the broken clouds. Just as he unbuckled his harness and prepared to bail out, he spotted land and was able to glide over the cliffs to a crash belly-landing.

"We should never have taken off in the first place, even though we had gone on many other missions regardless of the weather," Cook later reminisced. "The controller didn't know us, the wing commander didn't know us. We didn't have our squadron leader along.

"We had heard it was just a propaganda mission to give the American B-17 crews, newly arrived in England, some needed publicity. But when Brettell came back from the briefing and said we were going to go right now, we galloped for our planes and took off."

The B-17s, unable to find their target, had jettisoned their bombs. "Heaven knows where," Cook said. "After finally locating the bombers, we fighters had to zigzag, wasting precious fuel, in order to slow down so we wouldn't outrun them. We kept a safe distance from them. The B-17s were firing now and then to keep their guns warm, so we stayed fairly well away."

Spitfire pilots had a saying that after two hours of flying at 29,000 feet, about all the fuel left in the airplane was fumes. Cook heard a troubled Brettell consulting his deputy commander, Baker, one of the squadron's more experienced pilots.

"It was getting to be a long mission—we had been in the air two hours and 15 minutes—but I was not worried at all," Cook said. "I thought our commander knew where we were.

"I heard Baker say, 'I think we're supposed to go down.' Soon we could see a hole in the clouds, and Baker repeated, 'Gordon, I think we should go down.' Brettell said, 'Okay.'

"After we got down through the clouds and were being shot at, I heard someone say, 'Don't go down.' It was too late then."

Robert E. Smith recalled that the top of the overcast was at six or seven thousand feet of altitude and the bottom around three thousand feet above the ground. Although visibility under the cloud blanket was low, a southerly coast line soon came into view.

"What we didn't know was that this was the south coast of the Brittany peninsula, not the south coast of England," Smith said. "The low altitude and poor visibility made it impossible to see enough of the region to identify it. It did not look familiar—but the Bolt Head area was not our back yard either.

"Just as Gordon turned west (he should have kept on going) after crossing the coast, someone said, 'There's a city off to starboard.' Gordon reversed his turn and headed for the city.

"That city down there should have been Southampton or Plymouth or Portsmouth or anywhere except France. It was Brest—wall-to-wall antiaircraft guns and odd fighter bases here and there.

"No self-respecting fighter squadron is going to fly over a friendly city in a loose, unimpressive formation intended to give maximum flexibility and minimum vulnerability. No way. Tighten it up! Wing to wing! Nose to tail!

"That's what we did—close formation over Brest at about 2,500 feet. What a target! Those German gunners must have had a hundred casualties, stepping on each other, trying to get off the first shot. One of them finally did.

"As much as close formation flying permitted, I was looking for something that resembled a reasonable place to land, gear down. Preferably a runway with a petrol bowser handy, and an officers' mess with a bar.

"Instead I saw a muzzle flash, then another and another. I looked up and saw the familiar dirty gray-black puffs of flak. Radio silence went all to hell, starting with one demand I'll never forget: 'Tell those bastards to stop shooting at us!'

"In a moment the sky was full of bursts of flak, large, medium and small. They were throwing everything up at us but the ammo boxes. Immediately that precision formation exploded into 10 individuals desperately flying for their lives, all air discipline forgotten."

Sperry's account: "The entire squadron followed Brettell down through the overcast, breaking out at 1,000 feet right over the middle of Brest harbor. We all automatically broke into pairs, weaving like mad all around the harbor, with every antiaircraft battery throwing everything they had at us—and every member of 133 Squadron giving the wing leader a very pinpointed position report."

Middleton: "It seemed that every antiaircraft battery in the German army was stationed there that day, and they were all shooting at us. It was obviously an every-man-for-himself situation.

"We all scattered, some back into the clouds, some out to sea, some just blundering around trying to figure out what the hell had happened. I looked at the petrol gauge, which had stopped even wiggling by now, and at the rainy, wind-whipped ocean—it was getting dark, too—and decided to go as far into France as I could, and when the gas ran out I'd bail out."

Charlie Cook, again:

"Bob Smith says he heard someone call on the R/T, 'Tell those bastards to stop shooting at us.' That was me. Just three weeks earlier Spike Miley and I were chasing Focke Wulfs, and we almost got clobbered over the English coast by a Canadian mobile gun station. So this time I thought exactly the same thing was happening again. I had nothing left in my petrol tank, and I thought this must be England. I was preparing to set my plane down in a meadow when an Fw 190 suddenly appeared and shot my wings off. My shoulders felt really hot from the shells going by.

"I let the greenhouse—the canopy—go, put my foot on the stick, and got out of the cockpit. My plane missed hitting me by about a foot. I was so low my parachute barely slowed my fall, and I landed in a hedge. That's how I became a German prisoner."

Jackson recalls the day's events as "a panic mission all around—a makeshift deal. We just got clobbered. Our weather information was bad, we flew too far too long, and we ran out of gas.

"When we broke through the cloud cover, we were the immediate target of German antiaircraft and fighters. I went after an Fw 190 right on the deck and had my controls knocked out. I remember hitting the ground, but I don't remember getting out. I had pretty severe wounds in the front and back of my head and on the side."

Sperry recalls weaving the entire length of Brest harbor: "I saw Brettell get a direct hit on the wing root. He disappeared under me. Several months later I was greatly surprised when he arrived at prison camp. He had spun in minus a right wing and still managed to crawl out of the wreckage."

Enemy 40 mm. shells pounded Sperry's plane. "I lost my canopy, part of the windscreen, and most of the engine coolant. At about 500 feet I went between two Fw 190s taking off from Brest airdrome, so I headed for the protection of the clouds.

"The only radio transmission I can remember was Bill Baker saying, 'Am too low and have to ditch.' A few moments later the overheated Merlin engine seized up and quit cold. I pulled the nose up to slow my air speed, opened the side door, tossed my helmet and goggles and oxygen mask on the floor, unfastened my Sutton harness, and stepped out on the wing root.

"I had to reach back and push the spade grip to get the nose down. With a firm push against the side of the fuselage, I floated over the tail. As the rudder went by I pulled my ripcord. The chute opened, and the aircraft disappeared into the clouds below. Moments later I landed in a cow pasture."

Bob Smith remembers seeing a plane, above and off to one side, take a direct hit and blow up. "A second later a round exploded to the left of me, sending fragments into the aircraft," he said.

The explosion had put holes in the cooling system. The engine began to cough, and the temperature gauge started rising. Extended flight was no longer possible—"I hadn't the foggiest idea where I was"—and it became necessary to bail out. Smith later described the situation:

"So now I'm on the gauges, straight and level. Unstrap the

safety belt, disconnect the oxygen hose and radio cable, roll the Spitfire on its back and drop out. A small problem—the Spit is starting a split-S, and the G-forces keep me in the seat. I have forgotten to roll in enough forward trim to keep it in level flight upside down. So roll it right-side-up again, needle, ball and airspeed to get it level. The poor Rolls-Royce engine is really hot now. Take your time. Bags of forward trim, roll over again, and out you go, just like an old lady. No trouble at all."

George Middleton set a course southeast from the fireworks at Brest and was checking his map when two Fw 190s appeared from behind. "You learn to keep peeking around, no matter what else you're doing," Middleton explained. "As they started to shoot I wrenched around in a skidding turn and watched their tracers go by below me. They also had some shells—20 mm., I think—which exploded at a pre-set range, and they were popping around under me, too. I had never seen anything like that on an airplane, and I told myself how nice it would be if we had thought of it first."

Middleton darted back into the overcast and decided to fly until the engine quit, if necessary. "After a surprising 10 minutes with the engine still running I slipped down under the clouds to see where I was and flew right over a German airfield. What a reception! It looked like an explosion in a red ping-pong factory."

Middleton immediately headed back into the clouds. A few minutes later he took another look and found himself over flat, peaceful looking fields. "Farmers, walking their horses home after a hard day's work in the rain, barely looked up as I roared over them," he said. "Since nobody was shooting at me, I decided to bail out."

Middleton chopped the throttle, jettisoned the hatch, and then discovered he was unable to force his way into the slipstream. The airpseed indicator was registering 230 miles an hour.

He made a wide circle, slowing to about 160 mph, and shot straight out of the plane without difficulty. "Even my worry about banging into the horizontal stabilizer was unfounded. I went by it so slowly I actually reached out and touched it. Sort of like patting a dog so maybe he won't tear off your arm."

As the parachute lowered him, Middleton watched his plane, half a mile away, spiral down, hit the ground and explode —all in eerie silence. "When the sound of the crash reached me a few seconds later, it did not amount to much."

Middleton watched people running toward where the plane had come down. Apparently no one saw him descending. As soon as he landed he detached the parachute and hid it in weeds. Friendly peasants helped him evade capture for six weeks.

Jackson lost consciousness after the crash of his damaged Spitfire. When he became aware of his surroundings again, he was in a French farmhouse. Two or three elderly persons and a young girl were in the room. One of the adults was cleansing a shrapnel hole in his head. "I tried to talk them into giving me shelter," Jackson said.

"The girl, 12 or 13 years old, spoke a little English. She said they were afraid to hide me. A few months earlier some townspeople had been caught hiding a Canadian pilot, and the young people all had been taken away. The Germans said they had been killed.

"Some Germans came and took me to a hospital in Brest. The next day I was moved to a big hospital in Paris. I had a double concussion, a broken nose, and both knees were fractured. And then they brought in Brettell, also badly hurt.

"Later we were sent to the same prison camp, Stalag Luft III at Sagan, Germany. We Americans were moved to our own compound from which Middleton and I managed to escape for a short while.

"Brettell took part in the famous mass escape from the British compound. Of 97 or 98 prisoners who got away, all but a couple were rounded up again. Hitler was so enraged he ordered a mass execution. Poor Gordon Brettell was one of the 50 who were shot. The Germans brought the urns containing their ashes back to the camp and left them on display—a warning of what might happen to any other escapees. Our camp built a little memorial to these men."

Ryerson and D. D. Smith crashed and were killed in the same area where Neville had died just over an hour earlier. The three men and a German pilot shot down by Jackson were buried in the same cemetery at Guingamp. Baker's body and aircraft were not recovered.

Wright managed to evade capture for twelve months. Eventually he was caught and joined his squadronmates—Jackson, Cook, Sperry and Middleton—in Stalag Luft III.

─────

One of the English-speaking Germans who took custody of Cook and Sperry at Brest told them many hours later, "You must be important people. There are so many ships and planes out there on the Channel looking for you that we don't dare go near the place."

The German radio lost no time in announcing that a number of new British Spitfires had been shot down and that their pilots had been killed or captured. Among the prisoners were Americans named Jackson, Sperry and Cook.

Responding to press queries, Allied Headquarters in London acknowledged that some fighter aircraft and pilots had been lost "because of wing icing in adverse weather."

Said Middleton later, "There was no ice—wing or otherwise."

At Bolt Head the first notice of trouble, aside from an ominous silence from the wing, was the information that at 5:30 P.M. a Spitfire returning from Morlaix had crash-landed in England after running out of fuel. At 6 P.M., the estimated fuel time limit for fighters on the mission, a Canadian squadron "came in to land all over the field in all directions," in the words of the station logbook.

"An immediate security clamp was imposed on Bolt Head, and Gentile and I realized how lucky we had been," Dusty Miller wrote. "When we flew back to Great Sampford, we were amazed to hear the German radio using our call signs. We realized for sure that the Germans had breached our R/T security."

In London, Squadron Leader McColpin, newly commissioned a major in the U. S. Air Forces, listened in shocked incredulity to the German radio broadcast about his squadron's destruction and rushed back at once to Great Sampford. No one who had been on the mission was there or had even been heard from.

"All my queries were blunted both by the RAF and the USAAF, either because of security in the case of the RAF or ignorance in the case of U.S. officials," McColpin said. "There was no firsthand information at all at the base."

Word reached Great Sampford that an Eagle pilot identified as Smith had crashed in his Spitfire near Bolt Head and was in a hospital in critical condition. It was several days before the pilot was well enough to call squadron operations to find out what had happened. "This was my first news that the man in the hospital was Dick Beaty, not D. D. Smith," McColpin said.

"As far as I could determine, the fighter wing as a whole lost six other aircraft, from which four pilots were rescued off the English coast, in addition to our 12. Another four crash-landed, out of fuel. All in all, 22 of the 36 fighters taking off were lost or wrecked.

"As I recall, eighteen B-17s started the mission, and none was lost. Those that failed to complete the mission simply aborted.

"No bombers or fighters were intercepted by the enemy at altitude. The only action came when 133 Squadron descended through the clouds. No doubt the Germans couldn't believe anyone would be flying a combat mission in that area in that weather.

"The U.S. air leaders knew nothing of mission results in those days except the stories of their bomber crews. These were distorted beyond belief at that time.

"The timing of the B-17s was always off. They rarely found their targets. Carrying maximum fuel and minimum bomb loads—2,000 pounds, or less than most fighters—they could flounder around Europe for hours, trying to locate England."

McColpin said analyses of the ill-fated operation indicated that Brettell had asked the wing commander for permission to investigate through the hole in the clouds, and the Wing Commander told him, "OK, take a look." Because of a lack of orders, when Brettell started his descent the entire squadron followed, even though a full squadron had never before been sent to investigate an unknown situation. The wing commander's order to the squadron to stay at altitude came too late to be effective.

"Never before had the fighter squadrons flown beyond the range of ground control except at very low altitude," McColpin said. "The loss of communication contact at altitude, after but 20 or 30 minutes of flying on course, should have been the deciding factor in ordering a mission abort.

"In view of the loss of communications, leaving altitude to go low meant that the fighters never would be able to climb back to rejoin the other squadrons. Because of their shortage of fuel, once they descended they were committed to low altitude."

McColpin said the mission controllers at Exeter, the station handling the Morlaix operation, had had no experience whatever in running fighter sweeps or B-17 bomber attacks. "The mission was called on the spur of the moment, after days of waiting," he said. "The pilots thought, even up to start-engine time, that the mission would be scrubbed. The whole show was poorly run.

"The RAF suppressed mission details and results, but they did conduct an investigation. The commander was relieved, all senior controllers were sent to Malta or Africa, and the Exeter control area was restricted from all but air defense missions until new crews could be trained. This was rather stiff action for the RAF at that time."

Not until November 7 did the squadron learn definitely that Ryerson, Neville and D. D. Smith had been killed, that Jackson and Brettell were wounded and in the hospital, and that Sperry and Cook were prisoners. The news that Middleton was a prisoner and in satisfactory health came in February, 1943. In March the former Eagle pilots were delighted to learn that Bob Smith had evaded capture and made his way safely to England with Eric Doorly. In October, 1943, the news arrived that Gil Wright was a prisoner and in good condition. The fate of Bill Baker was never determined.

In the German prison camp Charles Cook bent over page one of a new logbook distributed by the War Prisoner's Aid Organization of the YMCA and laboriously penned this dedication:

> In Memoriam—1st Lt. Bill Baker, Cameron, Tex.; 2nd Lt. D. D. Smith, Redding, Cal.; 2nd Lt. Gene Neville, Oklahoma City, Okla.; 2nd Lt. L. T. Ryerson, Boston, Mass. Killed near Brest, France, Sept. 26, 1942, due to unforgivable circumstances while flying Spit 9s.

The adventures of the Eagles as prisoners of war, as escaped prisoners, and as near prisoners, would fill volumes. For most of the captured Americans, Stalag Luft III was the place of confinement.

Bill Geiger remembered life there as sheer boredom, devoid of really severe treatment, punctuated by "periods when we were very hungry."

M. E. Jackson and George Middleton escaped from the big prison camp by the simple yet daring technique of jumping from a rooftop, in daylight, into trucks laden with tree branches. Bill Nichols discovered a point in the prison fence that seemed to be a blind spot for the German guards and then, also in broad daylight, boldly walked out through it. All three were recaptured within a few days, however.

Barry Mahon and twenty-nine other RAF officers confused their guards and gained a few days of freedom. Mahon escaped again from another prison, Stalag VII A, by means of a key made of tinfoil melted and poured into a mold fashioned from soap.

Bud Wolfe went over the wall of his internment camp in Eire seven times, only to be recaptured. The eighth time he escaped to England. Dutch collaborators helped Bob Patterson hide out from the Germans for fifty-three days, until a turncoat in Amsterdam delivered him to the Gestapo.

Eric Doorly and Robert E. Smith, downed in France twenty days apart, had similar experiences. The French underground snatched them away before searching police could find them, hid, fed and sheltered them, and helped them escape to neutral Spain.

A windmilling propeller and other mechanical trouble forced Dixie Alexander to land at Lisbon. Weeks later the Portuguese released him, and he returned to England. Back in action once more, he was shot down over Austria and became an inmate of Stalag Luft III.

The Italians shot Harold Marting down over Egypt and released him to the Germans. He escaped in Athens from guards who were assigned to take him to Germany. Friendly Greeks helped him, and within two months he rejoined his squadron in Cairo.

────

As they prepared to exchange British uniforms and aircraft for American ones, the Eagles learned that the very first commander of an Eagle squadron had died in action. Group Captain Walter Myers Churchill, the original leader of 71 Squadron, crashed in flames while leading Malta-based Spitfires on an offensive sweep over Sicily on August 27, 1942.

EPILOGUE

"Shortly after the United States entered the war against Germany," said Red McColpin, "we knew that it was only a matter of time until the Eagles would be renamed and most of us would be wearing an American uniform. We knew that some of our American flyingmates would never leave their beloved RAF, even under the penalty of court-martial.

"Fortunately, when the big transition did come, we all had the option of remaining with the British or fighting for our own country. Although I liked the RAF very much, I knew I did not have much of a choice to make. The United States needed experienced fliers very badly. I felt it was my duty to meet a certain obligation."

The "big transition"—the change of command ceremony, the formal transfer of the Eagle squadrons to the United States —took place at Debden on a rainy Tuesday in late September, 1942. The three Royal Air Force units marched into the parade grounds: 71 Squadron headed by Squadron Leader Gus Daymond, 121 headed by Squadron Leader Jim Daley, and 133 headed by Squadron Leader Mac McColpin. When they marched out again a short time later, they were the Fourth Fighter Group of the United States Army Air Forces: the 334th Fighter Squadron led by Major Daymond, the 335th led by Major Daley, and the 336th led by Major McColpin.

Air Chief Marshal Sir Sholto Douglas presented the squadrons to their new commander in chief, Major General Toohey Spaatz. Looking on were Brigadier General Hunter of the Eighth Air Force Fighter Command; Colonel Anderson, Fourth Fighter Group commanding officer; and Anderson's deputy, twenty-two-year-old Lieutenant Colonel Pete Peterson, former longtime leader of 71 Squadron.

Sholto Douglas, later to become Lord Douglas of Kirtleside and president of British European Airways, addressed the Eagles:

"We of Fighter Command deeply regret this parting. In the course of the past 18 months we have seen the stuff of which you are made. We could not ask for better companions with whom to see this fight through to a finish."

Douglas took note of the Eagles who had lost their lives, calling them "those sons of the United States who were the first to give their lives for their country. Like their fathers who fought and died with that American vanguard of the last war —the Lafayette Squadron—so will these Eagles who fell in combat ever remain the honored dead of two great nations."

In eighteen months the Eagles had destroyed seventy-three enemy aircraft (the equivalent of about six Luftwaffe squadrons) and had probably destroyed or damaged a great many more. Douglas continued: "The actual official total is, I believe, 73 1/2, the half being part of a Dornier shared with a British squadron, a symbol of Anglo-American cooperation."

Of the aircraft destroyed, the RAF credited 71 Squadron with 41, 121 Squadron with 18, and 133 Squadron with 14 1/2.

"You joined us readily and of your own free will when our need was greatest and before your country was actually at war with our common enemy," Douglas said. "You were the vanguard of that great host of your compatriots who are now helping us to make these islands a base from which to launch that great offensive which we all desire. You have proved yourselves great fighters and good companions. We shall watch your future with confidence."

[As is the case with most initial war statistics, the preliminary figures about Eagle squadron combat results were inaccurate. Without question, the Eagles downed many more aircraft than the estimates quoted by Douglas. Accurate figures on kills and on aces never have been and probably never will be compiled. The Fighter Aces Association has worked up tallies, but these are challenged by many pilots and air combat experts. The armed services have declined to become involved in the controversy and have refrained from making "official" claims, particularly since all estimates tend to vary with the passage of time and the gathering of new information.]

The U.S. Fourth Fighter Group, built around the old Eagle squadrons and led by former Eagles—many of whom became aces, or double or triple aces—went on to become the highest scoring fighter group in the USAAF.

"The Fourth was the highest scoring wing in Korea and did an excellent job in Vietnam," says Major General Pete Peterson. "The few pilots who originally formed the Eagle squadrons were the progenitors of the finest fighter wing in the U.S. Air Force."

In 1964, eleven former members of 133 Squadron held a reunion in Los Angeles. In the following two years they met again at Hamilton Air Force Base north of San Francisco where their former skipper, now Major General McColpin, commanded the Fourth Air Force of the Air Defense Command. In 1967, veterans of the two other Eagle squadrons joined them to establish the Eagle Squadron Association. In succession McColpin, Peterson, and Dick Alexander served three-year terms as president of the exclusive fraternity. In 1976, the reunion was held overseas for the first time, in London, and Reade Tilley became president.

Together again in England, it became nostalgia time for the aging Eagles. Prince Philip greeted the former American fighter pilots, shook their hands, thanked them warmly. People on the street embraced them; autograph seekers hailed them in hotel lobbies. Taxi drivers provided free service, brushing tips aside with the comment, "You've already paid."

The visitors from America called at the graves of fallen Eagles at Brookwood Cemetery and at the American cemetery at Cambridge.

They attended Battle of Britain Thanksgiving services at Westminster Abbey, accompanying Winston Churchill's widow, proud and erect in her wheel chair. At St. George's Memorial Chapel at Biggin Hill they presented a silver chalice and paten. And during Sunday services at St. Clement Dane Church, they listened to these words from the pulpit:

"We consider the Eagles to be very special friends indeed. They went into the battle for liberty. This is their church as long as they are in London."

Before returning home they sent Queen Elizabeth a message of "warm and friendly greetings:"

> We flew with pride under the flag of England in your superb Hurricanes and Spitfires. We shared in battle the defeats, the victories, and the glory of the Royal Air Force.
>
> The Eagle Squadrons were a result of the force that motivates men who believe in freedom, to join in the fight for it regardless of when or where it is threatened. Let those who would challenge our way of life be warned that this force is enduring, and will characterize the relationship of Great Britain and the United States for all time.

McColpin capsulized the sentiments of the Eagles on one of his nostalgic visits to England: "I somehow felt that if I closed my eyes things would be the way they were at Debden, Martlesham Heath, Biggin Hill and Kirton Lindsey. When I opened them I would look out on a row of Spitfires with their shark-like bodies silhouetted against a foggy English dawn."

———End———

IN MEMORIAM

Compiled from data assembled and verified by the Eagle Squadron Association. The unit a pilot was flying with when killed is listed as the squadron of record. Other squadron service is shown in parentheses. KIA stands for killed in action, KOAS for killed on active service.

71 SQUADRON

ALEXANDER James Keith
Died 4 Apr 1976 A/C Accid.W.Va.

ANDERSON Newton
KIA   English Channel (S/L 222 Sqdn) Jun 1942

ANDERSON Paul Roger
KOAS   Cafe de Paris, London 8 Mar 1941

ANDERSON Stanley M.
KIA   Belgium 15 Apr 1943

ATKINSON Roger Hall
KOAS   North Weald 15 Oct 1941

AYER John Butler
KIA   English Channel 17 Apr 1942

BECKER Wayne A. (Engr.Off)
Died 1960, Ohio

BEESON Duane W.
Died en route Washington, D.C. 13 Feb 1947

BITMEAD E. R. (Br.S/L)
Died 1955, England

BOOCK Robert A.
KIA   Belgium 18 May 1943

BRITE William Oswald
KIA   England 27 Apr 1943

CHATTERTON Lawrence Albert
KOAS   North Weald 22 Oct 1941

CHURCHILL Walter Myers (Br.S/L)
KIA   Sicily 27 Aug 1942

DONAHUE Arthur Gerald
KIA   English Channel 11 Sep 1942

DOWLING Forrest P.
Died 1955, Auto Accid., Oklahoma

DRIVER William Richard
KOAS   North Weald 5 Aug 1941

EVANS Jack Elwood
KIA   Circus- St. Omer 27 Aug 1942

FENLAW Hillard Sidney
KIA   Sweep- Boulogne, France 7 Sep 1941

FISKE William M.L. III
KIA   Biggin Hill 17 Aug 1940

FLYNN John F.
KIA   Escort Bombers- St. Omer 27 Apr 1942

FRANCE Victor J.
KIA   Escort B-17s- Paris 18 Apr 1944

GALBRAITH C. O.
Further info. needed

GEFFENE Don (121)
KIA   Ceylon 5 Apr 1942

GILBERT Humphrey T. (Br.F/L)
KOAS   England 1 May 1942

HARRINGTON James
Died 3 Sep 1967, Saudi Arabia

HELGASON Joseph Field
KOAS   Debden 6 Aug 1942

HOLLANDER Walter John
KOAS   Helicopter Accid., Maine 9 Jul 1955

INABINET William Burness
KOAS   Martlesham Heath 9 Jan 1942

KENNERLY Byron F.
Died 1967, California

KEOUGH Vernon Charles
KIA   Kirton-in-Lindsey (No.Sea) 15 Feb 1941

KOLENDORSKI Stanley Michel
KIA   Sweep-Holland 17 May 1941

LECKRONE Phillip Howard
KOAS   Kirton-in-Lindsey 5 Jan 1941

LUTZ John F.
KIA   Belgium 4 May 1943

LYNCH John J. (121)
KOAS   B-52 Accident 1953

McGERTY Thomas Paul
　　KIA　Bomber Escort- No. Sea 17 Sep 1941

McGINNIS James Leland
　　KOAS　Martlesham Heath 26 Apr 1941

McMINN Richard D.
　　KIA　France 15 Apr 1943

McPHARLIN Michael G.
　　KIA　France 6 Jun 1944

MANNIX Robert Louis
　　KIA　Libya (Benghazi) 18 Nov 1942

MARTING Harold F. (121)
　　KOAS　P-40 Accid., So. Carolina 20 Sep 1943

MAURIELLO Sam
　　Died 23 Aug 1950, A/C Accid.

MAYS Ben Freeman
　　KIA　Circus- Hazebrouck, France 12 Apr 1942

MEARES Stanley Thomas (Br.S/L)
　　KOAS　North Weald 15 Nov 1941

OLSON Virgil Willis
　　KIA　Bomber Escort- North Sea 19 Aug 1941

ORBISON Edwin Ezell
　　KOAS　Kirton-in-Lindsey 9 Feb 1941

POTTER Eugene M. (121)
　　KIA　France 7 Jul 1944

PROVENZANO Peter Benjamin
　　KOAS　P-47 Accid., Alaska 1942

ROSS Gilbert C.
　　Died after war (1968)

SCARBOROUGH Ross Orden
　　KOAS　North Weald 15 Nov 1941

SEAMAN Anthony J.
　　KIA　Patrol- English Channel 20 Oct 1942

SPRAGUE Robert S. (121)
　　KOAS　Mid-Air, Debden 26 Nov 1942

TANN F. H. (Br.Adj.)
　　Died after the war

TAYLOR Kenneth Sampson
　　KOAS　North Weald 9 Aug 1941

TAYLOR William Douglas
  KIA   Rhubarb- Flushing 31 Aug 1942

TEICHEIRA George
  KIA   Circus- Bruges, Belgium 1 Jun 1942

TOBIN Eugene Quimby
  KIA   Sweep- Boulogne, France 7 Sep 1941

TONGUE Reginald (Br.F/O)
  Died after the war

TRIBKEN Charles Wallace (121)
  KOAS   Jeep Accid., Belgium 1944

VOSBURG Murray Slauson
  Died 6 Dec 1976, California

WALLACE Thomas Cherry
  Died 1971, South America

WEIR Jack Wesley
  KOAS   Magister, North Weald 28 Aug 1941

WHITLOW Gordon H.
  KIA   Belgium 21 May 1943

WOODHOUSE Henry DeC. (Br.S/L)
  KIA   Tangmere 1944

ZAVAKOS Frank George
  KIA   Air Sea Rescue- No. Sea 2 Jun 1942

121 SQUADRON

ALLEN Thomas Willcox
  KIA   Sweep- North Sea 31 May 1942

AUSTIN Frederick Carleton (133)
  KIA   Sweep- Boulogne 17 Apr 1942

BODDING Carl Olaf (133)
  KIA   Sweep- Dunkirk 28 Apr 1942

BOYLES Frank R. (133)
  KIA   Details Needed 8 Apr 1944

BROSSMER Robert Vincent (133)
  KIA   Sweep- English Channel 4 May 1942

CHAP Norman Richard
  KIA   Sidi Barrani, Egypt 7 Nov 1942

COFFIN Howard Macy
  Died after the war

COX Frank Mitchell
    Further Information Needed

DALEY William James
    KOAS   Near Paris 10 Sep 1944

EDNER Selden R.
    KOAS   Greece 22 Jan 1949

FINK Frank M.
    Died after the war

FREIBERG Ralph William
    KIA   Sweep- English Channel 4 May 1942

GAMBLE Frederick Arvon
    KOAS   North Weald 3 May 1942

GILLILAND Jack Dewberry
    KOAS   Ipswich 8 Jan 1942

GRIFFIN James Edward (71)
    Further Information Needed

GRIMM Chester P.
    KIA   England 22 Jan 1943

HALSEY Gilbert O.
    Died 1954, Oklahoma

HAPPEL James R.
    Died 1 June 1970, New Jersey

HOLDER Kenneth LeRoy
    KIA   Patrol- English Channel 12 Dec 1941

KELLY William P.
    KIA   Holland 5 Feb 1943

LAUGHLIN Loran Lee
    KOAS   Kirton-in-Lindsey 21 Jun 1941

McHAN Richard E.
    Died 26 Dec 1975, California

McLEOD Donald W.
    Died Oct 1946, Connecticut

MASON Earl Wallace
    KOAS   Kirton-in-Lindsey 15 Sep 1941

MATTHEWS Joseph G.
    Further Information Needed

MOONEY John Joseph (71)
    KIA   Rhubarb- Ostend 16 Jun 1942

OSBORNE Julian M.
  Died 5 Jul 1968 A/C Accid.

PATTERSON Richard Fuller
  KIA   Rhubarb- Belgium 7 Dec 1941

PECK James E.
  KOAS   P-38 Accid. Christchurch 12 Apr 1944

POWELL Peter (Brit.S/L)
  Died 28 Jan 1970, England

SLATER John T.
  KIA   Recco- North Sea 21 Sep 1942

SMITH Kenneth G.
  Died after war, Oregon

SMOLINSKY Frank J
  KOAS   P-47 Accid. England 3 Apr 1943

STEPP Malta L.
  KOAS   P-47 Accid. England 30 Sep 1943

TAYLOR Benjamin A.
  KOAS   Ramsbury, England 22 Dec 1944

TAYLOR James LaRue
  KIA   Sweep- Dieppe 19 Aug 1942

WILLIAMS W. Dudley (Brit.S/L)
  Died April 1976, Sussex

WILLIS Donald K.
  Died April 1977, Ocala, Florida

YOUNG Norman Dudley
  KIA   Circus- Berck Sur Mer 31 Jul 1942

133 SQUADRON

ARENDS William Albert
  KIA   Sweep- St. Omer 20 Jun 1942

AYRES Henry J.
  Died 24 Dec 1971, California

BAKER William H.
  KIA   Escort B-17's- Morlaix 26 Sep 1942

BARRELL Charles Sewell
  KOAS   Duxford 27 Sep 1941

BEATY Richard N.
  Died Feb 1965, New York

BICKSLER Edwin H.
  KIA   Tunisia 18 Apr 1943

BRETTELL Edward Gordon (Br.S/L)
   KOAS   Stalag Luft III Escape 28 Mar 1944

BROWN Hugh Card
   KIA   Weather Test- North Sea 16 Mar 1942

BRUCE George Russell
   KOAS   Eglinton 23 Oct 1941

COXETTER James Geiger
   KOAS   Eglinton 27 Oct 1941

DE HAVEN Ben Perry
   KOAS   Biggin Hill 28 Jul 1942

EICHAR Grant Eugene
   KIA   Escort Bostons- Abbeville 31 Jul 1942

EMERSON J. M. (Br.Int.Off.)
   Died after the war

FLORANCE Davis Ray
   KIA   Sweep- Fecamp 19 May 1942

FORD William Kenneth
   KIA   Sweep- Fecamp 31 May 1942

GALLO Tony
   KOAS   Texas 1943

GENTILE Donald Salvadore
   KOAS   Andrews AFB 28 Jan 1951

GUDMUNDSEN Dick D.
   KIA   Escort B-17s- Rouen 6 Sep 1942

HAIN Harry Clem
   KIA   Middle East 1942

HANCOCK Fletcher
   KIA   Sweep- Abbeville 5 Jun 1942

HARP Carter Woodruff
   KIA   Escort Bostons- Abbeville 31 Jul 1942

JOHNSTON H. A. S. (Br.F/L)
   Further Information Needed

KING Coburn Clark
   KIA   Escort Bostons- Abbeville 31 Jul 1942

McCALL Hugh Harrison
   KOAS   Isle of Man 8 Oct 1941

MAMEDOFF Andrew
   KOAS   Isle of Man 8 Oct 1941

MEIERHOFF Cecil E.
   KIA   P-47 Ie Shima 22 Jul 1945

MILEY Carl H.
    Died 26 Nov. 1968, Ohio

MITCHELLWEIS John
    KOAS   Debden 26 Feb 1943

MORRIS Moran Scott
    KIA   Sweep- Fecamp 31 May 1942

NELSON James C.
    Died 11 Jun 1971, Colorado

NEVILLE Gene P.
    KIA   Escort B-17s- Morlaix 26 Sep 1942

OMENS Gilbert Inland
    KOAS   Magister- Biggin Hill 26 Jul 1942

PEWITT Robert Lewis
    KIA   Sweep- Fecamp 19 May 1942

PUTNAM Hiram Aldine
    KIA   Malta 21 Apr 1942

ROBERTSON Chesley H.
    Died 15 Dec 1975, Florida

RYERSON Leonard T.
    KIA   Escort B-17s- Morlaix 26 Sep 1942

SCHATZBERG Seymour Morton
    KOAS   Biggin Hill 19 Jul 1942

SCUDDAY Fred R. (121)
    KOAS   India 14 Jun 1944

SLADE William C.
    KOAS   Further Information Needed

SMART Glen J.
    Died 15 Jan 1969, Wyoming

SMITH Dennis David
    KIA   Escort B-17s- Morlaix 26 Sep 1942

SOARES Walter Gordon
    KOAS   Duxford 27 Sep 1941

STOUT Roy Neil
    KOAS   Isle of Man 8 Oct 1941

THOMAS Eric Hugh (Br.S/L)
    Died 1972, England

WALLACE William R.
    Died 16 Feb 1976, California

WATKINS Vivian Eugene (121)
    KIA   Holland 24 Apr 1942

WHEDON Samuel Fisk
    KOAS   Kirton-in-Lindsey 3 Apr 1942

WHITE William Joseph
    KOAS   Isle of Man 8 Oct 1941

WICKER Walter Charles
    KIA   Sweep- Ostend 27 Apr 1942

ACKNOWLEDGMENTS

This book came about through the stubborn resolve of the American fighter pilots who served in the Royal Air Force Eagle Squadrons in World War II. These men felt deeply that their stories, and especially the stories of comrades who perished in that war, should be set down in printed form before it was too late.

Over the years, the Eagle Squadron Association has assembled logbooks, photographs, written anecdotes and taped narratives. Out of this reservoir, an informal accounting of the Eagles has been fashioned.

Reade Tilley, a retired Air Force information specialist, was a prime mover in this project. So many other persons—Eagles living and dead, family members and friends, representatives of military units in England, Canada and the United States —have also contributed generously in time, thought and effort that it would be difficult to single them out without slighting the similarly valuable assistance provided by others.

However, three couples should be mentioned specifically for their exhaustive research on correct dates, names, places and events: Dale "Jessie" Taylor, Historian of the Eagle Squadron Association, and his wife, Edith; James and Shirley Gray, frequent visitors to information sources in Great Britain; and Harold and Pat Strickland, essential fact-finders in the Pentagon and in the halls of Congress in Washington, D.C. Special thanks are due also to Denver Miner for finding and sending in the eloquent prayer attached to the dedication that opens this volume.

INDEX